PAINFUL PARTINGS

PAINFUL PARTINGS
Divorce and Its Aftermath

LITA LINZER SCHWARTZ
FLORENCE W. KASLOW

John Wiley & Sons, Inc.
New York • Chichester • Weinheim • Brisbane • Singapore • Toronto

Library of Congress Cataloging-in-Publication Data:

Schwartz, Lita Linzer.
    Painful partings : divorce and its aftermath / by Lita Linzer
Schwartz, Florence W. Kaslow.
        p.   cm.
    Includes bibliographical references and index.
    ISBN 0-471-11009-4 (cloth : alk. paper)
    1. Divorce. 2. Divorce—Psychological aspects. 3. Divorced
people—Family relationships. 4. Divorced people—Counseling of.
5. Life cycle, Human. I. Kaslow, Florence Whiteman. II. Title.
HQ814.S38 1997
306.89—dc20   96-19118

Printed in the United States of America

10 9 8 7 6 5 4 3 2 1

Series Preface

OUR ABILITY TO FORM STRONG interpersonal bonds with romantic partners, children, parents, siblings, and other relations is one of the key qualities that defines our humanity. These relationships shape who we are and what we become—they can be a source of great gratification or tremendous pain. Yet, only in the mid-20th century did behavioral and social scientists really begin focusing on couples and family dynamics, and only in the past several decades have the theory and findings that emerged from those studies been used to develop effective therapeutic interventions for troubled couples and families.

We have made great progress in understanding the structure, function, and interactional patterns of couples and families—and have made tremendous strides in treatment. However, as we stand poised on the beginning of a new millennium, it seems quite clear that both intimate partnerships and family relationships are in a period of tremendous flux. Economic factors are changing work patterns, parenting responsibilities, and relational dynamics. Modern medicine has helped lengthen the life span, giving rise to the need for transgenerational caretaking. Cohabitation, divorce, and remarriage are quite commonplace, and these social changes make it necessary for us to rethink and broaden our definition of what constitutes a family.

Thus, it is no longer enough simply to embrace the concept of the family as a system. In order to understand and effectively treat the evolving family, our theoretical formulations and clinical interventions must be informed by an understanding of ethnicity, culture, religion, gender, sexual preference, family life cycle, socioeconomic status, education, physical and mental health, values, and belief systems.

The purpose of the *Wiley Series in Couples and Family Dynamics and Treatment* is to provide a forum for cutting-edge relational and family theory, practice, and research. Its scope is intended to be broad, diverse, and international, but all books published in this series share a common mission: to reflect on the past, offer state-of-the-art information on the present, and speculate on, as well as attempt to shape, the future of the field.

FLORENCE W. KASLOW
Florida Couples and Family Institute

Preface

THE STUDY OF DIVORCE—its causes, the trials and tribulations that accompany it, the need for efficacious child custody evaluations, the roles and intervention strategies of divorce therapists, and divorce mediation as an accepted alternative dispute resolution strategy to adversarial, litigated proceedings—expanded greatly in the decade since our last book, *The Dynamics of Divorce: A Life Cycle Perspective* was published (Kaslow & Schwartz, 1987b). This new book represents comprehensive updating of our thinking based on reviewing the current literature, much additional clinical experience in therapy and mediation, discussion with thoughtful colleagues, and insights and knowledge gleaned from teaching about and conducting workshops on divorce in several dozen countries throughout the world.

We have incorporated much more on bicultural marriages and a more multicultural perspective as well as more on gender issues—particularly fathers' rights and the announcement of one departing partner that he or she will be living a homosexual lifestyle. A protocol for a full child custody evaluation is presented, along with excerpts from the recently promulgated American Psychological Association Child Custody Guidelines (1994), since this is an area of practice about which we are often queried.

We continue to be struck by how painful the partings wrought by divorce are; thus the selection of the title of this book. We also have been impressed with the enormous impact religion has on many people contemplating divorce, and how it can serve as a source of support and guidance or be a negative force that impedes the decision to leave an untenable marriage and/or interferes with the healing process. Because thousands of people who divorce desire, or are even required to obtain, a religious as well as a civil/legal divorce, an entire chapter has been devoted to religious and spiritual factors and to divorce ceremonies.

In this book, we attempt to provide a kaleidoscope of the divorce process, the feelings experienced during and after the marriage is legally terminated, and the transitions and tasks to be mastered. For many, the journey seems analagous to a prolonged roller coaster ride—at the beginning, climbing up and out is laborious and slow, followed by brief periods of respite and relief at the apex, and then a rapid descent into what may seem like a bottomless pit of pain and despair. As the months pass by, the ride becomes less turbulent as the highs and lows become less extreme, and ultimately the travelers alight from the tempestuous ride and establish a stable postdivorce existence.

Despite some daunting sequelae, we are convinced that life beyond divorce can be full of challenges and opportunities, and we try to balance the inevitable traumas with the possible great resiliencies.

To the couples and families we have treated and mediated, and to the graduate students and professionals we have taught and supervised, we express our appreciation for letting us enter their lives at critical points in their development and allowing us to learn so much from them. To our own families, we express gratitude for their love, commitment, and understanding—"the stuff" that enriches one's emotional life; and to each other—our gratitude for a long and productive friendship and collaborative relationship. To our talented and spirited editor at John Wiley & Sons, Kelly Franklin—we thoroughly enjoy working with you.

LITA LINZER SCHWARTZ, PHD
FLORENCE W. KASLOW, PHD

Wyncote, Pennsylvania
Palm Beach, Florida

Contents

PART I

What Precedes the Parting?

CHAPTER 1 SETS THE ENTIRE matter of divorce into context, for divorce, as is true for most processes and events, does not occur in a vacuum. The historical view of marital dissolution may vary by geography as well as by time, and cultural views also affect spouses who part.

In addition, we explain our professional orientation as we approach the issues of divorce. First, we both subscribe to a family systems orientation, since there is no question that divorce affects the entire family as well as the principal figures in such an action. Second, we remain committed to a life-cycle perspective, as we were in *The Dynamics of Divorce* (Kaslow & Schwartz, 1987b). The effects of divorce vary for both adults and children depending on where they are in their respective life stages at the time of the divorce (and later).

CHAPTER 1

A Family Systems Framework and Life-Cycle Perspective

LET THERE BE NO MISTAKE . . . divorce is painful. The pain may begin before the couple separates, is certainly evident for at least one spouse (if not both) from the time of separation and, over time, affects any children of the marriage as well as extended family members and friends as they become aware of the dissolution and chasm. The anguish may continue to be acute for two to five years after the divorce is final or, for a number of reasons, may persist many years at a chronic, if lowered level. Our goal is to portray the process as it unfolds, and to indicate ways that therapists and those experiencing the trauma of divorce can reduce and ultimately ameliorate the pains of parting for everyone concerned.

We believe that divorce has differential effects on adults and children alike. These vary according to age, personality factors, family relationships and alliances, religion, ethnicity, cultural heritage and attitudes, physical and mental health, socioeconomic status and resources, and many other factors that contribute to the uniqueness of each individual and family unit caught up in the crises and transitions evoked by divorce. Separation and divorce affect not only those in the nuclear family but also members of the extended family, friends, playmates, neighbors, and colleagues. Changes in all of these relationships are inevitable as the composition of the family and each member's respective roles shift.

HISTORICAL BACKGROUND

Until 200 or so years ago, divorce—when it occurred at all—had disastrous personal consequences. According to a British historian (Phillips, 1993):

> Married couples at all social levels lived and worked cooperatively, whether in agriculture, fishing, textile manufacture, or other artisan work, and the contribution of both was essential for the sheer survival of their family. Separation meant sundering their domestic economy, and the potential consequences could be seen in the hordes of wretched women and their children, cast into poverty by the death or desertion of their husbands and fathers.
>
> Moreover, there was little chance that a married woman alone could get work or accommodation, especially if she had children, and there was *no hope of charity if she was deemed to have chosen her fate by leaving her husband, no matter how abusive he might have been* [emphasis added by current authors].
>
> The result must have been that women especially, but also men, were effectively locked into marriages and tolerated conditions that we would find intolerable. . . .
>
> Husbands and wives were likened by one seventeenth-century writer to prisoners in a cell: there was no escape, and rather than beat their heads against the walls, they should resign themselves to their plight. (pp. 10–11)

In nineteenth-century America, marriage was defined as a lifetime commitment between husband and wife (Hartog, 1991). Following English rulings, American courts saw the marriage contract as an inviolate one and would not enforce any other contracts between husband and wife, even separation agreements. Wives were seen as the property of husbands and, like their British counterparts, suffered substantially if they lived apart from their husbands (whether by the wife's own choice or his). Nonetheless, a wife remained her husband's legal responsibility, even when he chose to ignore it. In the eyes of many, a lengthy separation, bigamy, adultery, and even a mutual desire for divorce on the grounds of incompatibility were insufficient reasons for the granting of a divorce. Marriage was perceived as an institution and contract that did not end "until death do us part."

As is true today, the states have historically varied in their limited provisions for divorce. Chief Justice John Marshall, in 1819, stated that divorce was permitted only to "liberate one of the parties" because the marriage contract had been broken by the other party (Hartog, 1991, p. 116). Clear and convincing evidence of adultery was often the sole ground for divorce, and was perceived as punishment for the guilty party in a society that valued the marriage contract. Unhappiness, sole or mutual, was no reason to break that contract in the eyes of society, also reflected in the law. Nonetheless, in some states, mental cruelty was also grounds for a civil divorce. No mention was made of physical cruelty or spouse abuse as being reasons to allow someone to extricate herself from an untenable union.

Legally and morally, traditional divorce required *a guilty party and an innocent one.* One spouse had to be "at fault." If both parties had violated the marriage contract, neither could obtain a divorce, for one of them had to have "clean hands." "To get around this rule couples who had decided to divorce would typically conceal the fact that both had grounds" and decide which one would confess to being the guilty party. "Technically their concealment constituted collusion or fraud, but it was nevertheless common practice" (Weitzman, 1985, p. 10) since it was the only route to legal marital dissolution.

Distress was evident in many marriages, even in the ensuing century and a half, with death the only certain release from abuse. The perception of wives as their husband's property and responsibility, unable to enter into contracts or claims in their own name, continued in many states well into the twentieth century (Tavris & Offir, 1977; Weitzman, 1985). Legally, women obtained some status with the passage of the Nineteenth Amendment (1919) and the later passage of civil rights legislation, but some men still treat their wives and children as chattel who can be pushed and ordered around. Change came slowly, and desertions, mainly by men, were the prevalent way marriages ended. Since this route gave the wife no claim to being legally divorced, however, she lived in limbo, unable to make any financial demands on her spouse and also unable to remarry.

DIVORCE RATES

Beginning with California's shift to "no-fault" divorce in the California Family Law Act of 1970 (Weitzman, 1985, p. x), almost every state has implemented some form of divorce reform law, and as a result, the divorce rate in the United States has climbed rapidly. Between 1962 and 1982, according to the National Center for Health Statistics (NCHS, 1985), the number of divorces more than doubled annually, from 2.2 per 1,000 in 1962 to 5.3 per 1,000 in 1981. By 1993, after the backlog of all those previously unable to divorce had been reduced, this rate had stabilized at 4.6 to 4.8 per 1,000 (NCHS, 1993). The 4.5 per 1,000 rate in 1995 was the lowest rate since 1974 (NCHS, 1996).

The changes in the divorce rates reflect a number of factors. First, the advent of no-fault divorce in the 1970s eliminated the need for legitimate or unfounded accusations of adultery, which was the major ground for divorce in earlier decades. Second, in some segments of society the attitude toward divorce has become much more permissive and accepting than it was a generation ago. Indeed, there is concern that divorce has become so prevalent in some geographic areas that it is the first option rather than the last when a couple has disputes. Third, women's status has changed. The millions of married women in today's labor force can be somewhat less anxious about being financially dependent on their husbands and therefore remaining trapped in an intolerable marriage, although they realize they may still experience a substantially reduced income after divorce and become downwardly mobile (Weitzman, 1985). Also, divorced women are no longer shunned or stigmatized in most communities in the United States and other liberal Western countries, and they are able to develop their own networks of friends. They are free to date and have romantic relationships, and to travel alone or with friends, in a way that would have been far more difficult for those in their mothers' generation.

A fourth factor is the greater longevity of people in general. Whereas in the nineteenth and early twentieth centuries, many marriages ended after 5 to 25 years because of the wife's death in childbirth or because of either partner's illness, people are living longer today and remaining more active at older ages. At some point, they may realize that they no longer have interests, values, and goals in common with a spouse of 20, 30, 40, or 50 years, and ask themselves, "Is this all there is?" The lack of compatability and/or feeling of pervasive ennui can become overwhelming and produce frustration, anger, or bitterness. In the view of some, "Marriage has become a choice rather than a necessity, a one-dimensional institution sustained almost exclusively by emotional satisfaction, and difficult to maintain in its absence" (Furstenberg & Cherlin, 1991, p. 7). Although this view may seem harsh, many people decide to change their life patterns at the 25-year-plus stage of marriage because they believe that since they have 20 or 30 more years to live, it is foolish to spend it in misery or in an unfulfilling relationship. The result is that long-term marriages, as well as those of shorter duration, are ending in divorce.

Staying together "for the sake of the children," as we indicated in *The Dynamics of Divorce* (Kaslow & Schwartz, 1987b), is less often considered essential today, except by those whose religions eschew divorce and advise them to "turn the other cheek" no matter how badly they may be battered and bruised. Nonetheless, for children in abusive or highly argumentative families, the parting of their parents may indeed lead to a healthier emotional environment than the tense one in which they had been living (Wallerstein & Kelly, 1980).

This positive impact of divorce on children who experience a sense of relief and greater safety when a violent and/or turbulent, highly dysfunctional parental union dissolves and they remain with the more stable parent, protected from the abusive or tormenting one, has been underestimated and underdescribed. This positive consequence is also observed when the person from whom one parent and the children separate has humiliated the family by onerous behaviors such as open philandering; embezzlement, rape, or other criminal behaviors; or sexual harassment. Therefore, it is crucial that this welcome aspect of divorce, reported to many clinicians in the postdivorce years, be highlighted here and be included in the overall conceptualization of outcomes.

For other children, the parting may lead to more painful situations as they become the pawns on the divorce chessboard and the weapons that their parents use to wage war with each other. What is abundantly clear, however, is that children of divorce are no longer unique in schools or among their friends. In many communities, there are simply too many such children for them to feel "different" and alienated, as was often the case prior to 1980.

From an historical point of view, the increase in the divorce rate began after World War II, or about 50 years ago. According to Stone (1990):

> The combination of modern technology, the rise of consumerism, and unparalleled affluence have made redundant the older need for deferred gratification, without which life in the not so distant past would have been intolerable, and which was inculcated by the practical problems of day-to-day life, as well as by religion, school, family, and kin. (p. 414)

The new demands for instant gratification of individual desires tend to erode the traditional sense of obligation and responsibility both within and to the family and society, and ultimately contribute to a rise in the divorce rate. "Although hard to document, there appears to be more stress on rights and less on duties. As a result, many marriages which would have been regarded as tolerable in the past are today seen as unendurable" (Stone, 1990, p. 414).

This perspective is echoed by Fine (1992), who wrote, "Compared to previous generations, behavior is based more strongly on what is best for the individual and less on what is best for the family" (p. 431). He added that a weakened sense of marriage as a permanent union has also contributed to the increased divorce rate. Certainly at least some of the factors cited by Stone and Fine contributed to the changes in circumstances and attitudes that led ultimately to revision of the divorce laws. In addition, one hears voices in social settings that advocate lack of permanency as desirable in life, or that suggest people should have two or three marriages—one for early enjoyment, one for childbearing and child rearing, and a third to share the postlaunch period of life.

FAMILY SYSTEMS PERSPECTIVE

Just as a husband and wife usually were economically interdependent in earlier centuries, so even today family members have interdependent relationships in emotional as well as financial spheres of living. What affects one ultimately affects all family members, whether an event is happy or sad. They have mutual needs and mutual commitments, whether or not these are recognized as such. A widely held systemic view among family therapists is that causality is curvilinear rather than linear: What A does (or feels) affects B, C, and D, and their reaction in turn affects A (Bowen, 1978; Minuchin & Fishman, 1981). Feedback loops are recursive, according to Dell (1982), with relationships having a multidirectional impact. Further, as Satir (1964) indicated so appropriately, if one member of the family is in pain, all members feel the pain in some way. This is easily seen when one member is ill, and the others must rearrange their schedules to include hospital visits or stints of nursing care, or when one loses a job and all family members must then tighten their spending belts or earn (more) money to pick up the shortfall.

Similarly, if one spouse or child is unhappy, there are repercussions within the entire family unit. Each member may respond differently, with one becoming hostile and aggressive, another exhibiting a behavior problem in school; yet a third withdrawing. If one member then enters therapy, the family systems-oriented therapist seeks to involve all family members at some points in the therapeutic process. The goal is for them to realize their multigenerational interconnectedness (Ackerman, Beatman, & Sherman, 1961; Boszormenyi-Nagy & Spark, 1973/1984; Framo, 1992; Kaslow, 1987).

LIFE-CYCLE PERSPECTIVE

The author(s) of Ecclesiastes in the Bible delineated an "appointed time" for everything in life: "To everything there is a season" (Eccl. 3:1). Shakespeare poetically described the stages in human life. Erikson (1950) introduced a psychosocial view of seven developmental stages for the individual, Levinson (1978) described patterns in men's lives, and Carter and McGoldrick (1988) delineated a family life cycle with various stages: (a) Leaving home: single young adults; (b) the joining of families through new marriage: the new couple; (c) families with young children; (d) families with adolescents; (e) launching children and moving on; and (f) families in later life (p. 15).

Hughes, Berger, and Wright (1978) adopted a similar multi-stage model but, like Erikson (1950) in his approach to individual development, postulated that as "families successfully meet needs at each stage, they become prepared to meet and resolve the tasks of the next stage more easily" (Kaslow & Schwartz, 1987b, p. 15). The emphasis of Hughes et al., is on the need to modify and adapt behaviors to the varying needs of each stage, rather than trying to force the tasks to conform to a behavioral pattern that was appropriate at an earlier stage. Couples need to maintain flexibility rather than rigidity as they approach new situations and periods of transition.

The stages of the family life cycle begin with the merging of two people into a new couple unit upon marriage while each partner maintains some individuality and separate identity. This initial stage calls for mutual adjustment even if the couple has cohabited for months or years prior to marriage. At that juncture, a new agreement needs to occur that recognizes evolving responsibilities and more formalized relations with others as a unit rather than as two individuals who are romantically involved with each other. Rhodes (1977), like Carter and Mc-Goldrick (1988), sees early parenting as a second stage, beginning with the arrival of the first child and ending when the youngest child enters school. For most new parents, the shift from the relative flexibility of couplehood to the 24-hour-a-day responsibility of parenthood brings new challenges, and new potential arenas for conflict, as well as new joys. As the number of children increases, the couple may relax some of their earlier rules for and expectations of their children, but may still find each child's uniqueness at times disconcerting and demanding. Parental expectations also may become a source of manipulation by the children.

Carter and McGoldrick's (1988) third stage parallels the preadolescent and adolescent school years, as family members restructure their relationship in light of the new nonfamily ties the children form and the changing roles for the parents. Adolescence, well known as a time of rapid changes—physically and emotionally—also can evoke crises within the family constellation as the "teenagers become more involved in peer networks and the parents must determine how far and in which directions to shift from the earlier more dominant parental authority role" (Kaslow & Schwartz, 1987b, p. 14).

Using a multistage perspective, Storaasli and Markman (1990) did a longitudinal study of problems occurring in early marriage, beginning when the subject couples were engaged or planning (first) marriage. The data they obtained over several years reveal some variation in the most intense problems. In premarriage as well as during the first two stages of marriage, money ranked first as a problem area for the participant couples. Jealousy, on the other hand, moved from second place before marriage to seventh or eighth after marriage, when the relationship was on firm legal ground. The shifts in problem intensity in a variety of critical areas can be seen in Table 1.1.

Other specific problems cited by Storaasli and Markman (1990) revolved around recreation and alcohol/drugs. However, correlational analysis suggested "moderately strong agreement between male and female ratings of [which were the major] problems at each stage. . . . The exceptions for individual problem areas were recreation and friends at premarriage, religion at early marriage, and recreation and children at early parenting" (1990, p. 87). Each area cited has the potential to create stress in the couple's relationship simply because each member has brought to it divergent constellations of experiences and values, which may overlap for the two, and that have to converge to some degree if the relationship is to continue with reasonable harmony and a shared rhythm. As the authors noted, for example, children are not a principal problem area at the early parenting stage, but

TABLE 1.1
RANK ORDER OF PROBLEM INTENSITY AT
THREE STAGES OF RELATIONSHIP ($N = 40$)

	Premarriage	Early Marriage	Early Parenting
Money	1	1	1
Jealousy	2	7	8
Relatives	3	4	4
Friends	4	5	7
Communication	5	2	3
Sex	6	3	2
Religion	7	10	9
Children	8	6	6

Source: Adapted from "Relationship Problems in the Early Stages of Marriage: A Longitudinal Investigation" by R. D. Storaasli and H. J. Markman. *Journal of Family Psychology,* 4(1), pp. 86–87.

"Many parents would probably agree that children become more of a problem as they get older and differences in child rearing practices become more apparent" (p. 94).

Carter & McGoldrick's fifth stage, in which the children begin to move away from home and the family unit, may bring even greater difficulties to the parents, especially if the younger family members adopt values and life paths at variance with those of their parents. The separation-individuation efforts of the adolescents are mirrored to some extent by the parents' efforts to metamorphose into a stage as a couple alone together once again, but with 20 or more years of experiences, a shared family history, and presumably greater maturity. It is at this point that many couples who have stayed together "for the sake of the children" decide to separate. Those who remain together must then enrich their relationship, value their shared life story, find new common interests and bonds, and incorporate a changed relationship with their young adult children (and possibly the children's spouses, children, and in-laws), and perhaps with their own aging parents—or, again, the prospect of divorce increases. Long-term satisfying marriages are characterized by these and other essential ingredients like mutual trust, shared values, love and affection, and commitment to marriage and their spouses (Kaslow & Hammerschmidt, 1992; Kaslow, Hansson, & Lindblad, 1994). It should be remembered that the husband and wife are also concurrently having to adapt to their own personal and separate individual changes in psychosocial and physical development, which may be occurring at different tempos and with varying success or lack of same for each.

Rhodes (1977) views the final stage (i.e., Carter & McGoldrick's sixth stage, 1988) as moving from retirement to death, with yet another alteration in the marital and multigenerational bonds as family ties are strengthened or weakened, or as role reversal occurs should one or both of the elders become dependent on the child(ren) because of ill health, financial need, lack of emotional resourcefulness, or absence of a friendship network. In terms of an Eriksonian perspective (1950), this is the time of ego integrity versus despair, and can be a period of satisfaction with a life that has been productive and fulfilling.

Awareness of individual and family life-cycle perspectives as well as the dynamics of the family system are imperative, in our view, for any professional who is attempting to help one or both members of the marital couple to resolve their differences and avert divorce. This is discussed in some detail by Colarusso and Nemeroff (1981), who combined childhood and adult development histories with stage-specific developmental tasks in their approach to psychotherapy.

Yet another approach to examining the stages of adulthood is to consider the questions individuals may ask themselves as they move into and through adulthood. Just as the resolution of major psychosocial tasks at each stage affects the perception and resolution of these tasks at later stages (Erikson, 1950), so the answers to each question will affect questions and responses in later years. The questions (and their answers) are affected by individual differences in socioeconomic status, abilities and talents, physical health, self-perceptions, and relationships (especially with immediate family members) in earlier years. Table 1.2 highlights issues that lead to the questions at different stages.

Early adulthood, as defined by Colarusso and Nemeroff (1981), has been divided here into "Young Adulthood," a period in which many young adults are pursuing higher education and are still financially dependent on their parents, and "Gaining Maturity," when most young adults have already or are in the process of assuming those activities usually associated with being an adult: marriage or cohabitation, parenting, settling into a job or career, and financial self-sufficiency. The latter stage is now attained several years later than was true for this generation's parents, who were often married by age 20, parents by their mid-20s, and on a lifetime career track by their mid-20s. Marriage and parenting in the mid-1990s are often delayed until the late 20s or early 30s, sometimes later.

In "Middle Adulthood," the issue termed "In the middle" refers to the self-characterization of adults at this stage as being in the "sandwich generation." This refers to their status as parents of nonadult children and caretakers of their own aging parents. In the last stage, "Mature Adulthood," the perception of oneself as a senior citizen varies markedly from one individual to another. Some people see themselves as old or "over the hill" at age 55; others resist the label even in their 70s. Some mature adults make every effort to retain their independence; others become emotionally dependent on their children, thus reversing positions in the family constellation—usually to the distress of the younger members of the family.

TABLE 1.2
ADULTHOOD STAGES: ISSUES AND QUESTIONS

Young Adulthood (Ages 18–25/30)	Gaining Maturity (Ages 25/30–40/45)	Middle Adulthood (Ages 40/45–60/65)	Mature Adulthood (Ages 60 to 70+)
Issues	*Issues*	*Issues*	*Issues*
Higher education vs. career	Settling into a career	Career matters	Retirement
Marriage/cohabitation vs. singlehood	Intimate relations	Marital status	Living alone
Relations with parents	Parenting, if married	Parent-child relationships	Money
Self-integration	Relations with others	"In the middle"	Friendships
	Redefining the self	Social responsibilities	Past, present, and future
Questions	*Questions*	*Questions*	*Questions*
Where am I going and how do I get there (goals)?	Am I in the right job/career for me?	Do I stay in my job or change careers?	When do I retire? And to what?
Do I live with my parents, alone, or with someone else?	How do I relate to my parents as an adult?	How do I care for my parents, children, spouse, and self?	Can I live independently?
What is my sexual preference?	Am I assuming adult responsibilities effectively?	If married, do I want to stay with my spouse?	How will I manage financially?
Do I want/am I ready to marry now?	If married, am I ready to be a parent?	How do I relate to my adolescent and adult children?	If alone, do I have family and friendship networks?
What do I believe (values, ethics, and morals)?	Have my values changed?	How can I be an effective mentor?	Do I feel like a senior citizen?
Who am I (sense of self and identity)?	What are my goals now?	How do I contribute to society?	Can I cope with physical ailments?
		What are my current and long-term goals?	Does the past look better than the present?
			What activities will enrich my life?
			How do I deal with death (mine and that of others)?

IDIOSYNCRATIC FACTORS

In addition to the unique perspective each partner brings to the marriage simply by virtue of differing personalities, backgrounds, values, and experiences, even if the man and woman come from very similar socioeconomic and religious backgrounds, there are differences in attitude toward marriage, the marital relationship, parenting, and postparenting.

The differences may be more marked among different cultural groups. For example, one must consider whether the couple, or one of the partners, is a first-generation immigrant from a tightly knit ethnic or national group, or is more acculturated to the larger society by virtue of longer familial residence in the United States or other nation to which the family migrated. Support networks vary in different families of origin by culture (ethnicity, religion, race), by socioeconomic status, and by community setting (e.g., urban or rural) for marriage and parenting as well as for divorce. These differences will be examined in the following chapters and are also elucidated in a continuous case vignette.

CONCLUDING COMMENT

Both authors work from a family systems perspective and are mediation oriented, seeking to defuse conflicts between parties rather than to escalate them. In most cases, this means trying to help divorcing couples recognize that each of them has contributed to the marriage and to its dissolution in some ways, and that therefore neither can be regarded as totally in the "right" or "wrong." Such a conceptual stance moves beyond the legal conception of no-fault and encompasses some modicum of shared responsibility. We also share a deep commitment to the well-being of children of parting parents, believing that they should not be victimized by their parents' inability to remain together. No one can eliminate the pain of separation and divorce, but professionals can try to reduce this through examining each situation in a realistic and mature manner. They can encourage the adults not to be destructive to one another nor to embroil the children in their battle or pressure them to take sides (Kaslow, 1990b; Schwartz, 1994a).

PART II

Stages and Phases of the Separation and Divorce Process

"I DON'T WANT TO BE MARRIED to you anymore, so let's get a divorce" sounds simple and final. It is not. The effects on the respective partners and their children vary based on numerous factors such as age, gender, length of marriage, health, self-concept, and sociocultural background and influences. In addition, divorce entails legal and sometimes religious considerations, economic concerns, and possible therapy with one or both spouses, and/or the child(ren) at various points along the separation-divorce trajectory. The following chapters examine each aspect of marital dissolution that can make the parting more or less painful.

Part II provides a different perspective, delineating the stages and phases of the divorce process, each of which is addressed in a separate chapter. A glimpse is offered into predivorce situations that provoke the ultimate step, and the range of reactions that may occur among the concerned parties. Chapter 2 includes a table that elucidates the aspects and stages of the divorce process. The roles of mediation, litigation, and therapy during the divorce process are addressed as are the individual differences that influence how the process unfolds and is resolved.

A clinical case, which is a composite of several similar cases from the files of one author (FWK), is presented to illustrate how a family goes through the divorce process and the changes that occur with the passage of time. We purposely chose a case of a divorcing couple in their older years, with grown children, since most of the literature covers dissolutions by couples when their children are under 18 years of age; the older population and its dilemmas and needs in the face of divorce have been somewhat neglected.

CHAPTER 2

Separation and Divorce: An Overview

SEPARATION AND DIVORCE ARE TWO aspects of the marital dissolution process, sometimes occurring years apart. In almost every state (except Alaska, Iowa, Louisiana, Massachusetts, and South Dakota), given bona fide residency or domicile, there is a preestablished waiting period between the time the initial physical separation occurs and the granting of a divorce. In some states and countries, there is even a legal condition called "marital separation" (Elrod, 1995). "Quicky" divorces may be obtained after only a few weeks of separation in some jurisdictions, such as Nevada, while at the other extreme, Italian divorce law requires three years of legal separation (Ceschini, 1994). The length of the physical and/or legal separation period required may vary as well depending on whether the divorce is contested or uncontested.

CONTEMPLATING PARTING

In many marriages, the rift leading toward ultimate separation ferments in someone's thoughts year by year, often without conscious awareness on the part of either spouse. This has been called a "devitalized marriage" and may be characterized as one in which there is "a pretense to oneself and others of having interests in common, as well as a pretense that the bond existing between the couple is alive and viable" (Crosby, 1990, p. 324). It

19

might also be viewed as a "cumulative divorce"—a "slow-brewing and long-term gestation of conflict wherein the decision to divorce arises out of a long series of stresses" (Crosby, 1990, p. 325).

Shapiro (1984) postulated 33 steps on the road to divorce, the first of which he labeled "unhappiness or boredom," which may be unilateral or bilateral. One spouse or both may confide the nagging discomfort to a close, empathic friend or family member. Incidents occur and resentment smolders; interests diverge; little conversation is made beyond banal questions and comments; the formerly loving partners move on to differing wavelengths and no longer find elements of their lives in common. Moving ahead a few steps in Shapiro's sequence, one or both may seek pleasure in a new relationship. Perhaps they argue vehemently, but having heard similar loud voices in their families of origin, they believe that they are communicating effectively and normally rather than moving apart. Gottman, a psychologist who has written extensively on marriage and divorce, has indicated that when divorce happens, it is almost anticlimactic; the emotional divorcing had been going on long before the actual legal divorce was undertaken (Bernard, 1994).

It is possible that only one of the partners is thinking about separation; the other may be oblivious to the growing gap between them or simply expect that any distancing is a natural function of their both being busy with other commitments. Perhaps one partner feels that the marriage was a mismatch from the start and that it is time to undo the error. From another perspective, one spouse may perceive fidelity differently from the way the other does and may become deeply involved with a third party. Divorce may be the inevitable result, either by choice of the unfaithful spouse or because the betrayed partner discovers the affair and cannot live with the cheating partner.

Infidelity, even in midlife, raises many issues (see Kaslow, 1993a, 1994; Schwartz, 1994b). Kirschner and Kirschner (1994) have even likened the need for reassurance in men as their bodies change at midlife to the anxieties and self-doubts of the adolescent male, and the boy's struggle for separation and individuation. "According to evolutionary psychology, it is 'natural' for both men and women—at some times, under some circumstances—to commit adultery or to sour on a mate, to suddenly find a spouse unattractive, irritating, wholly unreasonable" (Wright, 1994, p. 46). From this point of view, women may have affairs not only to seek reassurance of their desirability, like men, but also to gain economic favors.

Glass and Wright (1994), marital therapists, have worked with many couples where an extramarital involvement was revealed during therapy or was the impetus for seeking therapy. Whether the marriage can recover from such a revelation varies with each couple. They assert:

> The depth of traumatic reaction will be related to the basic assumptions about the marriage, the level of deception, and the vulnerability of the betrayed spouse. The data does not support the systemic view that the betrayed spouse colludes and is aware about an ongoing EMI. When involved persons are discreet, compartmentalize their extramarital relationships, and maintain a loving relationship with their spouse, the disclosure is met with shock and disbelief. The noninvolved spouse whose suspiciousness has been met by repeated denials may find disclosure a relief at first because their reality has been validated, but the pain and anger created by repeated lies and deception will make recovery more difficult. (From an unpaged handout at the 1994 APA convention)

For many betrayed spouses, whether suspicious or unaware, the pain and anger, but probably even more, the destruction of basic marital trust that accompanies the discovery or disclosure will make recovery impossible and divorce inevitable. Others are able to resolve the issues that led one to have an affair, and divorce may be averted if the affairee can accept responsibility for his or her behavior and work to reestablish trust, accept the affair and what it meant, and move beyond it to rebuild a more fulfilling marriage (Pittman, 1989).

Yet another reason for considering divorce is that one partner finds the responsibilities of marriage and parenthood overwhelming. Perhaps there is a chronically ill or disabled child whose care demands most of one parent's time, and a job that demands most of the other parent's time, leaving literally little time for the couple to enjoy each other's company, or to unwind and relax. One parent may even be in denial of the child's condition, making the situation more difficult for both the other parent and the child (Barbero, 1995). Either partner may feel unable to continue in this mode for the indefinite future, whether because of frustration with the situation or immature inability to cope with it, and decide that his or her only option is to leave the marriage. Research indicates that having a disabled child can make the marriage either stronger or weaker (Yura, 1987), so that a decision to separate would seem to be based on additional factors within the individual or relationship.

Are there factors that make some marriages more vulnerable to dissolution than others? In a review of research from the 1980s, White (1990) found several such variables:

- Second marriage (especially where there are children).
- Divorce of the parents of one or both partners.
- Premarital cohabitation.
- Young age at marriage.
- Premarital childbearing.
- Childlessness.
- Race (higher frequency among blacks than whites).
- Low marital happiness.

Gottman (1994), working from a social psychophysiological perspective, has found that he can predict with approximately 95 percent certainty what the eventual fate of a marriage is likely to be. Some of the key factors he evaluates in making his predictions are:

- Relative distance and isolation.
- Problem-solving ability regarding conflicts.
- Affect.
- Pervasiveness of discord and rebound.
- The couple's view of their marital history.
- Diffuse physiological arousal (related to autonomic nervous system reactions).

"The idea is that *dysfunctional marital interaction consists of inflexibility and a constriction of alternatives*" (p. 37). From the data gathered, Gottman says that he can predict whether his subject couples are on a high- or low-risk pathway to marital dissolution.

Bohannon (1970) has labeled this period of disillusionment and drifting apart the *emotional* divorce in his six-stage model of the divorce process. It is his model that Kaslow has adapted, greatly revised, and expanded into a seven-phase process in her work on divorce since 1981. Table 2.1 depicts the model in its

TABLE 2.1
"DIACLECTIC" MODEL OF STAGES IN THE DIVORCE PROCESS

Phase	Stage and Aspects	Feelings	Behaviors and Tasks	Therapeutic Approaches	Mediation Issues
Predivorce: A time of deliberation and despair	I. Emotional Divorce	Disillusionment Dissatisfaction Alienation Anxiety Disbelief Despair Dread Anguish Ambivalence Shock Emptiness Anger Chaos Inadequacy Low self-esteem Loss Depression Detachment	Avoiding the issue Sulking and/or crying Confronting partner Quarreling Denial Withdrawal (physical and emotional) Pretending all is fine Attempting to win back affection Asking friends, family, clergy for advice	Marital therapy (one couple) Couples group therapy Marital therapy (one couple) Divorce therapy Couples group therapy	Contemplation of mediated vs. litigated divorce

(continued)

TABLE 2.1 (CONTINUED)

Phase	Stage and Aspects	Feelings	Behaviors and Tasks	Therapeutic Approaches	Mediation Issues
During Divorce: A time of legal involvement	II. Legal Divorce	Self-pity Helplessness	Bargaining Screaming Threatening Attempting suicide Consulting an attorney or mediator	Family therapy Individual adult therapy Child therapy	Set the stage for mediation-orientation session Ascertain parties' understanding of the process and its appropriateness for them
	III. Economic divorce	Confusion Fury Sadness, loneliness Relief Vindictiveness	Separating physically Filing for legal divorce Considering financial settlement Deciding on custody/visitation schedule	Children of divorce group therapy Child therapy Adult therapy	Define the rules of mediation Identify the issues and separate therapeutic issues from mediation issues Focus on parental strengths and children's needs, and formulating best possible coparenting and residential arrangement

Stage	Feelings	Tasks	Therapy	
IV. Coparental Divorce / Issues of Child Custody and Contact	Concern for children Ambivalence Numbness Uncertainty Fear of loss	Grieving and mourning Telling relatives and friends Reentering work world (unemployed woman) Feeling empowered to make choices	Same as above, plus family therapy	Negotiate and process the issues and choices Reach agreement Analyze and formalize agreement
V. Community Divorce	Indecisiveness Optimism Resignation Excitement Curiosity Regret Sadness	Finalizing divorce Reaching out to new friends Undertaking new activities Stabilizing new lifestyle and daily routine for children Exploring new interests and possibly taking new job	Adults Individual therapy Singles group therapy Children Child play therapy Children's group therapy	

(continued)

TABLE 2.1 (CONTINUED)

Phase	Stage and Aspects	Feelings	Behaviors and Tasks	Therapeutic Approaches	Mediation Issues
	VI. Religious Divorce	Self-doubt Desire for church approval Fear of God's displeasure or wrath	Gaining church acceptance Having a religious divorce ceremony administered Making peace with spiritual self	Divorce ceremony for total family Adult therapy Pastoral counseling	
Postdivorce: A time of exploration and reequilibration	VII. Psychic Divorce	Acceptance Self-confidence Energetic Self-worth Wholeness Exhilaration Independence Autonomy	Resynthesis of identity Completing psychic divorce Seeking new love objective and making a commitment to some permanency Becoming comfortable with new lifestyle and friends Helping children accept finality of parents' divorce and their continuing relationship with both parents	Parent-child therapy Family therapy Group therapies Children's activity group therapy	Return to mediation when changed circumstances require a negotiation of the agreement

Source: For earlier versions see Kaslow 1984, 1988, 1995b. Table periodically revised and expanded. Copyright © 1984 by F. Kaslow.

most recent amplification and lists the disappointment experienced in this predivorce period as well as the numerous other feelings that are apt to surface at this time. The term "diaclectic" was created by combining dialectic to convey synthesizing various ideas with eclectic, conveying the judicious selection of ideas from a variety of possible choices.

ATTEMPTS AT RECONCILIATION

Whether before the word divorce is mentioned or after, one or both members of the couple might suggest that they seek marital therapy in an effort to remedy their problems. Either might feel that it is too late for therapy, or they might make an ostensible effort—with or without a real desire to make the marriage work. Both parties have to be willing to explore options other than divorce and to learn new techniques for maintaining their relationship if therapy and/or an attempt at reconciliation is to be successful. As has been pointed out, "We have become a society obsessed with instant gratification. Why work at a relationship in which we've invested so much time and effort when it's so much easier to just walk out?" (Rothman, 1991, p. 101).

Marital therapists may see the partners individually and together, only as a couple and/or as part of a group of couples who are trying to save their marriages. They not only seek the sources of each partner's dissatisfactions, but try to help each spouse perceive these as well, suggesting they "put themselves in each other's shoes" as it were. In many marriages, there is conflict avoidance, a denial that there are difficulties. This is potentially as damaging as constant conflict, for the spouses are not communicating effectively. Part of the therapeutic effort must then be directed to teaching the couple communication and problem-solving skills, to enhancing their ability to perceive body language as well as spoken language conveying messages (see Hahleweg & Jacobson, 1984, and Jacobson & Gurman, 1986, for broad coverage on marital therapy).

The reasons for trying to reconcile differences are varied. There is, as attorney Rothman has indicated, a relationship in which much time and effort has been invested. Is it worth saving? Vestiges of the original affection may remain. Can they be restored and enhanced? There may be children in the family.

What is best for them? Absent abuse or a third party, are there more reasons to stay together than to part? In Rothman's opinion, "Unless your divorce can serve as a foundation for future growth and increased self-esteem, I believe that you are better off holding onto your present marriage" (1991, p. 103). We agree that it is certainly a serious consideration.

THE DECISION TO DIVORCE

The decision to seek a divorce may be unilateral or bilateral. If it is unilateral, the rejected spouse may have protested and sought a reconciliation without success. The circumstances for the one-sided decision may be clear (the partner has found a new love) or vague ("you no longer make me happy"), leaving the rejected spouse with a mass of negative feelings such as guilt, anger, self-doubt, and insecurity. After the initial shock has abated, he or she may agree that the situation is irremediable and can only end in divorce. If both spouses have discussed their unhappiness and come to the conclusion that parting will be less painful than remaining together, the negative emotions may still exist, but the shock may not be as great, and the sense of loss of control over one's destiny will not be as overwhelming.

Once one or both spouses decide to seek a divorce, whether or not they have children, many other decisions have to be made. Will the divorce be filed on specific grounds such as adultery, cruelty, or abandonment, no longer required in many states, or on the no-fault basis of irreconcilable differences? How will it be handled—through litigation, arbitration, or mediation? Who will move out of the marital residence? Will it need to be sold, and if so, how soon? Does the more affluent partner, assuming there is one, seek to conceal assets in order to retain them? (If the initial decision is unilateral by that partner, concealment may have begun well before the decision to divorce is revealed.) If the wife has not been employed outside the home during the marriage, from what sources will she derive funds to live on after the marriage is dissolved? If there are children, who will have primary responsibility for their care? What will be the division of financial responsibility for them? The response to each of these questions has legal, financial, and emotional ramifications for the couple, their children, and their families and friends.

Isaacs and Montalvo (1989) reported a case in which the couple "separated" while continuing to live in the same house. (*Note.* This is not uncommon in Eastern European countries where housing shortages are acute and there are waiting lists of many years for quarters to become available.) This arrangement can exacerbate hostility and create additional problems for the children or, more rarely, may be reassuring (if confusing) to the children about the love their parents have for them. The bewilderment stems from both parents being present physically although one does not eat with the other, they have separate bedrooms, and they do not go places together. The parents "may be afraid that they will lose the house and their rights to the children if they move out, a fear sometimes kindled by a lawyer who recommends that one spouse stay put in order to protect his or her rights" (p. 44) and to avoid being perceived as guilty of abandonment.

We have had similar cases that are motivated by the family's limited finances; there is simply not enough income to support two households. In one case (LLS), there was, fortunately, a second entrance to the family home that provided access to a room that the husband could use as bedroom and living room. The children, who were both under school age, could not understand the situation at all and were suffering great anxiety as to where and with whom they should be when. In a second case (LLS), the couple and their preschooler were sharing a two-bedroom apartment. Under these circumstances, Isaacs and Montalvo describe a deliberately staged confrontation that they, as therapists, create to force the issue "so that physical separation would appear a desirable alternative to an intolerable situation" (1989, p. 46). The parents are reminded of their responsibilities to their children, who might be better served by such a physical separation. Nonetheless, the family has to work within its own reality, and it may take months to work out a suitable and affordable separate living plan for both.

When the reason for neither party leaving is punitive (e.g., "You want the divorce and I don't, so why should I leave?") or legalistic (e.g., a lawyer advises someone not to move out because it could be construed as abandonment of children or as giving up some possible claim to the marital home), then the resulting tension in the physically shared home can be enormous and very detrimental to the children, as well as the adults. In such instances, therapists and mediators can help the bickering pair to weigh the legal benefits of such ploys against the emotional costs to all concerned.

PAINFUL PARTING: RECOGNIZING THE INEVITABLE

Children's Responses to Separation

Children's reactions to the initial separation of their parents vary considerably, depending on many factors. These include chronological age, cognitive (Piaget, 1926) and moral (Gilligan, 1982; Kohlberg, 1981) development levels of the child(ren) at the time, presence of siblings and their ages (or being an only child), suddenness of the separation (in the child's eyes), presence or absence of abuse or tension in the family prior to and during separation, depression and/or hostility of the parents, and nature and degree of support by each parent (and perhaps grandparents) for the children. Figure 2.1 depicts these influences.

It is also important to recognize that the length of time of the separation prior to divorce, or even to the filing of intent to divorce, may vary in duration, so that research findings on these factors may not be comparable in the sense that the studies were conducted at different points in the time sequence. Children's responses immediately following separation may or may not persist six months later, or a year later, during which the family is in a "separation" status rather than already "dissolved."

Locus of control is another factor that may be related to children's adjustment to their parents' divorce. A study by Fogas and colleagues (Fogas, Wolchik, Braver, Freedom, & Bay, 1992), with children a short time subsequent to their parents' separation illustrates the time factor problem. The 78 children, aged 8 to 15 years, and their primary residential parents "were interviewed within ten weeks of the date of filing the petition for divorce" (p. 590), but the "mean length of physical separation was 12.1 months" (p. 591). No range for the separation period was given, but presumably it could have been 1 month to 24 or more months from the time of separation to the date of filing. Children mature substantially over the longer period, their perceptions change with level of development, and memory of the early separation events is altered to some degree over a longer passage of time. The differences between 8-year-olds and 15-year-olds are also marked in all developmental and personality areas.

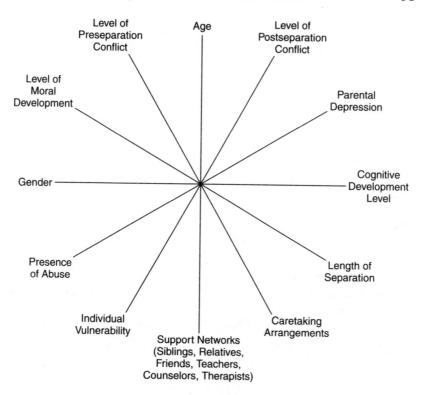

FIGURE 2.1
INFLUENCES ON CHILDREN'S PERCEPTION OF DIVORCE
(COPYRIGHT © 1995 L. L. SCHWARTZ.)

When the father "takes off," abandoning his wife and children, there is a real sense of loss for the children, particularly for the sons. This was described in a poignant essay by a mature professor:

> Fatherless boys gaze at the coach or scoutmaster with more than the hope of instruction. They look for approval of the ball dropping through the basket or of the merit badge earned with a bridge made of string and twigs. They hear, under the casual voice of instruction or the brief special attention focused by the mentor of the moment, a possible promise of filling a greater need. For the fatherless boy is ever seeking his lost father or the replacement who might stroll into his world. (Ray, 1994, p. 32)

Wallerstein and Kelly (1980) found, not surprisingly, that the children's adjustment is highly correlated with the parents'

adjustment. If the parents handle the grief and mourning associated with the separation well, do not malign the other parent,
and move on to recuperate and "survive the breakup," so, too,
will the children. If the adults continue the battle postdivorce
and remain embroiled in charges and countercharges, the children's recovery is severely impeded. This subject is elaborated
further in Chapter 7.

Parental Alienation Syndrome

There are, tragically, embittered parents who try to estrange
their children from the other parent. With some younger children, the alienating efforts of the caretaking parent may be combined with the child's anger at the absent parent. This young
child, who may not be capable of understanding why the one
parent has left the home (and him or her), feels abandoned and
strikes out, often expressing him- or herself by screaming "I
hate . . . [Dad or Mom]!" The alienating parent then defends her
actions (if it is the mother), such as denying visitation, based on
"respecting" the child's wishes. Gardner (1985, 1992), and Kelly
(1994) have termed this a parental alienation syndrome (PAS),
describing it graphically as a kind of programming or brainwashing. In some cases, the parent and child reinforce each
other's behavior, leading to a vicious circle that "becomes self-
reinforcing, complex to diagnose, and difficult to terminate"
(Cartwright, 1993, p. 208).

It should be noted that young children, fearful of being abandoned, may unwittingly contribute to this vicious cycle. For example, the 4-year-old who tells his father that the refrigerator is
empty and asks him to bring over some sandwiches, may precipitate a perception that the mother is spending support money
frivolously.

> From this perspective, it appears that the child, in attempting to
> get his or her needs met, initiates and participates in a behav-
> ioral sequence that results in overt parental conflict. The child's
> action is neither clearly willful nor clearly an instance of vic-
> timization, but partly both—hence the term *innocent but func-
> tional contributor*. (Saposnek, 1983, p. 120)

Although the anger and bitterness of the alienator may be
served in some ways, the children, especially some of the older

ones, may suffer an acute sense of loss, pain, guilt, and anger at one or both parents for putting them in such a position. Whether or not they are aware of the nasty nature of the parental brainwashing, the children tend to be deprived of contact with the absent parent or, if they do spend time with him or her, are miserable during the entire visit. The poisoning of the relationships with both the target of this manipulation (the nonresidential parent) and possibly the extended family of that parent may result in permanent damage to those important relationships as well as to the emotional stability and self-esteem of the children, who perceive themselves as being flawed because one of their progenitors (or adoptive parents) was or is such a horrible person. In extreme cases, the children are virtually being given permission by the programming parent to be manipulative of and disrespectful toward others, whether family members, peers, or teachers. In the long term, the children, as adults, may realize what was done to them and what they have lost in familial ties over the years, and suffer serious emotional distress at a later time, or turn against the residential parent for instilling hatred into their hearts and minds.

The success of the parental alienation depends on the time available for the parent to engage in this behavior and the vulnerability of the individual child, but it tends to be more effective with preteen and early teenage children who have psychological problems at the time of the separation, who are more dependent, and who have low self-esteem than with very young children or older adolescents. The time factor is now recognized as a critical element in parental brainwashing. The more delays in resolving child custody issues, the longer the bitter parent has to accomplish the estrangement. The alienator often "buys" time by making false allegations of sexual abuse against the other parent, "by assertions the child is in danger from contact with the lost parent, and by requests to the court for delays, continuances, and postponements" (Cartwright, 1993, p. 210). This is one reason custody arrangements should be settled by the court as early as possible in the separation/divorce proceedings; prompt decisions reduce the time available for the alienation process to occur. Lund (1995) asserts, "Time is of the essence in dealing with problems that may lead to PAS. If contact is stopped between a parent and a child, a pattern is likely to develop such that it will be difficult to mend the relationship" (p. 314).

One effort to forestall such alienation, with its concomitant ongoing litigation, is the program of the Family Negotiation Center of Central Indiana. Its program "was developed to address the needs of parents and children caught in the cycle of litigation and to break that cycle through education, negotiation, and counseling. Goals of the program are (a) to reduce court appearances; (b) to reduce parental conflict; and (c) to teach negotiation skills to families in conflict" (Hoff & Kramer, 1992, p. 34). Actually, judges may elect to refer families to the Center at any point in the divorce process. The entire process of initial assessment, counseling or negotiation, and monitoring a family may take several weeks or months. Some parents, particularly those who are substance- or person-abusers, may be required to attend therapy sessions. If they are not compliant with that order, they are referred back to the court where they may be held in contempt for their refusal. However, "when judges insist that visitation issues be agreed upon first and separately from financial settlements, a clear message is sent that children are more important than property or money" (Hoff & Kramer, 1992, p. 36). This is a most commendable point of view. In 63 percent of the closed cases, parents reported, "Conflicts have been reduced and children have exhibited improved behavior at home and in school" (Hoff & Kramer, 1992, p. 37). On the other hand, if efforts such as these are not introduced early, it may be almost impossible to bring the parties together for the kind of negotiation that is truly in the best interests of their children.

Another possible avenue to forestalling PAS is to have legislative and judicial support for development of a "parenting plan" (Tompkins, 1995). Such a plan emphasizes parental responsibility and residential care rather than "custody." It "addresses the specific functions of parenting and distributes responsibility for these functions to either one parent or the other, or both" (p. 292). Provision is also made for renegotiation of these responsibilities, usually through mediation, if needed in the future.

Florida has recently introduced a "Children First" program that divorcing parents are required to attend before the final divorce is granted (Dissolution of Marriage—Children Act, 1982) (see Appendix B for most recent revision of this Act). It stresses that the welfare of children must be the prime consideration of both parents and elaborates why this is so.

Coping Alone

Life is different when one adult is suddenly left alone. If the marriage is ending because one partner has had an affair and prefers to continue that relationship, he or she is moving into a new situation with positive expectations. The rejected spouse, on the other hand, initially has sleepless nights, loss of appetite or alternatively eating binges to compensate for the loss, a high risk for illness and accidents, difficulty concentrating, feelings of impotence about control over his or her life, and total bewilderment about what to do next. Individual therapy or, at minimum, participation in a support group is strongly recommended to minimize these effects and to maximize coping and planning skills (see Table 2.1, Therapeutic Approaches column).

The separation phase prior to the legal divorce is a critical time as the individual attempts to deal with the trauma (or pleasures for some) of marital dissolution and to reconstruct a lifestyle. Not only does the world suddenly look altered to the person who is alone, but that person also looks different to the world. Has he or she been revealed as a spouse abuser? As an abused spouse? As a roué or acting-out flirt? As untrustworthy? As naively trusting? To what extent do others help the one alone to recover? Does the abandoned one want to recover, or is he or she so depressed and self-pitying that contemplation of an independent future is impossible? Or is recovery impeded by the rejected spouse taking on anger and revenge as a raison d'être?

In rebuilding a life, or creating a new one, the individual has to be cognizant of his or her assets, social and vocational as well as financial; (e.g., appealing personality, attractive appearance, cash reserves) and of weaknesses (e.g., lack of work experience). Living arrangements, budgets, and employment are matters of practical concern. If there are children, arrangements must be made for their care and supervision while the residential parent is at work. In an increasing number of workplaces, usually larger companies, on-site child care centers are being provided that enable the parent-employee to be with the child for brief periods during the workday. This tends to reduce anxiety for both parties.

In a study of white and African American divorced and married fathers, 47 percent of whom had at least one child under age

18, Umberson and Williams (1993) analyzed psychological distress symptoms and alcohol consumption. The divorced fathers reported substantially greater strain in their parental role than the married fathers. Child care and child support were principal reasons for this among those divorced fathers with minor children, especially those who were not the primary residential parent, while fathers of adult children had less control over contact with their children. The very concept of being a "visiting" parent rather than an "in house" one upset these now-single fathers, while the responsibility for taking care of infants and preschoolers during visits overwhelmed many of them.

> The most important reason for thoughtfully considering the experience of fathers in divorce is not merely fairness to fathers. . . . It is to advance the welfare of children. . . . To better enlist fathers in advancing the welfare of children, therefore, it is essential to understand the obstacles and difficulties men experience in their efforts to remain involved and to appreciate why so many men abdicate their responsibilities to children after divorce. (Thompson, 1994, p. 211)

Thompson advocates that more effort be expended on facilitating ongoing interaction between the parents to emphasize their continuing obligation to their children rather than stressing the need to make a "clean break" after marital dissolution. He also points out that a major obstacle to their fulfilling their role as fathers is their uncertainty about the expectations, responsibilities, and options of that role. He is, if a visiting parent, a "parent without portfolio. . . . He often feels unneeded, cut off from the day-to-day issues in the child's life that provide the continuing agenda of the parent-child relationship" (p. 222). Stipulated times for contact, as in visitation schedules, further strain interactions with children, and often put the father in the position of being a "Disney Dad" or "Sunday Santa." (Some of the resulting problems could be reduced by frequent telephone contacts, letters, or audio- or videotapes that the father and child exchange—any of which may be initiated by either party.) Geography is another obstacle to maintaining that relationship, as distance (plus economic factors) may preclude frequent visits. Small wonder that some fathers feel at a disadvantage in relating to their children, even when, as many studies have shown, they are competent caregivers for infants as well as older children. Nonetheless, if the visitation/contact schedule is not pre-dictable, no one can plan and stability is further disrupted as too much is left to whim.

Midlife Divorce

As noted earlier, people live longer today, outlasting what used to be the normal marriage span. This is seen as a factor in the in-creasing number of mid- and later-life divorces. The transition to perceiving oneself as middle-aged or in midlife can be shat-tering to many people, precipitating the marriage dissolution.

> The middle-aged person . . . at the height of his or her powers, looks downward toward inevitable decline and limitations, and questions plans made, dreams deferred. The self-examination and reevaluation of life decisions that emanate from the aware-ness of middle age and of limited time inevitably have reper-cussions in the marital relationship. (Maltas, 1992, p. 123)

Instead of marriages ending in less than three decades by rea-son of death due to childbirth or illness, as occurred in earlier generations, they have the potential to continue for six or more decades. The sex-stereotyped roles of early marriage and par-enthood become less appropriate for many couples in the 50-plus age bracket. In some cases, communication is minimal; values and interests are no longer shared; there seem to be no reasons to stay together. As the children of the family reach late adoles-cence or young adulthood, and move out of the parental home, one or both spouses may recognize that the children provided the only glue or shared interest holding the marriage together.

Perhaps their earlier expectations of the marital relationship had diverged years ago, and even couples therapy cannot reunite them. One partner may be dreaming of a new (more relaxed?) life in retirement, while the other is looking forward to fewer do-mestic responsibilities but a long overdue chance to embark on or expand a career of some sort or engage in exciting new activi-ties. The disparity in dreams seems resolvable only by dissolving the marriage. Separation and divorce no longer bear the stigma that they did when these older couples married in midcentury—a second factor in the higher rate of these divorces. A third factor is the liberalization of divorce laws over the past 20 to 25 years. Dubin (1993) quotes a number of attorneys and social agency personnel who attest to the increase in their client case loads of middle-aged and older individuals who have chosen divorce over continuing in unfulfilling marriages.

CONTROVERSIES IN RECENT DIVORCE RESEARCH

Often, researchers in different studies come out with conflicting results. Not only do they have different-size samples, but the characteristics of the study populations may be highly dissimilar and the questions asked or data gathered may have varying bases. For example, studies of the effects of women's participation in the labor force on marriage (or divorce rates) are inconclusive (White, 1990). The "simple" matter of whether wives' employment contributes to higher divorce rates is really not so simple. As White has indicated, "Better attention to various dimensions of women's status (wages, hours, economic and social autonomy) and to the family processes involved (quarrels over the division of labor, and so on) are necessary to resolve this issue" (1990, p. 908).

Similarly, it is difficult to integrate the findings of studies that depend on court records from limited geographic areas, or from personal accounts. Many of the latter focus on factors that have been less studied in relation to divorce: "alcoholism and drug abuse, infidelity, incompatibility, physical and emotional abuse, disagreements about gender roles, sexual incompatibility, and financial problems" (White, 1990, p. 908). These reasons need not be stated in divorce records today, especially since it is possible to file on grounds of "irreconcilable differences." Furthermore, there is a need to study the interaction of a number of these factors across socioeconomic and ethnic groups if meaningful conclusions are to be drawn.

A third consideration is the point in the separation process at which the research subjects are at the time of a study. Studies of newly separated parties (or their children) provide quite different results from those done with people separated a year or more or those who are newly divorced and moving into the next phase of life. Many of the findings within the first three months after separation about problems of physical and mental health, financial status, and lifestyle may be ameliorated within three months after divorce, depending on how long it takes to reach

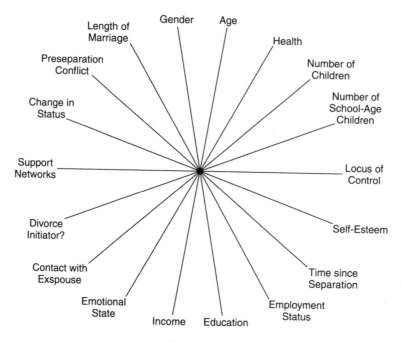

FIGURE 2.2
FACTORS AFFECTING THE DIVORCED
(COPYRIGHT © 1995 L. L. SCHWARTZ.)

that state of dissolution. These factors should be considered when seeking to understand the research literature on divorce.

Finally, a fourth area of concern has to do with the characteristics of the sample in terms of chronological age of the parties, length of marriage, presence or absence of minor children, socioeconomic status, and cultural background. Even here, one must be alert to whether a 2- or a 10-year marriage, for example, involves parties first married in their teens, 20s, 30s, or later. Or might one or both members of the couples be in a second or third marriage? Each combination of variables engenders different contexts and configurations for examining divorce, much as varying the quantities and kinds of ingredients in a recipe will result in different flavors in a stew (see Figure 2.2).

CHAPTER 3

Individual Differences and Their Impact on Resolution

DEPENDING ON THE CIRCUMSTANCES surrounding a marital dissolution, people may experience a variety of effects on their physical health, their psychological well-being, and their ability to relate to others. For some, the release from an unhappy and/or abusive marriage may be such a relief that they are reenergized and virtually ebullient. For others, the separation and divorce may be mind-numbing, depressing, and anxiety-producing (particularly if there are children, economic concerns, or fear of loneliness and feelings of worthlessness). To some degree, the effects may be shaped by the individual's self-image, gender, age, family of origin experiences, and sociocultural background, as shown in Figure 2.2 in the previous chapter.

SELF-IMAGE

If one member of the dissolving couple is rejected by the other, whether in favor of a new partner or for other reasons, what does that do to the self-image of the rejectee? Typically, the rejected partner feels unlovable, a failure in a major aspect of adult life. After all, from one point of view:

> Marriage can be thought of as a contract to affirm each spouse's sense of self and self-worth, though often in ways that are

paradoxically painful and growth-inhibiting. The mate must be able to affirm that one is lovable and worthy in the face of threats to self-esteem or to lend him- or herself to idealization. (Maltas, 1991, p. 569)

Whatever other emotions may emerge—anger, resentment, sorrow—the fact is that the person with whom the rejectee has chosen to share a major portion of their adult life has said, in effect, "You are unworthy of my time and my affection." The spurned person's self-image is consequently devastated, at least for some time.

The rejectors, on the other hand, perceive themselves as in control of the present and the future, able to make choices, perhaps at last able to satisfy their own wishes without regard for anyone else's desires. For those who are narcissistic, the act of rejecting their spouse seems to create no feeling of guilt or remorse (Kernberg, 1975). For those not so self-centered, there may be some awareness of and concern about the negative impact of the act on others. If there is a third party involved, feelings of being wanted by a new partner add to the rejector's positive self-image as being a fine and desirable person.

For the therapist, a major initial (and continuing) task may be to help the rejected partner develop a more positive self-image that is focused on being able to cope, to regroup, to be resilient, to move forward. Woven into the new pattern will be both the strengths and skills of the individual that existed before the marriage dissolved and the strengths being cultivated or accentuated in therapy.

GENDER

Just as males and females have different activities as children, when they reach adulthood, they typically perceive the world through different lenses. Carol Gilligan made that point clearly in her studies of moral development (1982), in which she was able to demonstrate that boys tended to make judgments based on a "law and order" perspective while girls focused more on relationships and needs. It is therefore no surprise that women and men have different expectations of and experiences in marriage and divorce.

On the physical level, for example, Hetherington has found that women are concerned with the quality of the sexual relationship while men are concerned with the frequency or quantity of sexual activity (Hetherington & Tryon, 1989). On another level, men's view of themselves as the "strong, silent type" may be perceived by their wives as lack of communication. Women tend to express their feelings, which their husbands may then perceive as nagging and whining.

In a series of longitudinal studies, Hetherington (1989) found two patterns that predicted the disintegration of a marriage:

> The first was the existence of a pursuing-distancing pattern in the relationship, in which one person indicates a complaint, to which the other responds by whining, denying the charges, or withdrawing. . . .
>
> The second pattern predicting divorce . . . , [occurred] in marriages with little overt conflict but significant differences between spouses in their expectations and perceptions about family life, marriage, and their children. Although these couples agreed about almost nothing, they actively avoided conflict, frequently leading parallel, but disengaged, social lives. (p. 59)

These patterns are also delineated in Gotman's recent work (1994), and in the bestsellers *Men Are from Mars, Women Are from Venus* (Gray, 1992) and *You Just Don't Understand: Women and Men in Conversation* (Tannen, 1990), which focus on the communications differences in depth.

The impact of divorce on these individuals, already so different in their perceptions of marriage, is again dissimilar. Where there are children, the wife is usually the primary physical and emotional caretaker and resident parent after the separation. The single parenting functions increase her responsibilities, while the resources she has to deal with this critical task are likely to decrease. She has less discretionary time, while her former husband has more. (Obviously, if the father is the primary caretaker of the children, this situation is reversed.) As Weitzman (1985), Kurz (1995), and others have found, her economic status tends to worsen, while his is either unaffected, changes far less than hers, or continues to improve.

In Hetherington's study (Hetherington & Tryon, 1989), some women found they had more resilience and more competence after working through the trauma of the separation than they had previously known, while she did not find similar qualities in nonremarried men. Women's friendship networks tend to change after divorce, with somewhat less contact with married friends because of mutual feelings that they have less in common than they did formerly (Guttmann, 1993). The single female is much more apt to feel like a "fifth wheel" with married couples than is the single male, who may be courted as a prospective date for their other single female friends.

In an Australian study, Jordan (1988) found that men whose marital breakup was instigated by the wife responded to separation and divorce differently from women in a similar situation. The men tended to seek a reconciliation and often saw themselves as powerless victims. Their sense of victimization might also lead them to view society as a source of injustice since it tends to focus on women as needing shelter, benefits, and legal assistance, but it does not provide these services for men. Initially, the men tended to have more difficulties in performing routine household chores, in making new friends and developing enduring intimate relationships, in concentrating on their work, and in saving money. One or two years later, they had more positive feelings, and fewer problems with daily living tasks as well as with financial matters than during the initial postdivorce stage.

Divorced men who are not emotionally involved with another person, particularly those who lose their parenting role, apparently engage in more health-compromising behavior, both physical and mental, than men in any other status (Umberson & Williams, 1993). Increased drinking and risk-taking behaviors, as well as higher rates of suicide are reported in several studies of divorced men (Guttmann, 1993). Divorced fathers of very young children seem to be especially ill-prepared to cope with their new situation, although they may be quite comfortable with their school-age children. These fathers need to learn nurturing and homemaking skills or hire a nanny/housekeeper to assist them if no female relative is available to help with the children.

One additional gender difference that must be recognized is the existence of gender bias in the courts. In a review of state and federal studies on this issue, Czapanskiy (1993) found:

State reports document substantive gender bias problems [in favor of the male] in areas such as custody, alimony, child support, abuse and neglect proceedings, and domestic violence actions. The reports also document gender bias problems in the process of litigation, that is, the ways that judges and male lawyers treat women lawyers and litigants. (pp. 248–249)

If a woman is a victim of spousal abuse and seeks not only protection but also a divorce from her abuser, she may be hampered in both efforts by a lack of funds with which to pay an attorney to represent her, and may not be helped by a court that refuses to order the husband to pay her temporary support and legal fees (Czapanskiy, 1993, pp. 250–251, n. 11). During the time she is trying to escape from an intolerable relationship, he may harass and/or continue to abuse her in an effort to maintain control and coerce her into keeping the marriage together as he cannot tolerate rejection or loneliness, and he may view her as his "property" and therefore not as someone entitled to leave him. If the threats, abuse, or harassment are severe, she may need to obtain a protective restraining order from a court. Sometimes such an order infuriates him and incites him to increased violence.

Cases have been cited in the media as well as the professional literature where the mother has either lost child custody or was forced to permit the abusive ex-spouse to have access to the children, often unsupervised, despite his documented physical or substance abuse behavior. The existence of judicial gender bias has an impact on the individual and, if present in a specific divorce matter, can cause additional grief, depression, and hardship on that individual.

SOCIOECONOMIC, RACIAL, AND RELIGIOUS FACTORS

Traditions and attitudes regarding marriage and divorce vary with religion, community mores, race, socioeconomic status, education and occupation, and country of origin as well as with the era in which one lives. Sometimes two or more of these factors interact to influence the individual, and may even conflict to some degree. The effect of these variables on marital quality and marital dissolution has not been studied as extensively as might be expected, especially among those of the red (Native Americans), yellow (Asians), and brown (Polynesian) races.

Nonetheless, some studies that have been conducted bear mentioning here.

"Since attitudes toward marriage and divorce are similar for blacks and whites, but rates of divorce are higher for blacks," Broman speculates that "there may be race differences in marital well-being, which may portend observed race differences in marital dissolution" (1993, p. 725). As might be expected, he found that within the black group poorer educational and financial status and potential than was true for whites (socioeconomic status) adversely affected marital quality, but so did less positive expectations brought to the marriage. Broman did not find that spousal emotional support, household task performance, or financial satisfaction explained the lower marital well-being of blacks, but estimated from his data that "Race has a direct impact on these intervening factors, and differing levels of spousal support and financial satisfaction by race have an impact on marital well-being" (p. 729).

Socioeconomic status affects black marital well-being differentially, as those at a higher income level are found to be working more hours to support less affluent family members, or expending time and emotional energy to integrate their family into the larger social environment. At the other end of the socioeconomic spectrum, poor couples may stay together despite marital discontent and strife to access any support that is available, particularly if there are children in the home. Broman (1993) concluded that this may be more true for black than for white couples at a similar socioeconomic level both because the former's income tends to be lower than the latter's, and because blacks are more likely to disapprove of divorce when there are young children.

In marriages at both the lower and upper socioeconomic rungs of the economic ladder, there may be unions that persist because the wife, no matter what her educational background, has no personal experience in the world of work. She perceives her chances of finding a job that pays enough to support her as virtually nil. She may therefore tolerate a less than satisfactory marriage for many years rather than lose her husband's economic support. When divorce does come, particularly if in midlife, she is not only ill-prepared to manage economically, but may have few prospects of being hired even if she acquires adequate training.

Religious views of divorce, ranging from liberal to prohibi-
tive, also affect the individual's reaction to marital dissolution.
Some people will remain in an unhappy marriage as "the lesser
of two evils" when compared with becoming estranged from
their religious practices. Atheists and agnostics, or those following a less conservative faith, on the other hand, may not have
to consider religious consequences as an added difficulty in divorce (see Chapter 8 for more on this variable).

Yet another group to be considered is the extended family.
One of our clients recalled being told quite firmly and proudly
by her then brand-new mother-in-law, "There's *never* been a divorce in this family!" Over the subsequent quarter-century,
three of her husband's cousins dissolved their marriages, and
in the client's case, it was her husband who initiated the move
to divorce, not she. So much for respect for the family "tradition." In other cases, the family of origin does not want to be
"embarrassed" in front of the neighbors (or at their church) by
a child's divorce, so pressure is put on the unhappy partner to
"stick it out." The family seems to disregard that the parent(s)
may be asking a terribly discontented or abused person to remain in an untenable situation, to spare them confronting the
anxiety about their own image.

PHYSICAL HEALTH

Family therapists and medical doctors alike are aware that the
shock of marital separation renders some of their patients
highly vulnerable to illness, and may so advise them. The crisis may make the individual's immune system less resistant,
for varying periods of time depending on their preseparation
health and stress history, to assaults by the assorted illness-
causing elements in the environment, so that more attention
needs to be paid to possible exposure to them. As Kressel
(1985) has indicated, a number of studies have shown that rates
of ill health and disability tend to be higher for the separated
and divorced than for individuals who were never married or
who were widowed. "Whether these health-related difficulties
are regarded as predating the divorce, as a reflection of the
stresses to which divorced persons are exposed, or as some

combination of the pre- and postdivorce conditions, they nonetheless constitute an additional source of stress in their own right" (Kressel, 1985, p. 46).

One element that is all too rarely considered in divorce is the physical health and well-being of the parties. In fact, our review of the indexes in several books written on divorce in the past decade failed to yield even one reference to (chronic) physical disability, except for the previously mentioned increased vulnerability to illness. There were few references to health insurance coverage except in the context of the ineligibility of a former spouse to continue participation in the plan that provided her coverage during the marriage beyond a mandatory extension period (usually 18 months) to allow her time to secure alternative insurance.

If one of the partners has a chronic health or disability problem, such as cystic fibrosis or multiple sclerosis, divorce evokes myriad issues not confronting healthier couples. At any age, there is a question of who will provide needed care for an ailing individual. For example, a not uncommon dilemma brought to a therapist is a case where one spouse's health continues deteriorating after a serious stroke or a spinal cord injury. After years of being the supportive partner, the caregiving spouse has reached the point where he or she has run out of sympathy, empathy, patience, and willingness to remain "tied" to an invalid while "life passes me by." Realizing the disdain others may hold for him or her for abandoning the needy spouse, even after many years of virtual servitude, and even working through in therapy the moral issue of treating the spouse as one would wish to be treated if the situation were reversed (see Kohlberg, 1981, on moral development), the drained partner sees divorce as the only recourse for his or her own survival. The therapist has to help such clients deal with the short- and long-term repercussions of a decision to leave. If they are still determined to take this step, they need to discuss the decision with the incapacitated spouse (and children), and make the best possible plans with and for him or her, absent their own presence.

Another scenario may be that the physically healthy mate decides to stay but withdraws emotional support from the ill or handicapped spouse. Such a withdrawal may exacerbate symptoms and contribute to serious depression and even suicidal ideation or attempts at self-destruction. The ill partner may come to feel so guilty of imprisoning the spouse that he or she believes death is the only solution.

If one spouse has a major life-threatening condition such as cancer or a heart condition and the other is either unwilling to cope with the situation or to take the drastic step of divorce, he or she may turn to a third party or become completely immersed in an outside activity or career for his or her comfort or escape. When this happens, the sick spouse's feelings of being rejected and undesirable will be increased tremendously.

If a divorce eventuates, in addition to the practical aspects of care for the nonhealthy ex-spouse, there are other considerations. Lifetime alimony is rarely awarded today, making support of the physically disabled in the long term a serious question. If a home has been modified to meet the needs of this person, will he or she have enough funds to stay there after the divorce, or might the home (if it is a house or family-owned apartment) be sold as the major or sole marital asset so that the parties can split the proceeds of the sale? At least one state, Indiana, in its no-fault statute "authorizes indefinite maintenance only where a spouse: (1) is physically or mentally incapacitated . . ." (Starnes, 1993, p. 99). This is also a provision in the Uniform Marriage and Divorce Act (UMDA), but states vary in the provisions of the UMDA that are incorporated in their own statutes. "Authorizes" becomes a key term, as "maintenance is not mandatory but depends on the discretion of a trial court" (Starnes, 1993, p. 99). In addition to the financial concerns, a corollary issue is how the individual's physical problems will affect selection of a primary caretaker for any minor children. If a partially disabled 30-plus mother of young children is divorced by her husband, does she have a chance to be the primary residential parent, and if awarded custody, can she manage without live-in child-care help? The answer to this question *should* depend on the extent to which she is able to care for herself as well as others, not on the simple diagnosis of disability.

On the other hand, if it is a child who is physically or mentally incapacitated and the primary caretaking parent must forgo employment to care for the child, the UMDA and the Indiana statute both authorize indefinite maintenance for the parent, although again this is at the discretion of the trial court

(Starnes, 1993). What must a departing-parent be like who would want to shirk all responsibility in such a situation?

In the case of ill, nonemployed wives who have been covered by their husband's medical insurance (or vice versa), there is a major concern about maintaining such coverage. However, "A dependent spouse can look to the Consolidated Omnibus Budget Reconciliation Act (COBRA—a federal requirement that the employer carry the spouse for a short time), but, after that, difficulties arise" (Schackman, 1994, p. 121), as the spouse may be unable to acquire or afford comparable insurance. For those who have a disability but are employed, it may not be available through their employer. Many employed partners are not willing to continue to pay premiums "for life" for an ex-spouse; it seems to them to be a lifelong sentence. Since the replacement cost of medical insurance, particularly when moving from a group policy to an individual one is very high, especially as the individual ages, this item needs to be considered in reaching an economic settlement that is fair to both parties.

Employed divorcées who are insured at their workplace may well feel the need to purchase additional insurance policies, such as disability income protection, since they no longer have the ex-husband's insurance as backup. Again, this becomes an additional expense to be taken from reduced funds.

Divorced men, 65 years and older, tend to have poorer physical health and higher mortality rates than their married counterparts. This is alleged to stem from two factors: first, ". . . they are without a spouse to provide the quality of care that later life married men seem to experience. Second, after divorce, men may have fewer contacts and a lower quality of relationship with their children" (Hennon & Brubaker, 1994, p. 54). The fact of this higher risk status may also make some older men less attractive to widows and divorcées as potential new mates, because many women tend to be reluctant to assume the role of a nurse to someone they will have known as a spouse for a relatively short time. However, if the man is extremely wealthy and appears to be generous, or is well-known and respected, he may still be deemed a desirable mate.

As already noted, little attention is paid to the health-illness and medical insurance issues in most mental health writings on divorce. (The insurance issues are covered in the family law literature.) Even less attention has been given in research to the whole matter of physical illness in relation to divorce, with the exception of vulnerability to illness early in the separation. If one of the parties is chronically ill, then this factor should certainly have high priority in any discussions of economic and child custody issues as the couple moves to divorce. Indeed, in New York, one of the criteria for determining equitable distribution is the health of each party (Schackman, 1994). Until everyone in our nation is guaranteed adequate health care, divorcing parties must attend to the cost of providing coverage of this need in their final agreements.

LENGTH OF MARRIAGE

"She (He) isn't the same person I married!" This lament by the departing marital partner, especially after years of marriage, might be humorous if it were not that the lamenter really believes that the partner should not have changed (and that he or she certainly has not). Two people can scarcely live together for a period of months or years without having an effect on each other's thoughts, behaviors, and feelings. So do life circumstances, the normal passages in one's development, and deliberate efforts to make changes. It cannot be otherwise if one is not frozen in time and space.

Just as individuals are affected in their development by a variety of internal and external factors, so are marriages and their dissolution. The duration of a marriage certainly has an impact on the people involved, if only because in longer marriages the people tend to have invested more of their feelings, energies, hopes, dreams, and expectations. Even those leaving short-term marriages may have invested a great deal of themselves only to end up feeling rejected or betrayed. When this is the case, they may swear off marriage as an institution forevermore. Most change their minds eventually as indicated by high remarriage statistics, but initially the bitterness makes such a prospect seem remote.

If the brief marriage has produced no children, it is relatively easy for the couple to part and to have no further contact for the rest of their lives. They develop new friendship networks and move on to a new phase of their lives. Some remarry fairly soon, while others find personal freedom more enticing.

When a longer childless marriage dissolves, there are more ties to the partner's family and to the couple's friends that may or may not survive the divorce, affecting those in these larger networks as well as the couple. A sense of great loss and disillusionment may permeate many people's lives as a result. There may also be more marital assets to divide, perhaps contributing to greater conflict, thereby adding to the difficulties of dissolution.

If the marriage, short or long, has produced children, their very being has an impact on the couple both in terms of the marriage during its lifetime and after the breakup. Usually each party has invested great effort and emotion over time, and they will have to continue to have some relationship (in most cases) after divorcing because of their offspring. The potential complexities of the postdivorce family situation are discussed more fully in later chapters.

Whether or not they have had children, women divorced in midlife or later experience the situation somewhat differently than do younger women. In a small study, Davis and Aron (1988) questioned whether midlife women (ages 35–55) selected causes of the divorce that had a self-serving attributional bias. They found:

> [There was] better divorce adjustment for those women who checked causes that are clearly the husband's fault (Husband's Alcohol or Drug Abuse) or due to neutral circumstances (Communication Problems and Financial Problems). And women who attributed the divorce to a cause that was more self-accusing (Husband's Lack of Interest in Me) had poorer divorce adjustment. (p. 52)

Looking at "later life" (age 60+) divorced persons, the problems differ somewhat from those of younger people. The divorce is a ruder shock to their sense of identity; they have less time to develop a new persona, and they tend to be apprehensive about the change in situation that makes them "receivers" of support from their adult children rather than "givers" to them (Weingarten, 1988). They may never have lived alone before or have been expected to be totally self-sufficient, and either or both prospects may frighten them. Their economic status may be more imperiled as those who had been primarily homemakers find it difficult to obtain a job that will adequately supplement their Social Security income. They may also have less support from and activities with others in their community than do younger divorcé(e)s. Gander and Jorgenson (1990), studying mid- and late-life divorced persons, found that those who were close to their adult children and to friends, as well as having a larger number of people in their emergency support network, had a better sense of well-being than those with more limited interpersonal contacts.

Case Example. "Saving Face"

An older couple, the Y's, were referred to author FWK for mediation by the wife's psychiatrist. The story that unfolded was that the husband, after long deliberation, definitely wanted a divorce. Before the explanation of mediation could be given, the wife blurted out, "You cannot have a divorce! I will not be openly shamed by your rejection. I must remain Mrs. Somebody, not Ms. Nobody. You can live in another city [he did work in a northern city while she resided in Florida], you can have a girlfriend, and you can live a separate life—most of the time. But you will come home one long weekend a month, for holidays, and for family celebrations."

When he responded, "I can't live a dual life any longer; this is not a satisfactory marriage and I don't want to live with you ever again," she shrieked, "I cannot face not being married. I will call the children immediately and tell them good-bye, that you drove me to this, and I will kill myself. Then you won't need a divorce!"

When I calmed her down enough to explore this, she had a well-thought-out plan and relished the idea of endowing him with a huge burden of guilt. Since both her husband and I took her seriously, I asked both to take some time to think about their positions before we proceeded, and to see if either one or both could be negotiated. Mr. Y called two days later to say he had decided to stay married legally, live an almost totally separate life physically and detach emotionally, and not risk having his wife carry out her threat. He felt too much of an obligation to his children and to his wife of 40 years.

Gander and Jorgenson (1990) also found that "older divorced persons tend to have a poor relationship during and after marriage with their former spouse's family" (p. 49). In both the Weingarten (1988) and Gander and Jorgenson (1990) studies, the positive influences on postdivorce adjustment of a support group of divorced persons are mentioned and seem to be very helpful to older divorced persons suddenly cut adrift from long marriages.

A composite case has been developed from the files of FWK for presentation that illustrates some of the dilemmas older couples face when divorce eventuates. An older, long-married couple was selected since, as indicated earlier, most of the literature addresses divorcing couples much earlier in their life cycle and we wanted to fill in this gap. In this particular case, the issue of poor physical health surfaced, not for either spouse, but for the wife's live-in mother, and this had to be addressed along with all the other pressing issues. This case will be presented illustratively at different junctures in this book where its unfolding is most relevant.

Case Example. The Royale Family

Predivorce—The Emotional Rift

When Mr. and Mrs. Royale first came for divorce therapy in Florida, the family gestalt was comprised of the people listed in Table 3.1.

Luigi was a hard-driving attorney who specialized in personal injury cases. A self-made man, he had worked his way through law school, "clawed" his way up from an associate to a senior ranking partner in his firm (his self-depiction), and become known as a rough-and-tough adversarial lawyer, an ego-syntonic description.

The Royale constellation presented numerous factors to be considered in the therapy. Mrs. R. needed permanent alimony, as the likelihood of her entering the paid job market was negligible. For

TABLE 3.1
ROYALE FAMILY COMPOSITE (AT TIME OF ENTERING THERAPY)

Name	Age	Gender	Occupation	Religion	Race	Other Key Variables
Luigi R.	63	M	Attorney	Catholic	Caucasian	Desires freedom
Sylvia R.	58	F	Homemaker	Protestant	Caucasian	Highly dependent and undifferentiated
Lauren	36	F	Teacher	Protestant	Caucasian	Peacemaker
Philippe	34	M	Architect	Catholic	Caucasian	Success-oriented
Margo	30	F	Homemaker	Undecided	Caucasian	Very attached to mother
Mrs. S. (Sylvia's mother)	80	F	None (never worked)	Protestant	Caucasian	Some memory loss and mild Parkinson's

years, Luigi had refused to let her work as he "wanted her to do his bidding and be available to him as needed," as his mother had done/been for his father. Now he regretted it. Short of becoming a domestic or a companion to an aged, sick person, Mrs. R. saw no job possibilities, and these two were onerous to her. Besides, her own mother was an invalid who she believed she had to care for in her own home.

Luigi realized that legally he would be considered obligated to provide for his wife of 39 years "forever" and resented this as a "life sentence" now that he finally had the time and money to "have some fun." When everyone with whom he discussed his situation stressed a "moral obligation" to continue to help support his near destitute ex-mother-in-law as well as his wife, he was outraged. He had already done this for many years, although it had not been part of the original "marital contract." He decided to consult his priest. The conservative priest not only disliked that (a) originally he had married out of the faith, and (b) now he was getting divorced and abandoning his wife, but (c) told him it was shameful to desert Sylvia and her elderly mother so he could more fully pursue his own selfish pleasures. He was chagrined at this response!

On entering therapy, he heard something different: that the choices were his within the parameters set by law, and he would have to live with the consequences of whatever decisions he made. He was supported in the idea that just as his wife and mother-in-law had "entitlements," he, too, had some entitlements, including the right to get more enjoyment from his life. In an individual session, he and the therapist explored likely outcomes, and he decided to "contribute" half of what was being requested by his wife and her attorney. In a conjoint session, Mrs. R.'s other options for her aged mother were explored, and she was encouraged to inquire about Medicaid and about programs at a nearby Center for Seniors.

The older children were irate at Dad's childish, "selfish" behavior. The three adult children and their respective spouses came to see the therapist as a family subgroup for two sessions and voiced their major concerns: (a) Dad was being self-centered and insensitive, (b) their parents' divorce would upset *their* children and set a poor example regarding family commitment and continuity, (c) they would be expected to comfort Mom and Grandmom and spend more time with them—both immediately and over the long haul—which would disrupt their already too busy lives, (d) they might be expected to chip in to make up the financial slack although they were already overextended, and (e) Dad might remarry a younger woman and embarrass them. Further, this woman "might be a gold digger" and eat into their anticipated inheritance (Kaslow & Schwartz, 1987b).

In the first session, each person's primary concern was "what will this mean for *me?*" They saw Dad's selfishness, but not their own; they wanted to continue taking his financial support and prestige for granted. They vented their fury and confusion and exhibited little compassion for their father's perspective and his desire to break away from his quiet homebody wife, especially since they saw their Mom as largely a creation of their Dad. After having their views and feelings heard, and having a chance to discuss these from various angles, they asked for time to mull it over and then return.

By the second session, they had shifted their positions slightly and could see how incompatible their parents had become, and could identify with their Dad's quest for an expanded, more interesting lifestyle. They agreed to talk with their father and express their fears and feelings to him directly. A session was scheduled with Luigi and his three children the next week. Following that, all of the children met with their mother in a session to convey their love, loyalty, and concern; to discuss her expectations of them; and to relate what they thought they could provide.

[To be continued . . .]

HOMOSEXUALITY AND DIVORCE

Women divorced from husbands (or husbands from wives) who belatedly admitted their homosexuality are a special group in today's society. Smith and Allred (1990) suggest that contemporary thinking identifies these women as having been attracted to these men "by personality traits . . . that promote deep friendships, such as ease of communication, and by their similar intellectual values, such as similar interests in politics or the arts" (p. 274). When the husband admits to or leaves because of his homosexuality, the wife not only loses a spouse but a close friend, leading to great anger at the husband for what she perceives as fraud on his part and anger at herself for being naive and unperceptive of his orientation. This will be seen more clearly in a case presented in Chapter 4. There is also a problem for these ex-wives in that there are no societal norms relevant to such marriages and their dissolution. Smith and Allred, on

the basis of their study of this cohort of women, hypothesized
that they had a codependency problem:

> Every one of these women reported in her interview that she felt
> she had been married to a child. [They] found themselves doing
> such things as making decisions for their homosexual husbands,
> handling financial crises, and intercepting and smoothing out
> their husbands' problems at work. The underlying codependency problems these women may be required to deal with in
> treatment include that of seeking out men whom they view as
> less able than they in order to achieve a sense of being needed,
> valued, and important. (p. 281)

Some women may leave their marriages because they feel
more content in a lesbian relationship. Upon learning their sexual preference, their husbands feel similarly outraged and deceived, as well as very embarrassed by this "supreme betrayal."
In either case, if there are minor children in the marriage, the
homosexuality factor may be utilized to sway the judge's decision about custody arrangements, or his or her own biases may
enter into the final decree. In addition, if there are children,
minor or adult, they may be totally bewildered by their parent's
revelation.

WIDOWHOOD VERSUS DIVORCE

Although there are some external similarities in the state of
being widowed or divorced, there are also many differences.
Some of these variations may be attributable to the individual's
age, gender, personality, length of marriage, and sociocultural
background; others are due to the legal and economic ramifications of the event itself.

Except for persons who are genuinely joyful at being released
from a marriage, either to escape from an intolerable situation
or to move into a more appealing relationship, people in
the throes of separation and divorce tend to suffer from sadness
and depression for a year or two in much the same way as
widow(er)s do. The sense of loss may be pervasive. Some studies indicate that widowers are more vulnerable to depression
than widows because of their dependence on "their spouses for
intimacy, social participation, and social support" (Umberson,

Wortman, & Kessler, 1992, p. 11), not to mention the more practical aspects of daily living such as cooking, laundry, and such domestic tasks. Although divorced men may have had similar circumstances in marriage, in many cases they may already have a new "significant other" with whom they are getting more involved; this attachment may reduce their feelings of anxiety, anger, loneliness, and depression. On the female side, both widows and divorcées may also suffer depression; however, relatives and friends are more likely to gather round in support for the first than the second. True or not, "The widow is presumed to have had a relatively happy marriage and therefore legitimate reason to mourn its end. The divorcée is perceived to have failed at marriage and to be suffering the consequences" (Schwartz & Kaslow, 1985, p. 73).

Widowhood and divorce have a differential economic impact as well. Typically, widows are left with the family home or other marital property, income from life insurance policies, and benefits from Social Security (if appropriate), and most other existing assets. "Divorcées, on the other hand, frequently have to negotiate and/or litigate for spousal support (alimony), property settlement, and child support payments" (Schwartz & Kaslow, 1985, p. 75). In both cases, however, the women may have to learn to deal with financial decisions and budgets that had previously been their husband's province. From the point of view of the male, the economic strain tends to be greater also in divorce, as he must divide his income and assets with his ex-wife (and children) and possibly later with a new spouse and family.

Where there are minor children involved, again the widowed individual faces a different situation than the divorcé(e). Although both may be thrust into primary responsibility for child rearing and decision making, there are no externally imposed constraints on the widow if she chooses to move to another community, to raise the children in one faith rather than another, to place them in private school, to take them for psychotherapy, to allow elective surgery for a child, and so on. She also has no one close at hand to aid in setting limits on child behavior or to share in being with the children and in making decisions with and for them.

The divorced mother, to the contrary, unless she is the sole legal and physical custodian of the children, must either conform to judicially stated limits for matters, such as relocation, or consult her ex-husband in making many decisions, such as whether a child should have therapy or music lessons. She may, if she is on reasonably amicable terms with him, seek his advice or assistance when problems arise, but, where they have a negative relationship, she may find herself confronted with even more conflicts in child rearing as he and she differ in their permissiveness, limit setting, disciplinary techniques, and philosophies. They need to share in their children's life events, whether or not they welcome the renewed contact (equally true if the father is the custodial parent). None of these are factors in the life of widowed parents.

Yet another contrast between widowhood and divorce lies in the realm of contact with the late/ex-spouse's family. The widowed individual is likely to have continuing emotional (and perhaps other) support from the late spouse's family, as they all shared affection for the deceased and mourn his or her loss together. The surviving spouse also has the option finally to disengage from them if she does not wish to see them. In the case of divorce, however, unless there is great genuine affection between the individual and the ex-spouse's family, it is unlikely that the in-law family will provide a support network since their stronger loyalty is to their son or daughter (Schwartz & Kaslow, 1985).

CONCLUDING COMMENT

Although the effects of divorce on people can be stated in generalizations, the foregoing discussion indicates that, in reality, individual differences—stemming from the idiosyncratic to sociocultural backgrounds—influence the ways in which individuals resolve the events and tasks of separation and divorce. Therapists and other professionals need to attend carefully to these differences as they assist their clients through the painful parting process.

CHAPTER 4

Therapeutic Issues and Interventions during the Divorce Process

WHETHER "OPPOSITES ATTRACT," complement each other's personality and habits, and remain married, or find that their differences outweigh their joys in each other's companionship leading to persistent conflicts and thus to divorce might seem to be a matter of maturity, of chance, or of any combination of several factors. As part of a 20-year study that focused on factors predicting divorce, Buehlman, Gottman, and Katz (1992) found that an oral history interview had approximately 94 percent accuracy in discriminating between couples whose marriages were stable and those who were likely to separate or divorce. The interview was coded on seven dimensions: Fondness/Affection, Negativity toward Spouse, Expansiveness versus Withdrawal, We-ness versus Separateness, Gender Sterotypy, Dealing with Conflict (Volatility, Chaos, and Glorifying the Struggle), and Marital Disappointment and Disillusionment. (Subject couples, all of whom had a child in the 4- to 5-year age range, were also observed for problem-solving interaction and for affect in a laboratory setting, and a number of physiological measures were done at the same time.) The couples were seen again three years later:

Compared to stable marriages, couples who separated or divorced in the intervening 3 years had been characterized as follows at Time 1: husbands had expressed less fondness for their wives, greater negativity, less expansiveness, and less we-ness;

couples had described their lives as more chaotic and were less likely to glorify the struggle, and both husbands and wives had expressed more disappointment in the marriage. (p. 307)

The problem-solving behavior, affect, and physiology in the laboratory setting correlated consistently and significantly with the data from the interview.

Although one would hardly advocate a mandatory premarital interview, use of an oral history is a familiar part of the initial therapeutic sessions. In the case of those seeking help to weather the storms of separation and divorce, an interview including the elements described by Buehlman et al. may enable the therapist to suggest constructive new directions to a client that may avert further distress in future relationships.

PREDIVORCE STAGES IN THERAPY

As a practical matter, when a client experiencing marital distress comes for help, it is important to caution the individual that separation and divorce can literally be harmful to one's health. Sleep patterns and eating behavior can be so altered that resistance to illness may be greatly reduced, and heightened distractibility can elevate the risk of accidents.

Case Example. Disturbed Behavior Patterns

One female client lost 25 pounds within the first three months postseparation, and said that she was trying to function on her job with as few as two or three hours' sleep each night. She also reported at a therapy session the upsetting recognition of her perturbed mental state when she sat at a Stop sign for several minutes waiting for it to turn green. Although her doctor wrote prescriptions for medication for her, she chose not to take any drugs because she feared their possible side effects, and within a few months was functioning on a healthier basis. (case notes of LLS)

The cost of psychotherapy may be borne by health insurance for a time, but many managed health care plans today limit the number of visits for which they will pay to 10 or 20 sessions. These may be too few therapy contacts to enable the client to move forward in a healthy fashion, yet the cost of professional care may be too great for the client to pay it personally. It would be appropriate to include financial responsibility for psychotherapy needed as a by-product of the divorce in the initial financial agreement governing asset allocation during the separation period, and perhaps into the first years postdivorce. Where the couple's finances are not ample to cover this, mental health and social agencies may provide sliding-scale fees and/or low-cost group therapy sessions. The trauma for one or both parties in a marital separation is sufficient to warrant such professional support.

Throughout this book, we discuss divorce as a process with seven phases or aspects (see Table 2.1 in Chapter 2). The dynamics of Stages 1 through 6 have been discussed in preceding chapters, and the final stage, the Psychic Divorce, will be covered in Part IV. The composite case study of the Royales is interspersed where appropriate to illustrate what is apt to unfold at each protracted juncture. Until now, however, the most efficacious therapeutic approaches for each stage have not been elaborated, that is the focus of this chapter.

A different case has been selected for summarization here to exemplify how and why different treatment modalities should be utilized, depending on what is being presented and by whom. It is a complex case that represents some of the typical problems confronted by a subsegment of divorcing couples who are coming to therapists' offices with increasing frequency and about whom we are asked to comment in our lectures and workshops.

In 1970, Bohannon promulgated a six-stage model that he called "the stations of divorce." I (FWK) have built on his model, incorporating the ideas of others (Kessler, 1975; Turner, 1980) and adding my own ideas into the model to make it more inclusive and comprehensive (Kaslow, 1981b, 1984, 1987; Kirschner & Kirschner, 1986). I have also added another stage and material on mediation (Kaslow, 1990b, 1994; Kaslow & Schwartz, 1987a), and subjected the model to periodic revisions to keep it current.

THE DIACLECTIC MODEL OF THE DIVORCE PROCESS

The "diaclectic" model integrates theories of human growth and development, mate selection, marital disillusionment and dissolution, and family systems. The constructed term *diaclectic* combines the concepts *eclectic* (selective) and *dialectic* (seeking a

synthesis that continues to evolve as new data emerge) to encompass numerous theories of behavior dynamics, family dynamics, and humanistic-existential ideas (Kaslow, 1981a, 1981b;
Kaslow & Schwartz, 1987b).

The stages do not necessarily occur in an invariant sequence,
nor do all individuals go through every stage. Rather, the stage
conceptualization provides a broad framework that helps to
sensitize therapist and patient alike, and perhaps attorneys
and judges, to the core issues, and suggests useful strategies at
different phases. Despite the purported growing acceptance
of divorce on the part of some segments of society, most individuals faced with divorce initially view the event as a disas-
ter. It is, for most such people, highly traumatic. The clinician
seeks to help the family to move through and beyond this crisis and to develop new skills to meet this intense, even if temporary, volcanic situation.

PREDIVORCE

Stage 1. The Emotional Divorce

The *emotional divorce* can be brief or protracted. It occurs when
one or both members of the pair become aware of their discontent. One partner may sense his or her dissatisfaction before the
other does, and convey it to the spouse. This usually evokes a
strong emotional response and some turbulence.

People initially select a mate for many reasons, including a
strong attraction and because each perceives a "fit" with the
other. As they grow and change, however, their emotional
needs may also change, and they may come to believe that their
mate is no longer the appropriate choice. Often, a couple may
have a seemingly satisfying, adequate marriage for a long period and then find, when a major crisis or transition occurs,
that their emotional resources are too depleted to meet it. Or
they may gradually go their separate ways, pursuing divergent
interests and pathways, each wanting someone new, different,
and more exciting.

The intense anxiety stirred up by talk of a possible breakup
may propel the couple into therapy. Couples are more likely
to be able to resolve their marital conflicts if they enter treatment conjointly than if one or both begin individual therapy

(Whitaker & Miller, 1969). If both enter couples therapy with the desire to improve their marriage and keep it afloat, the likelihood of success is far greater than if either one feels he or she is the identified patient who has been designated as such because of the need to seek individual treatment. *Couples therapy* at this stage often focuses on the history of the relationship, conflict resolution, exploration of anger, improved communication, and reflections on what is positive.

When children are involved, the therapist may attempt to sensitize the couple to the upheaval their children are likely to experience if a divorce occurs. The therapist may talk about the wrenching pain they will feel as parents in the event of a divorce because they will no longer be part of their children's lives on a daily basis, nor will they be able to celebrate all birthdays and holidays with them. Some practitioners find it useful to recommend books for both parents and children, such as Gardner's *The Parent's Book about Divorce* (1977) or Ricci's *Mom's House, Dad's House* (1980), which provide a clear picture of life after divorce for parents and their children.

Sometimes, couples who have been helped to explore their feelings of rage and disapproval are able to renew their commitment and revitalize their marriage. This is possible primarily when they still profess love and caring, despite continuing disagreement, and if neither is already seriously involved in an extramarital affair.

An alternative approach to single-couple therapy is *short-term psychodynamic couples group therapy* (Kadis & Markowitz, 1972; Kaslow & Lieberman, 1981). Because this is a time-limited therapeutic approach and has a focal theme, most couples in the group are able to decide within the 10 to 12 weeks allotted whether they wish to stay together. Group members support, mirror, and confront one another, thus intensifying the impact of the therapy. Usually, within these closed-end groups (preferably made up of five couples), some bonding occurs within both the male subsystem and the female subsystem, which members perceive as providing them with a network for identification and empathy. For the men, group meetings may provide the first forum they have ever participated in where people expressed emotions and men acknowledged and talked about personal problems.

Since the focal themes tend to be dependence versus independence and individuation and/or connectedness and commitment, all participants have common concerns and much growth is likely to occur in a relatively short time span. When a heterosexual cotherapy team serve as coleaders, and they are mutually respectful and equal in terms of the power distribution, group members may see and experience a different example of parenting, of cooperative couple interaction, of good communication, and of the kind of united front that does not foster or allow for splitting (Slipp, 1988). Members also view the unattractive aspects of others being critical, disparaging, self-effacing or self-pitying, and may gain the ability to see what happens when they exhibit similar behaviors, thus developing a more realistic view of why they are difficult to live with or how they precipitate the problems they want to avoid. Group members are often effective in giving direct feedback, and serve as auxiliary therapists (for a fuller discussion of short-term couples group therapy, see Kaslow, 1982). For many couples, this modality gives impetus to the making of the key decision—whether or not to stay married—and illuminates how others, besides their spouse, perceive and react to them. Under the guidance of skilled cotherapists, couples group therapy is a very powerful treatment modality.

We have found that:

> Rarely is there anything anyone can do to dissuade a spouse who is determined to sever the marital ties. Nonetheless, the rejected spouse may be able to coerce the mate into staying temporarily by becoming depressed or physically ill or by threatening or attempting suicide or homicide. In such instances, the therapist should attempt to guide the couple in exploring the probable implications of remaining married versus getting divorced. The therapist may suggest a trial separation, which can serve as a cooling-off period during which to make more rational choices. Clearly, the choice must be the couple's and not the therapist's. (Kaslow, 1995b, p. 274)

During the course of treatment, the couple may decide to discontinue conjoint sessions. At that juncture, one or both may enter separate individual or group therapy. Issues of concern to the rejected partner are desertion, fear of loneliness, loss, fury, and failure. For the departing spouse, guilt and sadness may be major concerns. One or both may choose to stay in treatment with the original therapist, or continue with a different one. The advantage of staying with the initial therapist is that she or he is already familiar with the situation and the former partner. If occasional conjoint sessions are deemed necessary—for example, around parenting and visitation—these are manageable. If both trust the therapist, splitting maneuvers can be minimized and handled (Singer-Magdoff, 1988; Slipp, 1988).

When working with couples in conflict who are likely to pursue divorce, the therapist should indicate unwillingness to shift roles from therapist to mediator or expert witness at a later time, and should include an agreement about this as part of the initial therapeutic contract. Nonetheless, records should be kept in such a way that the therapist is prepared if a subpoena arrives. Should this occur, the therapist must attempt to acquire a written release from both parties. If this is not forthcoming, the therapist's options include (a) asking the attorney of the unwilling patient to have the subpoena quashed or to have a protective order issued; (b) contacting the judge and indicating why, on ethical grounds, he or she is reluctant to testify; (c) explaining to the lawyer of the patient who requests the testimony why it might not be to the patient's advantage.

Once the decision to divorce has been made, the therapist's role may shift to helping the spouse who feels abandoned to take charge of refashioning his or her future, and urging the couple to make the divorce process a constructive, growth-oriented experience rather than an adversarial, destructive battle. Sometimes it is appropriate to recommend that the client(s) consider mediation rather than litigation, as this process is more conducive to a constructive divorce and more consistent with the goals of holistic and humanistic therapy (Gold, 1992; Kaslow & Schwartz, 1987a; Marlow & Sauber, 1990). Couples who enter mediation may find that continuation of therapy, concurrent with but separate from mediation, provides for the ongoing resolution of highly charged emotional issues.

Case Example. The Jacksons*

Session 1. Intake and Brief History

Jerry and Sally Jackson (J) had been married ten years and had two children—Glen, age 8, and Susie, age 5. Mr. J was 31 years of

---

* Case is an amalgamation of several similar cases from the files of FWK with all identities disguised.

age and a decorator by vocation. Sally was 29 years of age and had worked in public relations before the children were born. Jerry worked for a busy decorating firm in a South Florida community. When they entered therapy, they were nearing their tenth anniversary. Sally was discontent because Jerry spent less and less time at home, always using work as an excuse. He never played ball with Glen nor participated in the children's school or other activities. Their social life had dwindled and they rarely had any sexual contact—unless she initiated and insisted, and then he might reluctantly oblige.

Sally definitely wanted the marriage to continue. She loved J, admired his ambition and talent, knew he could be a good father if he devoted time and energy to it. She knew he had changed and was detaching from them, and was frightened. As a staunch Catholic she was opposed to divorce, so at the outset of therapy she indicated this was not an option.

Conversely, J stated he still "cared about Sally and the kids," but his real satisfaction came from his work, his clients, and being with his buddies. He didn't enjoy the children's world and had come to dislike the restraint marriage placed on his freedom. He indicated that although he did not want to hurt her, he had little hope that the marriage could survive and meet his needs.

Session 2. The Story Unfolds

Because Jerry had been so outspoken about his discontent in front of a third neutral person in the prior therapy session, Sally had taken him seriously. She was dejected over the prospect of a physical separation leading to divorce, and indicated she was willing to work hard and do whatever it would take to "make the marriage work." She stated she would fight on behalf of herself and the children, and beseeched Jerry to tell her what she needed to do to make herself and the marriage more appealing to him. She was teary, contemplative, and distraught, and almost too willing to take full responsibility for whatever had gone amiss and to rectify it. She asked for clarification of what she had done wrong.

Since Jerry was reluctant to tell her, and just said, "It's over and there is nothing you can do to make it better; it isn't you, it's the combination of us that is not working," and the therapist realized how important it was for Sally to have something less nebulous so she could comprehend what was happening that was so out of her control, she asked if he could be more specific and explain why. He retreated into a painful silence and shook his head "no."

Sally couldn't contain her rage and anxiety. She screamed, "Is there someone else? How long has this been going on? How could you do this to us? Whoever she is, she can't love you as I do nor need you as your children do. I won't let you or her do this to us."

Unable to handle this barrage and the pressure Sally was putting on him, Jerry blurted out, "There is no other woman, and never has been." He paused, lowered his voice and added, "But there is a significant person in my life and it's a man. I didn't want you to know because I knew you would call this sick, perverted, and against God's will, and it would hurt you terribly. And I did not want to hear your harangue and your demeaning statements." Sally seemed dumbstruck; her disbelief was almost palpable. She shook and sobbed, and all she could say was, "How could you? You are a disgrace!"

The session was drawn to a close after each was a little more composed, and they were asked to think about "where to proceed from here?" It was suggested that no hasty physical move or legal action be taken until they each had a chance to sort out the developments that were unfolding and their reactions to them.

Session 3. Achieving Clarity

Jerry came in determined to establish that he needed to finally "be true to myself," which meant coming out of the closet and living as a gay male (Myers, 1989). In response to further queries from Sally, he indicated that he had begun to suspect he might be gay some years earlier, but had attempted to squelch his feelings and inclinations so as not to disrupt the family, upset his parents, or cause upheaval at work. Over time, his attraction to and for men had grown until he felt he could no longer negate it. Then Kevin had come on board at the firm as a designer, and they were often thrown together. Kevin was out of the closet and Jerry found that this was accepted by his clients and the other staff at the firm. Their relationship blossomed, became sexualized, and they had "fallen in love." He told Sally he wanted to be able to be candid with her at long last, that the pretense had been costly for him, and he was actually relieved that he could disclose his secret (Imber-Black, 1993).

Sally was enraged. During the week, she realized Jerry had been living a double life and had thoroughly deceived her. She could not believe that he had been so skilled at duplicity and wondered if she could believe anything else he had told her or "if it was all a lie." She felt hurt, rejected, angry, disillusioned, and nonforgiving. She had gone to a local bookstore to see if they had anything she could read on the subject of a seemingly straight spouse suddenly revealing he or she is gay, as she sought to understand this strange world into which she had been thrust. The clerk had suggested *The Other Side of the Closet* (Buxton, 1991), and she was planning to buy it. She told Jerry she could never forgive him for his dishonesty, his transgressions, and the humiliation he was going to cause her, their children, and their respective families of origin (Kaslow, 1995c). She told him to "pack and move immediately."

The therapist expressed understanding and empathy for each of their positions, actions and reactions, and was careful not to take sides. She asked them to think about what they would tell the children, and when, and urged that they consider how to do this in a way that would be least disturbing to the children—suggesting they do it together and without blaming one another or saying much more than "Mom and Dad are no longer happy together and our marriage isn't working any long. We will be separating and probably divorcing each other, but we will each continue to love you and be part of your lives." Sally doubted she could do this, saying "It's time for the whole truth, and the children have a right to know who and what their father really is." Jerry said, "Let Sally do what she wants; I just want to be free to be with Kevin openly and as much as possible." He said he could understand if the children wanted no part of him, and if that was the price he had to pay, he would. Neither seemed to be able to act "in the best interest of the children" at this point in time; their own personal agendas were too compelling. Neither could even begin to contemplate a lasting mixed orientation relationship.

DURING DIVORCE

Stage 2. The Legal Phase

This period encompasses the *legal, economic,* and *coparental-child custody* aspects of divorce. It starts when either the husband, the wife, or both initiate legal action. Until the mid-1970s the only route to divorce was adversarial, and usually entailed the stirring up of further embitterment.

The American Bar Association's (ABA) Canon of Ethics (1981) states that an attorney can only represent his or her client; the other party to the dispute must have separate legal counsel. Although many states rewrote their laws in the 1970s and 1980s to reflect a shift from fault to no-fault divorce, from sole custody to shared parental responsibility, and from contested to noncontested divorce proceedings, many divorces are still bitter, long-drawn-out, and costly battles.

The options of litigation, arbitration, and mediation are discussed in Chapter 5. Whichever path toward settlement is selected by the pair, the function of the clinician during divorce therapy includes helping them to sort through what's happening, to face their multiple losses, and to grieve sufficiently to be able to cooperate in reaching a divorce agreement.

A therapist who is able to help the couple to utilize a noncombatative problem-solving approach may continue to help the couple periodically thereafter. They may return as coparents to deal with various developmental issues in the lives of their children. Later, the clinician may meet with the original pair as divorced coparents, or with one parent and his or her new mate in a stepfamily situation, or with both parents and their new partners. Such an integrative, expansive approach (Kaslow, 1990b) is consonant with the thrust toward interventions in the larger family ecosystem.

Sessions 4 through 11. The Battle Rages

At the beginning of Session 5, Sally announced, "I've been to an attorney. He says I have a strong case (Green & Bozett, 1991). You'll pay plenty and you will not be entitled to joint parental responsibility because the judges here are conservative and don't think kids should have to be with a gay parent. If you fight me, I'll ruin you!" She was dripping with venom, her fury fired up by her attorney and her friends from church who shared her belief system that homosexuality is a sin. Jerry again apologized for the hurt he had caused, and said he wished it had been possible for him to be comfortable as a heterosexual man, but it hadn't. The therapist asked if Sally might reconsider and try mediation, which is a calmer, fairer, and less costly process (Kaslow, 1990b), but Sally was irate and determined to retaliate against Jerry for his betrayals.

Since conjoint therapy was now counterproductive, given that their life process was about separating and not about improving their way of being together, it was agreed that separate individual therapies would be more beneficial at this time. However, both acknowledged that they did care about the children, and therefore would come to therapy together for sessions dealing with them. They were complimented on their sensitivity, rationality, and willingness to go beyond personal wrath and disillusionment.

Sally used her first few individual sessions to continue ventilating her horror, humiliation, bewilderment, and disbelief. She obsessed over why she hadn't seen what had now become so obvious

(Buxton, 1991). She wanted to strike back, and vowed that she would never trust another man. Fortunately, her dad was available and was gentle and supportive, and she was encouraged not to generalize that "all men are b_____ ." Concurrently, she was working with her attorney to serve papers to Jerry and was quite agitated about what was transpiring.

For his part, Jerry had moved out of their marital home and went immediately to live with Kevin. The two men simply could not wait to establish their identity as a couple. Jerry derived peace, contentment and fulfillment when he was with Kevin, and he was doing well at work where clients and colleagues who knew about his personal journey appeared supportive. But he dreaded every encounter with Sally. And he was surprised at the strong negative reaction he received from his own parents and siblings. His folks were shocked and outraged, and talked of disowning and disinheriting him. They clearly sided with Sally, as did her parents; they did not want to lose contact with their grandchildren or be blamed for their son's "affliction." He could not believe that his happiness counted for naught and was reeling from their rejection. In his quest to find a lifestyle congruent with his self-image, he had not given much thought to how his significant others would react to and be affected by his coming out (Bozett & Sussman, 1989).

Added to all this turmoil was the realization that he was soon to be served divorce papers and that he needed to engage an attorney to respond and to handle his case. Reluctantly, he engaged a well-known matrimonial lawyer and soon realized how expensive the forthcoming battle might become. This was not what he had intended. He wanted a quiet, personal settlement and was dismayed that his difficulties were escalating. He again asked Sally to reconsider mediation, but she was tenacious in pursuit of her day in court before a judge to whom she could tell her story of his disloyalty and transgression. During this month and a half, Jerry called the children weekly and saw them for two brief Sunday outings. He felt uncomfortable with them and did not know what to say to them. Sally had told them "Daddy doesn't love me any more and does not want to live with us. He'll come see you once in a while." Both sets of grandparents continued to visit and to be involved with the children, and since Jerry had often worked late in the past and not come home for dinner, on the surface the children's lives did not change markedly.

Stage 3. The Economic Divorce

Fears about financial survival cause some people to cling to an unsuccessful marriage. Most realize that when assets are divided, each will have substantially less than they did in tandem. For those who decide to divorce, it is ironic that at the same time they are under the greatest emotional pressure, they must cope with thorny money matters. These include payment of debts, the division of assets, insurance concerns, and child and spousal support. When there are few assets to be divided, the process may be simpler, but everyone is apt to emerge with much less than they need. When there is substantial wealth, the divvying up can be complex and each partner may continue fighting for his or her rightful share—even if the amount to be agreed on is sufficient to continue his or her lifestyle. Women and children tend to fare worse than men, economically, and they often become downwardly mobile (Kurz, 1995; Weitzman, 1985), while men remain at the same level or move upward in the future (see Chapter 6 for fuller discussion of these issues).

Therapists treating individuals going through divorce can intervene by accepting their fury, outrage over betrayal, and desire to punish. Having validated their feelings, they can then guide them toward seeing each other's real financial needs and toward engaging in fair, nondestructive negotiating. They may be able to help interpret the complex economic issues, while encouraging them to request information and clarification from a lawyer, accountant, and/or mediator. They can stress the importance of long-range financial planning, because the marital separation agreement (MSA) becomes the map for their financial futures and that of their children. The economic divorce is not coterminous with the legal divorce, but ends with the final transfer of funds from the payor spouse to the recipient spouse, often many years later if a young child is involved and child support is granted. If permanent alimony is ordered, the couple is bound together until either former spouse dies. Thus, the financial settlement has long-term consequences that will influence the future of all family members.

Sessions 12 through 15. Money Issues Come to the Fore

During this time, there were two conjoint sessions, and each party had one individual session. Their attorneys were negotiating the terms of the financial settlement, and both were displeased with what was going on. Sally had told her lawyer she thought Jerry had stashed away some undeclared income and that if he didn't give her all that she wanted, she would report him to IRS. Her lawyer advised her that this ploy rarely works since whoever attempts to use it implicates herself (i.e., she had knowingly cosigned tax returns and previously enjoyed a standard of living based on the utilization of this hidden income). Next she tried to bargain using chips that would reveal both adultery and homosexuality by calling a reporter for a gossipy newspaper. Her attorney and the therapist both explored with her the consequences of publicizing their private lives by going to the newspaper and providing them with a scandal story. Both asked her to think about the impact on the children, on extended family members, and on her ability to coparent with Jerry long into the future. Such rational responses did little to mollify her belief that he should pay heavily to compensate for the misery he had caused, and to offset information she received from female friends that some of the judges came down hard on adulterers and on gays in terms of ordering long-term and higher alimony to atone for their transgressions. She wanted to drive the hardest bargain she could, and by and large had a tough attorney who relished the challenge. She indicated she was deriving much satisfaction from seeing how gaunt and unhappy Jerry looked, and from the fact that his family was on her side.

Jerry had not anticipated the storm of resentment and the many losses his disclosure of (a) his desire for a divorce, (b) his being gay, and (c) his being involved with a male lover would unleash (Strommen, 1989). He could not fathom the rejection from his previously loving and approving family of origin, and he felt bereft. Slowly he, along with Kevin, was reaching out to gay acquaintances, but this was not a substitute for severed family bonds. While trying to deal with his pain, hurt, and bewilderment, he was informed by his attorney that he would have to produce many financial records and substantiate his assets as well as his debts. He was overwhelmed by the task and felt paralyzed. All of this, combined with Sally's uncharacteristic demands and sarcasm, led to his feeling depressed and caused him to question his self-worth. He could not fathom how he could manage to survive financially and meet all of Sally's requirements for herself and the children. This was a trying period for him; the only relief he found was in Kevin's steadfast support and affection, in adulation of his work by pleased clients, and in individual therapy sessions. In joint sessions, he felt he was attacked and belittled; it was rarely possible for Sally to curb her vitriolic monologues, despite the therapist's attempts to help her gain some control and to be less critical.

Stage 4. Coparenting Schedule and Concerns

The lives of children change dramatically when their parents dissolve their marriage (Ahrons, 1989; Ahrons & Rogers, 1987). To ease this painful transition for their children, parents should (Kaslow, 1995b, p. 278):

- Explain, preferably together, that they are divorcing and assure the children that it is not their fault, and there is nothing the children can do to get them back together.
- Decide on a primary residence based on the best interest of the child(ren) and not on their own wishes.
- Reassure the children that each parent will continue to love them and remain actively involved in their lives.
- Refrain from deprecating the other parent and his or her family of origin.
- Refrain from placing children in loyalty conflicts.
- Arrange adequate financial support for the children.
- Work out a cooperative parenting schedule based on children's needs, activities, and preferences.
- Make as few changes as possible in the child(ren)'s life.

When rapid changes are unavoidable (e.g., relocation, a parent's change of job or entry into the labor market, change of schools, or a new partner coming into the picture), parents should explain what is happening and why the changes are necessary, and work to soften the impact of the unexpected new events and/or unanticipated new people.

Older children of divorce, like their younger counterparts, also experience an open heart surgery of the family when their parents divorce. Their loyalties may be challenged, and they may feel angry and alienated from one parent, particularly if they are expected to take sides. Contact with one set of grandparents may be abrogated. In some states, such as New York, grandparents have visitation rights granted to them by law that are incorporated into the final agreement. However, rarely do they have the right to prevent someone from moving out of state. The loss of the attention and love of nurturing grandparents is another sad occurrence that compounds the other major losses and disruptions. Cutting grandchildren off from grandparents is often experienced by youngsters as cruel and devastating. Unless there is good reason to do so, such as a grandparent who has been abusive, the relationship should be fostered by therapists and parents alike.

Therapists treating children of divorce should have a solid knowledge of individual and family development and life-cycle issues, and also understand the typical and idiosyncratic responses to divorce of children of all ages. The therapist may be the only adult in the child's life who can listen sympathetically and attentively to the child's story. Treatment of choice may be play or art therapy; individual psychotherapy; sibling group therapy to strengthen the bonds and diminish the rivalries (Bank & Kahn, 1982); or groups for children of divorce. The latter have proven beneficial in minimizing feelings of alienation and the sense of being alone, augmenting problem-solving skills, and reframing and normalizing the experience (Farmer & Galaris, 1993; Kessler & Bostwick, 1977; Roizblatt, Garcia, Maida, & Moya, 1990). Group sessions can be lively and even occasionally be perceived as fun, and attendance does not stigmatize the child as "sick."

How children survive a parental divorce is partially contingent on the degree of conflict they witness during and postdivorce. Other factors include the child's personal resilience and the parents' level of emotional recovery. Longitudinal research (Wallerstein & Blakeslee, 1989) indicates that effects may be long lasting and that repressed feelings may resurface years later. This "sleeper effect" may become visible in the reluctance of an adult child of divorce to make a commitment to a permanent relationship; they may wish to avoid the risk of having to face a second divorce. Thus, therapy that takes place close to the time of the original family breakup or when it is first evident that a child is distressed, is most likely to avert future unhappiness or pathology.

Sessions 16 through 20. They Are My Children Also

When Jerry finally consulted an attorney, he was told that he was misinformed in that he was and always would be the children's biological father and therefore would have a continuing right to see his children and be involved in their lives. The lawyer cautioned him against making further comments implying he would bow out of their lives, except for supporting them financially, unless that was truly what he wanted to do. Jerry brought this issue up in therapy and indicated that he had realized how important the children were to him and he wanted to see them more often and truly be involved in their lives. He hoped they would come to understand his dilemma and accept his identity. Further, Kevin wanted to get to know the children, after the divorce was final, and thought he, too, could have a constructive and nurturing role with them. Jerry saw some books on homosexuality in the waiting room and asked to borrow several. He found parts of *Lesbian, Gay and Bisexual Identities over the Lifespan* (D'Angelli & Patterson, 1995) particularly illuminating. He also read *The Other Side of the Closet* (Buxton, 1991) to gain a more objective understanding of what was going on in and for Sally, and to try to "tune into" her perspective.

In a joint session, he tried to gently tell Sally that he missed the children much more than he had expected to, and that he wanted to play an active role in their lives. He tried to assure her that being gay did not impede his ability to be a good father and that, under law in Florida, he was entitled to share joint parental responsibility. Sally was nonplussed and started to sob, gasping, "You've hurt us enough; can't you stop screwing up our lives? I won't let you do this to them. They'll be ridiculed by all their playmates! Why don't you just go away and leave us some modicum of peace?" Jerry had no idea of how to resolve this impasse. Sally was too unnerved for the therapist to intervene much beyond, "It's obvious you did not anticipate this and it hurts terribly. You will need time to integrate this possibility into your thinking, and we can continue to discuss it here at the same time you are dealing with the legal ramifications of this new development."

The issues raised in all of these sessions are fairly representative of the concerns expressed and agonized over during the course of divorce therapy by the majority of couples seen clinically. The additional dilemmas alluded to herein which are confronted when one partner announces he or she is "coming out of the closet" concurrent with seeking a divorce seem to typify the extra layer of crisis that couples and families in this group experience and must address.

Gay couples who dissolve their unions, whether or not they have had and shared children brought into the relationship from prior relationships, or acquired during their partnership by artificial insemination, an agreed upon external liaison, or adoption, confront the same problems that arise from the trauma of separation for heterosexual couples and couples where one leaves to lead a homosexual lifestyle. In addition, state laws vary regarding parental rights of "divorced" lesbians (Matza, 1995) and gays, and must be checked in each specific instance.

For the children, particularly if they are raised to hold the values of the dominant culture and the major religions, that heterosexuality is normal and homosexuality is not, accepting a homosexual parent and his or her same-sex lover may be a confusing and difficult task. Homophobic attitudes will need to be unlearned and all of the adults involved will have to encourage acceptance and help the children cope with their own questions and reactions, as well as those of their playmates, classmates, and the other children's parents if the ambivalence is to be overcome. Patience and a strong support network will enable parents to bear the transition phase. Much re-education will need to occur. In communities with many gay couples and an ethos of acceptance, the adjustment may be somewhat easier for the children than in one in which homosexuals are generally ostracized and/or dismissed as invisible. Despite the conservative, even reactionary pronouncements by some politicians and legislators in the mid-1990s, who are trying to ban and disenfranchise homosexuals, another trend is also visible; that is, "society appears to be more open to gay parenting" as data become available that children raised by gay couples "prove to have the same level of adjustment as offspring from traditional families" (Cavaliere, 1995).

In the case of Sally and Jerry, the impact on the children is not clear since the case is still unfolding and the final agreement has not been reached. As of this writing, the children have not been told of their father's gender orientation. He has begun to call more often and is negotiating for more frequent visitation. Sally and both sets of grandparents are opposing this. Currently, the children do request "more time with daddy" and enjoy their visits with him.

Stage 5. Community Divorce

Sometimes one's extended family, friends, colleagues, and neighbors provide much-needed support during and after divorce. Having others available to listen, to sympathize, and to validate the unhappy person's worth is extremely helpful. Wallerstein and Kelly (1980) found that women with a strong network of friends and family who can provide financial assistance, temporary housing, and child care during the crisis and transition fared much better than their counterparts who were lonely and isolated. For adults, receiving understanding at work, and for the children, receiving compassion at school, can make a huge difference in whether they feel valued by others or experience the world as a hostile, insensitive place.

For men who move out of the family home and lose their daily involvement in family life, the support system may be more amorphous. It may include their parents, siblings, and/or colleagues. Some men maintain contact with both single and married friends either by telephone or in person. Lacking this, or perhaps in addition, they may seek comfort or escape in alcohol, drugs, or gambling, or look for any available companionship at a bar. Some men become workaholics to fill the emptiness, and others increase time in recreational and athletic pursuits. Some ask friends to introduce them to potential dates, and others find themselves pursued. Often what is missing, and for a long time, is someone to talk and share with who really cares.

The social and community stage begins during divorce, and like the economic and coparenting phases, continues long beyond the legal divorce. Those who are criticized and rejected by significant others are apt to have the most difficulty forgiving themselves and/or the former partner for choosing to divorce. Those who are invited in a genuine way to participate in activities by others will find their pathway made easier. The divorcée should ask friends and relatives not to push them to date, nor to restrain them from "too much" socializing. Each person needs to find his or her own rhythm. It takes months, or even years, to become comfortable again in the singles world and to adjust to current psychosexual mores, which no doubt have changed markedly since the person was last single.

At this stage, individual therapy may constitute the treatment of choice. Some conjoint parent-child sessions may be advisable to keep lines of communication open, and to ensure that children's needs and feelings are being heard and met. Participation in a divorce therapy group can also be beneficial. Members can share their concerns and receive reflective feedback, both confrontative and supportive. Self-help groups for single parents provide a forum in which to address and normalize common issues. Group meetings can become a place to socialize,

acquire new friends, and plan activities that may involve the
postdivorce family as a unit.

Sessions 21 through 24. Responses of Family,
Friends, and the Community

Sally and Jerry each had two separate sessions during this time.
Generally, Sally felt that her friends and family were supportive
and sympathetic, but that they could not truly comprehend what
she was going through and all the shock waves she kept experiencing, as they had never had to cope with this specific disillu-
sioning and horrific life event. Like others in this predicament, she
talked about how her little dream world had totally unraveled
(Gabriel, 1995) and that she was really having a tough time getting
hold of herself and trying to put her life back together without
Jerry. She was reassured that this is an expected reaction, and that
it often takes several years of sorting things out before a person
can equilibrate and begin to feel back in charge of her own life.
She was encouraged to live each day as fully as possible, enjoying
whatever gave her pleasure.

The therapist asked whether Sally might consider going back to
work in the near future, as she had had a thriving career in public
relations before the children were born. The therapist underscored
that this would probably be good for Sally's sagging self-esteem,
and would also enable her to supplement the child support and alimony she would be receiving. Sally concurred and said this was
exactly what she had been thinking, and it was good to have her
idea validated. However, her attorney had adamantly advised her
against doing so until *after* she received the final decree since, in
Florida, any income she earned would be computed along with
Jerry's, and based on this, an amount would be deducted from
what Jerry would otherwise be ordered to pay in child support
(Dissolution of Marriage; Support; Custody, 1992). [Such legal advice, based on realistic economic considerations, often runs
counter to what might be preferable in terms of promoting emotional well-being.] It was agreed she would start making inquiries
and perhaps be able to line something up to begin to work as soon
as the divorce became final. As she began to build some enthusi-
asm about resuming her career, Sally became more willing to move
toward a settlement.

She had checked to see if there was a group in the community
for partners deserted when their spouse came out of the closet, but
found none available (Parents, Families, and Friends of Lesbians
and Gays [PFLAG], 1994). She considered this unfair, but accepted

the recommendation to attend several different Parents Without Partners groups until she found one in which she felt comfortable. She was encouraged to read about homosexuality and its effects on families (see, e.g., Bozett, 1989) to increase her understanding of what was happening to her internally and externally, and as another aid to her own healing.

Conversely, Jerry had been dropped by former friends of the couple; he realized when he called them and saw them unexpectedly that they were uneasy with him. None called just to keep in touch. His parents and siblings, who had initially berated him and beseeched him, "Don't do this to yourself and to all of us," found that their pleas were in vain. They could not accept that Jerry felt he had no other choice. At this point in time, they were shunning him and he did not feel they would relent. Despite how deeply their attitude hurt and bewildered him, Jerry still missed them. However, unlike Sally who could find no special group support in the community, he and his lover joined a gay social and advocacy organization and derived validation and a stronger sense of the meaningfulness of their commitment to each other in this context (PFLAG, 1994).

Stage 6. Spiritual and Religious Considerations

These are described in detail in Chapter 8. Here we will only discuss their manifestations in this specific case.

Religious Involvement

Sally remained active in her conservative Catholic Church. The prevailing doctrine, strictly adhered to by her pastor, was that homosexuality is totally unacceptable to God and the Church. This belief reinforced Sally's position and made her feel justified about the stance she had taken. She was glad she had enrolled the children in Bible School and that they were being indoctrinated with a similar belief system.

The pastor made it clear that Jerry was no longer welcome. He tried talking to the priest, who counseled him to relent, give up his transgressions, and pray for forgiveness. Since Jerry could not do this, he left the Church and sought a spiritual haven elsewhere. Many of his new gay friends belonged to the Metropolitan Church (a religious organization with affiliates in many cities; it has predominently gay and lesbian congregations), and he and Kevin had to attend only a few services and events to realize this was a place where they could feel connected and not damned.

Their now separate church affiliations became yet another schism between Sally and Jerry that seemed likely to get larger. It was much too early to approach the idea of a divorce ceremony (Kaslow, 1993b), and at this point it seemed unlikely that this might ever be possible.

POSTDIVORCE

Stage 7. The Psychic Divorce

Many individuals going through divorce describe the process as having entered a dark and narrow tunnel on a roller coaster. The tunnel has no windows near the entry, and they have no idea how long it is or when they will see light. Once the legal divorce is final and they begin fitting the pieces of their life puzzle together in a new way with different proportions allocated to the pieces, some light filters in and the tunnel widens. Anywhere from two to five years after the actual physical separation, they emerge from the tunnel, climb off the roller coaster, and realize there is life beyond divorce.

During this interval that it takes for even reasonably well-balanced people to reequilibrate, little can be done to hasten the healing. The length of time depends on several variables, including who initiated the divorce and who was the rejected partner, whether one party was still struggling to save the marriage while the other was pressing to pull apart, the length of the predivorce separation, whether the grief work was well under way before the physical breakup, resiliency of personality, financial resources, age, gender, strength of support network, level of self-confidence and optimism versus pessimism about the future, and the nature of the larger family constellation (Kaslow, 1995c, p. 280).

When individuals have been moderately to severely dysfunctional before the breakup, the restabilization will probably take longer and be accompanied by more bitterness. For disturbed individuals, divorce becomes the critical life event that colors their entire future; the former mate continues to be viewed as a villain on whom all of their problems are blamed, and resentment continues to influence many of their actions. From this group come the patients who attempt to keep their children (of all ages) embroiled in postdivorce struggles about money, visitation, and emotional bonds. Those who cannot grieve and then relinquish the now defunct marriage are destined to remain caught in a web of their own hurt and venom. They are not free to *go forward and lead a meaningful and productive life.*

The Immediate Aftermath—A Bumpy Road

As this is being written, Sally and Jerry are still in the throes of divorce. It is too early to predict how quickly and fully each will arrive at their psychic divorce. However, prior to the inception of the decision to divorce, each exhibited considerable ego strength and self-confidence; each has good vocational skills and prospects, with Sally's in abeyance but likely to blossom within several years; each has a substantial support network; and there are and will probably continue to be adequate financial resources. The prognosis, therefore, is good for the long term. In the short term, the divorce path is strewn with roadblocks that the therapist is attempting to help them to eliminate, or at least minimize. Despite some resistance and defensivenesss, both are responsive in therapy and growth oriented, so an overall positive outcome can be anticipated with cautious optimism.

The postdivorce period can be one of new challenges and opportunities, at least for those who have the energy, spirit, time, and money to open up and travel new pathways or to reactivate old friendships and past hobbies. However, during the early postdivorce period, many divorced persons experience acute anxiety and/or depression. Their adjustment may be more difficult because they lack time (because they are working harder), hope (because their future appears dreary), and money (either the woman, who bears the economic crunch that comes from a divorce, or the man whose former income proves insufficient to cover child support and alimony and still afford him a good standard of living).

It is beneficial to ask the adults and children what gains they might derive from the divorce. Answers may include (a) freedom from abuse; (b) no longer fearing humiliation from their partner's alcoholism, drug abuse, gambling, or derogatory comments and behavior; (c) cessation of arguments and criticism, and "a more peaceful household; (d) space to think one's own thoughts and be one's own person; (e) freedom to make one's own choices and be in charge of one's own life" (Kaslow, 1995c,

p. 281). The therapist can stress that it sounds like the benefits may outweigh the losses, and can focus upon how to harness their strengths and resiliency to enhance their postdivorce adjustment.

Some people come into postdivorce therapy feeling hurt, angry, distressed, pessimistic, and desirous of revenge. They may still be demeaning their former partner and trying to turn family and friends against him or her. They may be mired in self-pity. When this is the situation, individual and/or group therapy should focus on decreasing the anger, and later toward exploring the person's own role in continuing to provoke conflict. Such individuals should be helped to decrease their sense of helplessness and hopelessness and to release their children from any "parentified" role they have taken on, and/or from an overly enmeshed relationship with them that hinders the children's ability to individuate (Kaslow, 1988).

Unless these situations are mastered, one cannot reach closure on the psychic divorce. Evidence of completion of the emotional tasks can be seen when there is a return of hope, willingness to enter into a new relationship and to trust again (if a relationship is something the person wants), a marked decrease in the rage, the lack of preoccupation with the past, and the ability to think about the present and future with optimism.

CONCLUDING COMMENT

Therapists would do well to be aware of the various stages of the divorce process. They must realize that the chaos and turbulence are experienced differently by each member of the nuclear and extended family, and that there are also reverberations with friends.

This chapter has attempted to describe the elements that affect a family's ability to cope successfully with divorce. Those mentioned include age and developmental level, personality, gender identity, religion, financial resources, and social and family support system. Other key variables encompass education and occupation, mental and physical health, race and ethnicity, and level of self-confidence.

It is crucial that the therapist assess correctly where in the transitional process from marriage through postdivorce each member of the family is. This is true throughout the therapeutic process. Working from a family systems perspective is urged because changes in one family member will affect all other family members. Consideration of the two postdivorce subsystems—mother and children and father and children—also requires sensitive attention. Interventions should be age and stage appropriate, and should be modified as patients pass from phase to phase.

The therapist will need to be concerned not only with the family gestalt, but with multisystemic issues also. Often one should cooperate with other involved professionals, such as attorneys, mediators, physicians, clergy, and school personnel, but only with the full informed consent of the clients. Such collaboration augments the benefits of professional guidance and can reduce tensions. In times of strife, patients do not need a replication of their own conflicts among the professionals from whom they have sought assistance. The therapist is usually in a pivotal position (with patients' permission) to initiate contact with other involved professionals, and to build a cooperative team approach. Sometimes it is necessary to request that the various professionals meet together to avoid splitting, working in opposition to each other, or duplicating of services. The competent professional should decide whether it is advisable or contraindicated to include the patient(s) in team-style meetings.

A comprehensive (Kirschner & Kirschner, 1986) approach to divorce, such as the diaclectic model utilized herein, provides a theoretical frame in which to view family members' feelings and coping strategies, and affords flexibility of choice in treatment methods. In the case presented in this chapter, the case formulation combines psychodynamic, existential, life cycle, and family systems constructs. The interventions draw from structural, strategic, systemic, psychodynamic, intergenerational, problem-solving, and cognitive-behavioral approaches.

Divorce therapy is most successful when treatment is sought quickly after the traumatic process begins. Informing patients that achieving resolution may take several years helps them live with their ambivalence, procrastination, and occasional emotional outbursts or withdrawals, and enhances their patience with the slowness of their own progress.

Therapy for children and adolescents is preventive in that the resolution of current despair can preclude delayed reactions such as bitterness, fear of commitment, inability to achieve emotional intimacy, and prolonged anger over abandonment and the sense that divorce has been an unforgivable disruption to their lives. [The therapist] can help to normalize, interpret, and ease the painful divorce process for children, parents, and grandparents. (Kaslow, 1995b, p. 282)

Atwood (1993) has enumerated several factors in attaining what she calls the "competent" divorce, all of which are tied to the parental role in one way or another. Perhaps one of these factors is the key to all of the others—"Parent's own sense of well being":

One of the most important predictors of children's post divorce adjustment is the single parent's sense of well being. If the single parent mother/father has adjusted in a healthy way to the divorce, the children will also. This process can be facilitated through counseling and support structures. (p. 17)

To achieve such a sense of well-being, the therapist needs to encourage reduced parental conflict, a nonadversarial divorce, effective parenting, and the development of a strong support system. The therapist also needs to try to counter such unproductive factors as learned helplessness, feelings of being a victim, and a personal and/or societal view of single-parent families as being pathological.

In a society in which there are millions of postdivorce, single-parent families, creating an ethos in which such families are accepted and perceived and treated as normal, will lead to their having a more wholesome context in which to reequilibrate and thrive.

CHAPTER 5

The Legal Aspects
of Divorce

THROUGHOUT THE WORLD, marriages MAY be considered legal only if the couple undergoes whatever is required by their country's law. For the marriage to be recognized and sanctioned, the couple must conform with the civil procedures mandated by their society. If they wish to have, or are obligated to have, a religious ceremony to consecrate their marital vows, this is in addition to the civil requirements.

So, too, with divorce. A couple cannot just decide to dissolve their union and do so on their own. They must again fulfill the civil and legal requirements before the court awards a formal decree, since ostensibly the state maintains an interest in the welfare of families, including their coming together and splitting apart. If a religious divorce or annulment is also sought, this is again separate from and in addition to the legal divorce.

Thus, it is impossible for a divorcing couple to avoid contact with the legal system at a time when they are already likely to feel out of control in many facets of their lives and to be experiencing great emotional upheavals. Engagement with the legal system all too often exacerbates the sense of confusion, anger, depersonalization, loss of control over one's destiny and that of one's children, and fear of additional financial woes. Analysis of the various routes to procuring a divorce is essential for therapists who want to help clients/patients, colleagues, and friends select the pathway most suited to their personality, needs, and financial situation.

> Between 1969 and 1985 divorce law in nearly every Western
> country was profoundly altered. Among the most dramatic
> changes was the introduction of civil divorce in the predomi-
> nantly Catholic countries of Italy and Spain, and its extension to
> Catholic marriages in Portugal. Other countries replaced or
> amended old, strict divorce laws. (Glendon, 1987, pp. 66–67)

In Ireland, a vote on a constitutional amendment to permit divorce and remarriage of divorced persons was narrowly passed
in November 1995 (KYW radio, Philadelphia, Nov. 25, 1995).

In the United States, the movement toward change began in
California. Until 1970 in all states in the United States, one spouse
sued the other for divorce because of some "fault"; grounds included adultery, prostitution, and mental cruelty. The presumed
innocent party had the responsibility to prove that there was indeed "cause" for divorce, that the other was guilty of some noxious behavior, and, if (s)he won the suit, gained the bulk of the
marital assets in payment for being so aggrieved. In making such
an award through the judicial system, society punished the guilty
party and rewarded the presumed innocent victim. As noted earlier, mere unhappiness, mutually agreed upon, was insufficient
cause for divorce and, indeed, any consensual agreement bespoke
a collusion that was unacceptable in the courts as a basis for divorce (Weitzman, 1985). In the past quarter-century, however, all
states have moved to permit no-fault divorce, frequently with "irreconcilable differences" given as the basis for such a suit. This
legal premise is much more compatible with and influenced by
systemic thinking in mental health/family theory—that in a marriage, as in other relational systems, neither party is all guilty nor
all innocent regarding contributions to the demise of the marriage (both parties play a role in determining its continuation vs.
its termination). Even no-fault actions, however, may be contested
or uncontested, usually thereby influencing the length of time
between the filing of the suit and the granting of the divorce.

The impact of the changes in the divorce laws can be seen in
Figure 5.1, where an increase in the divorce rate is visible from
the mid-1960s on, with the slope of the curve climbing sharply
in the ensuing 15 years. The only other marked increase between 1925 and 1981 occurred in 1946 when servicemen and
women returned from World War II and dissolved marriages
that may have been made in haste during the war and were no

longer compatible after the years apart and the very different life experiences of the spouses.

Conversely, from a peak of 5.3 divorces per 1,000 population in 1981 (NCHS, 1985), the rate dropped (provisionally) to 4.4/1,000 by 1993 (NCHS, 1994a), and actually to 4.5/1,000 in mid-1995 (NCHS, 1996), suggesting several possible explanations. The drop may indicate that divorce and being single again might be being perceived less optimistically now than in the prior decade or two; alternatively, the higher rate in the early 1980s might reflect a rush of long-disaffected couples to take advantage of the new laws, with a tapering off once this initial group had been processed. The present rate still reflects the current expectation that one of every two marriages occurring will end in divorce.

This high rate distresses social conservatives, however, who have begun movements in several states to revoke no-fault divorces under some circumstances, such as when one spouse opposes the divorce (Johnson, 1996). Supporters of such proposals

FIGURE 5.1

ESTIMATED NUMBER OF DIVORCES AND CHILDREN INVOLVED IN DIVORCES: UNITED STATES, 1950–1990 (*Source:* National Center for Health Statistics. (1995, March 22). *Monthly Vital Statistics Report, 43*(9S), p. 3. Hyattsville, MD: Public Health Service.)

deplore both the breakdown of the family and the poorer state of women and their children (financially and otherwise) as a result of easy divorces, while opponents point out that making divorce more difficult may increase the frequency of unmarried couples/families living together without the protections of marital responsibility and prolong the agony suffered by the battered spouse and children in an abusive marriage by placing almost insurmountable obstacles in the exit route.

Currently, the grounds for divorce, if they must be stated, represent one of the major legal variables to be considered in reaching a settlement and dissolving a marriage. Where the parties agree that they wish to divorce, their respective attorneys may suggest the grounds that meet the state's laws as well as the couple's situation. A second variable is the state's position on child custody, with most states at this time having a statutory preference for joint custody. Third is the "prevailing rationale for alimony (supportive of a dependent former spouse or temporary payments for rehabilitative purposes)" (Brinig & Alexeev, 1993, p. 281). The final variable is the division of marital property, depending on the state's legally defined regulations and preference for community property versus equitable distribution. The second, third, and fourth variables, in contrast to the "grounds" variable, can be resolved in one of three ways: litigation, arbitration, or mediation.

FAULT VERSUS NO-FAULT

Until the early 1970s, divorce was based on the fault or marital misconduct of one partner, or a pattern of behavior that posed a danger to the other spouse through physical and/or emotional abuse ("cruel and inhuman treatment"). Today, such abuse grounds may include drug or alcohol abuse by one spouse, or the potential for a tort action based on the need for treatment of herpes or AIDS transmitted by one spouse to the other. The other principal grounds for divorce in most states are incarceration of the defendant spouse for three or more consecutive years after the marriage, and abandonment for one or more years (Samuelson, 1988).

There is also *constructive abandonment* (also known as *constructive sexual abandonment*) [italics in original]. This ground is often used when both parties want to divorce as quickly as possible.

One spouse without opposition will serve a complaint stating that the other spouse has refused to have sexual relations for more than one year. (Rothman, 1991, p. 127)

The advent of no-fault divorce was the result of lawmakers' recognition that some couples no longer want to remain together and meant that something as vague as "irreconcilable differences" or "incompatibility" could serve as the basis for marital dissolution. Although this sometimes reduces the adversarial nature of the divorce and even some of its trauma, critics of the no-fault laws point out that the accompanying economic concepts of community property, equitable distribution, and (impermanent) rehabilitative alimony or maintenance have proven to be inequitable for women, although they were intended to balance the scales of justice for them (Rothman, 1991). Proponents disagree and the arguments continue nationwide in legislative, judicial, and mental health forums.

Florida built on California's law, and in 1982 promulgated its own Dissolution of Marriage—Children Act (Chapter 82–96), which has been amended several times since. The revision from December 1992, known as Ch. 61—*Dissolution of Marriage; Support; Custody,* specifies "that no dissolution shall be granted unless the marriage is irretrievably broken or one party is mentally incapacitated" (p. 22). However, if one party is incapacitated, the other may be required to pay alimony. Specification of fault is not sought. In many cases, one member of the couple would like to allege abuse or adultery as the cause of the breakup, to get this on the record and receive some recompense to offset the injuries the person has sustained, but this is currently not essential or central in no-fault divorce. This law is considered one of the most advanced in the country and has been a model for subsequent legislation in other states. The Florida Act will be alluded to later in several places as it pertains to other salient issues. The 1994 Revisions to the Florida Statutes 1993 are included in this book as Appendix B.

CONTESTED VERSUS UNCONTESTED DIVORCE

If one party wants to be free of the marriage and the other does not, the divorce action may be contested, that is, fought out against the other party in court. Why would someone want to stay in a marriage when his or her spouse does not want to, and therefore contest the divorce? Spite or anger at being rejected is one reason. "If I can't have you, no one else will!" is the accompanying angry attack statement. Indeed, even after a divorce has been granted, such a spouse may spy on the former partner, try to break up any budding new relationships, or physically abuse the ex-spouse.

> Continued love for the rejecting spouse may also play a role. Anxiety about letting go and starting anew is another consideration. The desire to hang tough in order to extract a bigger piece of the economic pie or more favorable child-care privileges also can motivate a rejected spouse to impede a divorce action. (Rothman, 1991, p. 125)

Other reasons include extreme dependency, fear of being alone, desire to be married and fear of not finding another partner, an unrealistic belief that this is a whim that will pass and that the departing partner will come to his or her senses.

If, on the other hand, both parties agree that divorce is the answer to their unhappiness, today the divorce can be uncontested. In several states, an uncontested divorce can be granted after a short period of separation, such as 90 days in Pennsylvania, whereas a contested divorce may take one to three years to be granted (Elrod & Walker, 1994).

PATHWAYS TO MARITAL DISSOLUTION

As stated earlier, there are three principal pathways to divorce: litigation, arbitration, and mediation. Individual situations and personalities, as well as relatives, friends, and legal counsel, direct couples to choose one path over the others. Both litigation and arbitration involve a third party—the judge, a divorce master, or the arbitrator—as ultimate decision maker. In mediation, by contrast, the third party—the mediator—acts as a neutral and a facilitator, for the couple themselves are the decision makers. It is also possible that some attorneys may be willing to negotiate a settlement when requested to do so by their clients, but this is less common than any of the other routes to divorce.

Litigation

Litigated divorces are the stuff from which captivating dramatic scripts are made for theater, television, and film. The parting spouses cannot come to terms on one or more issues involved in the divorce, and determine to "have it out" in their day in court, with each hoping for a favorable decision by the judge. They do not want to be responsible for the decisions and the subsequent repercussions or "fallout." Even when their respective attorneys urge compromise, they refuse to be seen as "giving in." In some cases, one spouse is so angry with the other that he or she is determined to have revenge by airing the dispute and any related embarrassing accusations in court. Perhaps one party, or both, forcefully accuses the other of physical, emotional, or substance abuse; or exorbitant wasteful spending, for which substantial compensation is sought. Or, if they are prominent in the community, one partner may want to smear the other's reputation by having the sordid details of an affair or of shady business dealings come out in the media. If the issue revolves around the children, litigation may be instituted several times, as support, visitation, alleged mistreatment, and other areas of contention are raised repeatedly between the embattled parents in their continuing war for control of the children's bodies, souls, hearts, and minds.

Most familiar to the general public are scenes of aggressively fought cases in the courtroom, with each spouse and his or her witnesses testifying to the brutality, adulterous behavior, neglect, or unfitness of the other. Litigation is costly in time, energy, and dollars, although the public exposure of the errant spouse's behavior may fulfill the other spouse's need to vent anger, frustration, jealousy, and hostility. *War of the Roses,* a movie from the 1980s, depicted the terrible lengths some spouses go to in waging a debilitating, destructive, and tragic war against each other.

If the two parties are at odds on property division or child custody (or both) and cannot be in the same room without displaying rage or coming to blows, an adversarial divorce may be the only avenue to take. On the other hand, in some cases, depending on state law and the "pugnacity" of the attorneys, a custody battle may be threatened to coerce the other parent into accepting a reduced property settlement, even where the litigious parent really does not want full or joint custody. It is important to recognize that lawyers who aggressively represent their client's positions and interests are functioning as they are trained to do in their role as an advocate; they are not supposed to be concerned about what happens to the other spouse, as this is the province of the other attorney. In fact, the ABA Canon of Ethics enjoins attorneys to represent only one party to a dispute (ABA, 1981).

Assuming that the parties do litigate their divorce, where is the less economically favored party going to find the funds to pay an attorney? Will he or she be able to recover the fees paid as part of the distribution of assets, and if so, is it "fair," particularly if this was the party who wanted the divorce? What if the person's attorney has said, "We'll figure out some way for you to pay me including putting a lien against your house." We have had women patients postdivorce where this has occurred and they did not comprehend what it meant. They did not understand until the attorney insisted the house be sold to pay legal fees if the woman had meager savings and the judge would not approve recovery of those fees. Such a course of action adds markedly to her many troubles and overwhelming feelings of abandonment and dislocation.

If children are involved, has the couple considered the potential harm of publicly airing the marriage's "dirty laundry," especially in cases of marital misconduct? Are the psychic, financial, or custodial gains of a prolonged battle likely to outweigh the emotional, financial, and time costs? Are the gains sufficient to warrant abdicating control of the future of one's life to a third party?

Arbitration

Arbitration is a second option for resolving disputes about property and other matters as part of dissolving the marriage. First, the arbitrator seeks to determine on which issues there is agreement and then proceeds from there with the controversial points to achieve agreement. On those issues on which the disputants cannot reach an acceptable agreement, in binding arbitration, the arbitrator makes the decisions. Arbitration has the neutral third-party decision maker aspect of litigation, but tends to be more private than a full-blown court battle, and is usually a faster process than a court proceeding. While similarly dealing with apparently unresolvable issues, arbitration occurs in a less formal setting, and usually includes some attempts at negotiation within the process. This may be a particularly effective way to handle disputed property assessments, where each party's evaluator has arrived at a different figure. It is a less appropriate modality for dealing with children's lives from the time of the parental separation until the children become adults. It differs from having a judge in that "In an arbitration, the parties get to choose their arbitrator or at least have a veto over possible choices. In judicial proceedings, a judge is assigned by the court" (Rothman, 1991, p. 183). Each party will be heard, and supporting documents and witnesses examined, as in court, but without the opportunity to make a public scene in which to exhibit rancor and vengeance. Although there is somewhat more control over the proceedings, each party in arbitration still gives away to a third party some control over decisions that vitally affect his or her life.

Mediation

The late 1970s witnessed the evolution of divorce mediation as an alternative dispute resolution strategy after the publication of Coogler's seminal book (1978). The rapid expansion of mediation theory and practice during the 1980s and early 1990s (Erickson & McKnight-Erickson, 1988; Folberg & Milne, 1988; Haynes, 1981, 1982; Kaslow, 1988) has enabled couples to participate directly in making key decisions about parenting, child support, and property distribution, rather than turning these crucial choices over to lawyers and judges. Mediation can prevent the need for costly and contentious litigation and stresses empowerment, self-direction, concern for the best interests of all family members, cooperative problem solving, and equitable distribution of assets. The effort to fashion a mutually acceptable agreement while minimizing anguish enhances one's sense of self-worth and leads to forging an agreement that truly belongs to the two parties, and of which they can be proud. Because it is theirs, they are far more likely to abide by it and implement its provisions.

In contrast to the adversarial nature of litigation and arbitration, mediation brings the divorcing parties together to hammer out their own agreements. Mediation is the choice of those who wish to end their marriage with minimal legal procedures, cost, and hostility, and at the same time with maximum personal input and control over agreements about property settlement and child caretaking arrangements (Kelly & Olin, 1992). Even where the parties are extremely angry with each other, those who select the mediation option usually have recognized the benefits to themselves and to their children of determining their own futures rather than having a third party do it for them (Erickson & McKnight-Erickson, 1988; Marlow & Sauber, 1990). As one well-known mediator put it, hostile parties in mediation "will only agree to a settlement if they feel the other is not getting away with something" (Grebe, 1989, p. 17).

The third party in mediation—the mediator—is usually an attorney, a psychologist, a social worker, or a retired judge who has been trained in mediation techniques and who serves as a facilitator, generator of options, negotiator, and information provider rather than decision maker. Sometimes a team of an attorney and a mental health professional works with the couple as comediators; in other cases, the team may be a female and a male of the same or differing professions of origin who share a common philosophy as mediators. The mediator must remain abreast of changes in the relevant tax code; in divorce, child custody, and child abuse legislation; in regulations about what constitute distributable assets and other pertinent data on profit-sharing and pension plans if he or she is going to provide appropriate information to serve as the basis for a settlement. Whenever it is necessary to venture into arenas in which evaluations are needed before decisions about the distribution of assets can occur, such as appraisals of houses, boats, or businesses and professional practices, specialists should be utilized. The mediator may develop a list of experts he or she can recommend for couples who request this information.

Despite all of its positive elements, mediation is not a panacea. When there is a huge power differential in a relationship, or if either is prone to chicanery, an attorney's services may be needed for the couple to obtain a fair settlement. Then, too, if parting spouses are so infuriated that fairness is the polar opposite of what they want, they may need to fight ferociously as a way of venting their fury en route to letting go of the relationship and healing psychologically. If one partner has been untrustworthy or one craves vengeance, then the adversarial process may suit their needs better.

The initial session serves as an introduction to the mediation process for the couple and enables the mediator to learn what is involved in the dissolution of the particular couple's marriage (Folberg & Milne, 1988; Gold, 1992). The five areas included in the mediation process are division of marital property, spousal support, parenting, child support, and tax consequences of possible decisions (Grebe, 1989).

Confounding mediation with individual or family therapy, as some mental health professionals may do, is not advisable or appropriate. Mediation is not therapy and it calls for a different knowledge and skills base while incorporating information about child development, family dynamics, the stages of the divorce process, and the impact of divorce on children and adults. (Attorneys who become mediators need to acquire knowledge in these areas just as the mental health mediator has to become conversant with salient family law concepts and content.) However, the mediator can reduce the power imbalance that may characterize the marriage by establishing rules for the pair's behavior in the session, like listening to one another's statements of need, and by artful questioning (Neumann, 1992).

If there is a history of family violence, the mediator needs to be aware of this as an abused wife not only may have low self-esteem and therefore feel as if she has little leverage in the mediation process, but may need legal protection from her abuser. Protective orders may or may not be sufficient to assure her safety during and after the divorce depending both on the husband's compliance with the order, and on the jurisdiction and its enforcement of such orders. Sometimes the order serves to incite the abuser to further violence. Some mediators believe that cases where there has been domestic violence can still be mediated if a protocol is followed regarding treatment for the abuser and there is an agreement to a no-abuse contract (Erickson & McKnight-Erickson, 1988); others believe they can not. (There has been ongoing dialogue about this explosive issue in the Academy of Family Mediators *Newsletter* for the past several years.) Mediators in non-court-based practices may be apt to accept such cases on a selective basis if they have expertise in dealing with domestic violence cases from other arenas of their professional activities.

However, the Family Law Act specifies: "Family Court mediators will not offer a service to clients where violence is currently a feature of the relationship or where a manifestly unequal power relationship exists between the couple" (Nicholson, 1994, p. 143). This precaution is one that all mediators might well follow, although it should be noted: "While some advocates for abused women favor voluntary mediation, all strongly oppose requiring victims to mediate and some have gone so far as to insist that women who have been abused *cannot be allowed* to mediate" [italics in original] (Thoennes, Salem, & Pearson, 1994, p. 3).

Mediation requires cooperation on the part of each spouse, and the determination of both not to escalate their conflict by airing private matters in court. It seeks "win-win" rather than "win-lose" solutions and posits that neither one gets all that he or she wants and that both should get most of what they want. It also requires honesty and "full disclosure" on their parts and a willingness to compromise; there is to be no hiding of assets, no inflation of living costs, and so on. It requires negotiating "in good faith." Two checklists (Child-Related Agreements and Spousal-Related Agreements) can assist both partners to be certain that all items they need to consider are indeed examined (Koopman, Hunt, & Favretto, 1994). In the area of child custody specifically, "part of the custody mediator's task is to help transform the initial presentation of contending spouses into that of problem-solving parents and to direct their energies into essential child-focused activities" (Koopman & Hunt, 1988, p. 383).

The mediator, using financial affidavits and other information supplied by the couple, seeks to help them reach an accord with which they can live, since the final document represents a map for their future and that of their children. Drawing this up is the couple's responsibility, and they are more likely to abide by it if they have arrived at their own decisions and believe the terms are equitable.

Commentary on the Options

Of the three means of resolving conflicts arising from the desire to divorce, mediation offers the most privacy, the greatest degree of confidentiality, and, from all evidence, the highest likelihood of follow-through after the divorce. This is because the parties themselves agree on custody and property matters, albeit with the help of a neutral third party—the mediator. A small survey of people who had mediated their divorces in Ventura County,

California, gives one clue to feelings six months to more than three years after reaching agreement: "Long-term satisfaction with agreements was demonstrated by the continued compliance with the original agreements and changes by mutual consent, modifications that were reached through constructive private discussion or by a return to mediation" (Meierding, 1993, p. 169). A survey of more than 250 fathers, divorced an average of five years, similarly revealed more positive long-term satisfaction for out-of-court settlements compared with litigated proceedings (Dudley, 1991).

A third study, comparing families that had accepted mediation with families who had litigated their settlements, was conducted nine years (range 8.3 to 10 years) after settlement (Dillon & Emery, 1996). The results suggested more favorable outcomes for the mediation families in terms of interparental communication and frequency of contact between noncustodial parents and children, with no more frequent return to the courts than was true for the litigation family subjects.

We highly recommend that all agreements should include a postdivorce remediation clause for the mediation of problems that arise later if the couple cannot resolve these on their own, despite having learned good problem-solving skills in the prior mediation. This will prevent the disagreement from escalating and being fought out in court (Kaslow, 1990). For example, remediation to modify some provisos of the agreement may be advisable if the payor spouse becomes incapacitated due to a stroke or debilitating disease such as multiple sclerosis and can no longer pay the stipulated child or spousal support. In a similar vein, children's needs may change in unanticipated ways and the child support or contact schedule may need modification. Sometimes the recipient spouse's financial situation improves markedly and this, too, may mean that renegotiation is warranted.

In choosing to mediate, the parties are exhibiting an ability to look beyond their immediate differences and emotions to long-term needs as well as the effects of their decisions on others, such as their children. This takes intelligence, an ability to articulate needs, and foresight (Kaslow, 1988). There is a growing movement in many states to require mediation in divorce cases, especially where child custody and visitation issues are involved (Rothman, 1991, p. 191). It must be recognized, however, that not all people are suitable candidates for mediation, so that such a requirement may be inappropriate for some (e.g., persons who are severely mentally ill, mentally retarded, or actively abusive).

A variation of the mediation approach is the use of a conciliation service with multidisciplinary staff such as the one authorized in Australia's Family Law Act 1975. Restricted to married litigants when originally passed, one of the service's four goals was "to protect the rights of children and to promote their welfare" (Nicholson, 1994, p. 138). Later legislation, the Courts (Mediation and Arbitration) Act of 1991, provided a legal mandate for mediation and permitted a child or the child's biological or adoptive parent, in addition to one of the marital partners, to request mediation to settle a dispute in which he or she is a party. Follow-up interviews 6 to 10 months after the conclusion of mediation revealed that in "86% of cases where agreement had been reached the agreement was being carried out or followed with only minor changes" (Nicholson, 1994, p. 145). Chief Justice Nicholson regarded the program as successful in that it provided emotional and financial savings to the divorcing parties and their children.

No one pathway constitutes the optimal choice for all divorcing couples. We believe mediation is the preferable option for those who wish to participate in making and being responsible for their own choices and who are willing and competent to gather the financial data needed on which to base an equitable distribution of assets, and rational and considerate enough to fashion a shared parenting arrangement that is truly in the best interests of their children—based on recognizing (and learning if need be) sound child development principles. Arbitration may be best suited to those who can reach partial agreement, but need a neutral third party to make some of the final decisions in a more private atmosphere than the courtroom. Litigation is the route that should be pursued by those who do not trust their partner to fully disclose assets and therefore need to have a complete discovery process undertaken and someone to advocate staunchly on their behalf because they are unable to do so themselves for emotional, intellectual, or physical reasons. It might also be recommended for those who are so angry that only preparing for and having their "day in court" might give them a chance to slowly express their fury and thereby resolve it. Mediation might be too peaceful and gloss over the emotional trauma.

It is essential that professionals working with divorcing individuals and couples, such as therapists, judges, clergy, and accountants, be aware of these alternative dispute resolution strategies and which might be preferable for whom so they can make appropriate referrals.

When therapy is occurring concurrent with the legal divorce, many of the emotional and substantive issues are also being dealt with there. This is the time when the parting partners may be being seen separately most of the time and conjointly when that appears to be more advantageous for both. When necessary, children of all ages may also be in treatment, individually, as a child subsystem (Bank & Kahn, 1982), or with one or both parents in family therapy.

Although in our diaclectic model, the legal and economic aspects of divorce are separated for purposes of analysis, they proceed together and in reality are quite intertwined. We return now to the Royale family case to illustrate this.

During Divorce—The Legal and Economic Phase. The Royale Case

Through the mediation process, everyone's level of tension began diminishing. As Luigi felt "heard," he became less of an antagonist and asked his attorney to soften his approach. Subsequently, his lawyer and his wife's were able to reach a relatively fair settlement. A reasonable amount was included to support his mother-in-law in the alimony he would be sending to his ex-wife each month. Plans were made for supplementing this amount by utilizing her Social Security checks and applying for other aid to which she would become entitled.

After some discussion in therapy of what "equitable distribution" meant to him personally and how he wanted his family to continue to perceive him, Luigi realized he could enjoy his life, postdivorce, much more if he believed he had been considerate and generous, and that he recognized this would help him absolve some of the sense of guilt he really did feel—underneath his "toughing it out." Luigi agreed to leave his ex-wife as the beneficiary on a rather sizable life insurance policy, even though this was not part of the original marital settlement agreement.

CHAPTER 6

The Economic
Issues in Divorce

INTERTWINED IN THE TURBULENT legal aspects of the divorce are all of the financial concerns. Dividing assets invariably means each party will have less than they did when they were a combined unit. There is no rebuttal to this disturbing reality!

Many of the difficulties confronting divorcing parties today, especially the women, result from the changes in divorce laws that have made divorce easier through no-fault, but that have also largely eliminated payment of lifetime (permanent) alimony. The related concepts of "equitable distribution" of marital assets or of equal distribution under community property laws (as in California and some other states) bring further complications. The economic issues emerging from divorce are complex, with both spouses usually having some validity to the arguments supporting their positions.

For example, if the wife has contributed to a lengthy marriage principally through unpaid labor at home, chauffeuring of children, and being supportive of her husband's career, she is less prepared to enter the labor market after divorce. Even short-term rehabilitation alimony designed to enable her to acquire marketable skills may be insufficient to gain her employment at a salary sufficient to maintain anything near her prior standard of living.

If the couple has subsisted on a tight budget prior to divorce, there may be almost nothing to divide. If the woman has been working part- or full-time for meager wages in the past, chances are she will either have to find a way to earn more, or her financial plight will sink from bad to worse. As Weitzman (1985) pointed out, the financial condition of women and children tends to plummet after divorce, while that of men tends to remain the same or to improve. An additional factor that needs consideration is that if the mother is the primary residential parent and is attempting to keep the children's life as stable as possible and not also be away more, because the father is now absent from their daily lives, taking on additional job responsibility means more hours out of the home. This can be detrimental to the children's sense of security and can compound the losses being experienced; therefore "the best interest of the children" is an essential factor in any planning undertaken regarding distribution of assets and future supplementation of income.

If the woman is over 55 years of age and has not been employed outside the home since being married, the possibility of obtaining employment diminishes even further. However, some women in this category do come up with creative solutions such as turning a hobby or avocational interest into a vocational one and ultimately open a small business, perhaps with a talented friend in similar circumstances. Others parlay their homemaking and child-care background into becoming qualified nannies for the young, companions for the sick or elderly, or housemothers in a variety of programs. Therapists and mediators can explore these kinds of possibilities with divorcing women who will need to supplement their income from alimony and other sources. Creating or finding a revenue-producing position is also likely to have emotional benefits—such as increasing self-esteem, and broadening the person's friendship network and view of the world.

On the other hand, if the woman remarries a person of affluence within a few years, the economic impact of the divorce will likely be minimized (Duncan & Hoffman, 1985), unless her bridegroom insists on having her sign a stringent prenuptial agreement, even if reluctantly (Kaslow, 1991). If her new spouse's income is marginal, remarriage may not mitigate her financial woes.

For the men, long-term child support, which continues until the child is 18 years old in most states and 21 years old in New York, places a strain on their financial well-being, as well as on any subsequent marital relationship. If alimony payment is also mandatory, the ex-husband may be continuously strapped financially and resentful emotionally. However, without adequate financial support, the children of the first, and possibly the second, marriage may well be deprived of the life-style and the kind of education that they could have anticipated had their parents remained together. How to divide the "financial pie" to maximize it for all poses some major dilemmas.

As Mahoney pointed out in her address to Association of Family & Conciliation Courts members (1995), family law is based on a male point of view and on the norms of white males. She asserted that ex-wives' entitlement to support is based on false assumptions of the wife's equality in preparation for and opportunities in the labor market. Further, although Canada (Mahoney's home nation) has legislation that makes child support the top financial priority for the payor and stipulates that the children's standard of living should not fall below that enjoyed during the marriage, in reality practice does not match these policies. Rather than basing child support awards on the children's needs, they tend to be based on the payor's ability to pay and do not match the cost of raising children. The Hon. Alastair Nicholson, Chief Justice of the Family Court of Australia, echoed her sentiments, pointing out that treating men and women equally at divorce leads to inequalities after divorce (1995). He advocated changing the laws to create a more level playing field. A third speaker in this symposium (Barrasso, 1995) alleged that men rather than women were at a disadvantage in the legal system because they were programmed (by women) to be workers, not nurturers, and that the law is hostile to men who want to be responsible fathers. These disparate views underlie the issues discussed in the next several pages.

DISTRIBUTION OF ASSETS

On the surface, it would appear that the principal economic issues to be resolved at divorce focus on dividing the marital assets—tangible and intangible, present and future. If the couple resides in a state like California with a community property system, each spouse owns one-half of all earnings and property acquired during the marriage (other than by inheritance or gift from a third party). "The community property system assumes that both spouses have contributed equally to the economic assets of their marriage, whether by homemaking or by earning a salary, and that each is entitled to an equal share of the total assets" (Weitzman, 1985, pp. 53–54). In the majority of states, on the other hand, *equitable distribution* is the means for dividing marital property. It is intended to be fair to both parties, and in some states, such as Florida, tends to approach a 50/50 distribution. In other states, "The starting point for an 'equitable distribution' is typically one-third of the property to the wife, two-thirds to the husband. The underlying assumption is that the property really *belongs to the husband* because he was the one who earned it" [italics in original] (Weitzman, 1985, p. 54). In addition to this assumption, homemakers' contributions (whether in lieu of or in addition to outside employment) are typically undervalued by judges, who are mostly male, as shown in a number of state task force reports (Starnes, 1993). For military couples, divorce settlements (especially retirement pay) are subject to the Uniformed Services Former Spouses' Protection Act (Public Law 97-252), enacted in 1982, and its subsequent modifications.

What marital property might there be to divide? Depending on length of marriage and level of income, a list might include the following:

Present Holdings

- Marital and other personal home(s), farms.
- Household furnishings, including sterling silver, furniture.
- Vehicles such as cars, motorcycles, boats.
- Savings and checking accounts.
- Horses, show (or pet) dogs, cattle, and other animals.
- Investments (stocks, bonds, mutual funds, other real estate holdings).
- Family-owned businesses and goodwill.
- Jewelry.
- Works of art or other valuable collections.
- Professional practices, professional education, and licenses.

Future Assets

- Profit-sharing plans.
- Military or other pension.
- Social Security pension—each party may have a claim on it.

- Retirement plan.
- Future earnings (as in a professional practice).
- Medical, life, and other insurance benefits.

Each of these assets can represent a sizable sum of money at the time of divorce or in the future. Their value will also vary with the state of the economy, especially with respect to real estate and other investments. The value of medical insurance can be expected to change if and when a national health care plan is voted into law, but it is an appreciable asset when one is included in a group plan, and a very costly obligation if one is insured as an individual.

In many marriages, one spouse has worked to enable the other to complete graduate or professional education only to be confronted with an action for divorce shortly after the degree is attained. In *O'Brien v. O'Brien* (1985), a New York case where Dr. O'Brien sued for divorce after his wife had worked for seven years to support the couple while he attended college and medical school, the "court considered his license to be marital property and awarded his wife a share of the enhanced earning capacity the license afforded" (Schackman, 1994, p. 119). This decision helped reduce the inequity inherent in this situation, although Starnes (1993) states that the appellate court's ruling in *O'Brien* was an "extraordinary departure from tradition" (p. 90). However, everyone needs to be aware that the O'Brien decision could be replicated in other states and that professional practices can no longer be considered immune from distribution.

ALIMONY OR SPOUSAL SUPPORT

Some maintenance payments may be paid during the period between separation and divorce (alimony *pendente lite*), but post-divorce support (i.e., permanent alimony until remarriage or death) has been awarded more infrequently since the advent of the no-fault divorce, community property, and equitable distribution concepts. If a marriage was relatively brief and there are no children to support, an award of permanent alimony is often perceived as inappropriate (see, e.g., *Geddes v. Geddes*, 1988). This is the reality today no matter what the disparity in spousal incomes, especially where the mates are young.

Even where permanent periodic alimony is awarded, whether it should enable the wife to maintain the standard of living enjoyed during the marriage (assuming the husband's ability to pay it) has been subject to recurring debate and varies within and among judicial jurisdictions. If there are substantial assets to be divided, this may be done by a lump-sum payout, perhaps over a period of one to two years, or by an award of lifetime alimony, which is what no-fault divorce is partly designed to avoid (Starnes, 1993, p. 97). There are emotional as well as financial risks in having lifetime or long-term alimony: (a) The paying party may fall behind or decline to pay as scheduled, which can lead the parties back to the courtroom; (b) contact between the two parties is maintained, usually much to the displeasure of at least one of them, if not both; and (c) if the payor spouse dies soon after the divorce, alimony payments cease. The estate is not responsible for continuing the payments. In either arrangement, tax consequences have to be considered carefully and should be spelled out as appropriate in the final agreement. The advantages and disadvantages to each spouse of an up-front settlement versus long-term alimony should also be discussed so that wise decisions can be made.

So-called rehabilitative alimony for a limited term may be awarded to enable a homemaker to acquire marketable skills for self-support, but, as indicated earlier, this is really ineffectual if it is unlikely that anyone will hire her because of lack of experience and/or advanced age. In *Mundy v. Mundy* (1986), the First District Court of Appeals in Florida observed that "rehabilitative alimony is appropriate only in those instances where the evidence indicates the recipient spouse has the potential or capacity to be rehabilitated to the financial stature that would permit her to become self-supporting." Not all judges recognize this practical problem. If they did, and if the husband could afford it, there might be a supplemental lump-sum payment that the wife could invest to produce future income, or a reduced permanent periodic alimony.

EMPLOYMENT FOR THE DIVORCED WOMAN

The publication in 1985 of Weitzman's study of the effects of no-fault divorce laws in California, based on a review of 2,500 cases recorded between 1968 and 1977, was an eye-opener for many people. Her conclusion that, one year after divorce, the men's standard of living had risen by 42 percent and the women's had dropped by 73 percent (Weitzman, 1985, p. 338) has been repeatedly cited as authoritative by many writers in the field. Even if the figures are cut in half for a larger population, the decline in standard of living suffered by ex-wives is regarded as not quite "right," and as perhaps even immoral. It is certainly not equitable, and this was in a state that dictates *equal* division of community property rather than *equitable* distribution of marital assets. What a distressing, vexing portrait these data present!

A sample of 108 mothers in a southeastern community, with 79 percent working 40 hours per week, reported a median net monthly income of $915 (range 0–$5,000) with most of them defining "their economic situation as 'struggling' (37%) or 'doing okay' (45%)" (Buehler & Legg, 1992, p. 183). The uppermost income range typified only about one in five of the caretaking mothers. According to these figures, none were in the over $60,000-a-year bracket based on their own earnings, yet we know some single women and many single and married men achieve earned incomes above this figure.

It is apparent that the economic impact of divorce varies with age of the parties, length of marriage, education, occupation, employment history, geographic locale, and socioeconomic class. Although younger women tend to have more currently marketable skills, and may have combined child rearing with employment, they are still confronted with the gender gap in wages, a slowly growing economy with fewer jobs in service areas and greater competition for available positions (Morgan, Kitson, & Kitson, 1992). At the same time, if they are single parents, they may not be hired by a company that must abide by the Family Leave Act of 1993 which would have to permit them extended absences from their job in case of a child's illness or future pregnancies.

As Kitson and Morgan (1990) concluded, even where middle-class women do not become poverty-stricken, their income may be seriously reduced after divorce. They may have to relocate to a less desirable neighborhood, with poorer-quality schools for their children, lose their own and their children's support networks of neighbors, friends, and playmates, have less adequate healthcare, and have fewer opportunities to enjoy those facets of life that they had during marriage. The poorer quality of education in itself may produce potentially negative consequences in terms of the children's future.

By contrast, women married in the 1950s and 1960s whose marriages dissolve in the 1990s tend to have less education and a shorter employment history than those married in the 1980s or later. It is also more difficult for them to obtain employment even if they are granted rehabilitation alimony and acquire marketable skills. If they had been employed prior to or early in their marriage, perhaps until having children, their knowledge in almost any field would be seriously out-of-date 25 or more years later. Many lack computer and other essential electronic skills for today's working world. As a result, at a time when, now that the children are finally grown, they had been thinking of a less pressured life, perhaps "retirement," or travel and other sources of active pleasure, they find themselves struggling economically to maintain a semblance of the lifestyle they had enjoyed during the marriage—until their personal D-Day occurred.

ECONOMIC STATUS OF THE DIVORCED MAN

Men tend to have higher educational levels and higher incomes than their wives.

> So long as they remain married, men are content to trade their higher income for the nurturing, child-care services, cooking, and housecleaning they receive from their wives. When the relationship dissolves, this exchange of benefits ceases. Accordingly, many men feel justified in withdrawing their economic support from their wives. Why, they ask, should they pay for benefits that are no longer being provided? (Furstenberg & Cherlin, 1991, p. 29)

In litigating or negotiating the divorce, they tend to downplay these spousal services and benefits to reduce the amount awarded to the former wife whether in a community property or an equitable distribution jurisdiction. As her share of the marital assets and any alimony decrease, however, so does the economic support available for the couple's children, if she is primary residential parent. If he is granted legal and physical custody, and if his income increases, the children may fare well financially, and even be overindulged with all kinds of sports and cultural activities as well as all the accompanying equipment—skis, ski trips and lessons, ballet or tennis camp, horseback riding lessons and their own horses, and so on. This can be an expression of caring and being willing to provide the children with the many advantages he can afford and/or a way of bribing them to stay with him because life with Mom would not be anywhere near as luxurious.

Where the husband has acquired substantial assets during the marriage, he may have purchased securities or real estate of which his wife is unaware, or may have separate bank accounts and safe deposit boxes that he has kept secret. Some of these men have conducted their business affairs in this way in anticipation of a future divorce, and manage to keep these assets hidden throughout the discovery process and even under court order to reveal all their assets. If their wives are not suspicious that such sequestered assets exist during the marriage, it is unlikely that they will look for such property at the time of divorce (which was the idea in the first place). This leads to further imbalance in the equitable distribution of marital assets. Even if a woman has stashed away some of her household allotment or of her own salary, the amount she has accumulated is likely to be minuscule in comparison. If either has participated in such deceptive shenanigans, the level of trust for negotiating cannot be high, as each is likely to attribute similar underhanded behavior to the other partner—an interesting use of projection as a mechanism of defense.

If, in addition to an essentially inequitable distribution of assets, the man remarries and subsequently has children in the second (or third) marriage, in what ways do his new obligations intrude on the economic support obligations to his earlier marriage(s)? Although the answer to this question obviously has importance for his (first) ex-wife, the impact of his decision tends to weigh even more heavily on his children.

In contrast with many other Western nations, the United States has until recently favored a voluntary approach to child support. In effect, fathers have been allowed to put their money where their heart is:

> [Many of them have invested most if] not all of their resources
> in their current household rather than their former one. If all
> women reentered marriage soon after divorce, this arrangement

would work well enough [assuming the new spouse is willing to support her and her children]. But fewer women than men remarry, and our society has begun to realize the high costs to children of letting fathers decide whether their first loyalties are to their present or past families. (Furstenberg & Cherlin, 1991, p. 60; material in [   ] added by current authors)

This is not to say that men should not provide adequate support for their new families. Clearly, they should. However, existentially and morally, the children from the first marriage did not ask to be placed in their present position and should not be penalized because their parents chose not to stay together. To the contrary, their existence and claim on their father for affection and support predate his new commitments and have a compelling ethical validity that should not be ignored or minimized. Second, there is a need for the man to recognize that he is assuming additional, rather than simply different, financial obligations when he remarries. He has ongoing prior and continuing obligations, and should have loyalties to his children of prior marriages. If he is very wealthy, this is less of a problem than it is for the great majority of modest-income divorced men.

Nevertheless, one can understand his new wife's resentment of continuing payments to his first family. This matter seldom is actively considered prior to the remarriage, or, if considered, it may be glossed over as "manageable, so don't worry." Prenuptial agreements and the future spouse's reading of the divorce decree, which spells out financial commitments and responsibilities to children of the first marriage, can ground the new marriage in reality and avert some of the postmarital disputes over this issue, although they may not reduce feelings of resentment.

CHILD SUPPORT

Although many marriages are no longer entered into "until death us do part," parenthood is rarely as disposable. This means that parents have an obligation to support their children at least until they reach age 18. Although each state was supposed to have state-specific child support guidelines in place by October 1987 (Public Law 98-378, 1984), there is no guarantee that attorneys or judges will follow those guidelines (Ellis, 1991). Usually, the amount of child support awarded is determined by a formula that includes the gross income of *both* parents and the number of children involved (see Appendix A for the Florida Child Support Guidelines and Worksheet).

At the time of separation, and again when the divorce is finalized, the parents must deal with the basic question of who is going to contribute how much to the support of the couple's children and how many dollars will be allocated for that support. Whether court-ordered or decided by the parents, the support arrangements, with or without a formula such as that described, will likely include consideration of the wage earners' salaries and other financial resources as well as the needs of the children. In addition to rent, food, and clothing, who will be financially responsible for medical care? Unreimbursed psychotherapy fees? Day care? Tuition, if the child attends a private school or is in college? Religious education? Extracurricular programs such as music lessons, or sports equipment and opportunities?

According to Kurz (1995), "Nationwide, child-support awards have been so low that they have not met even half the costs of childrearing. For many custodial parents, the cost of childcare currently exceeds their entire child-support award" (p. 82). Kahn and Kamerman asserted, in their discussion of child support in the United States, that the central components of the child support problem are "how to assure children an adequate income and standard of living, and how to ensure that parents fulfill their support obligations to their children" (1988, p. 11). In countries of continental Europe, "the problems of adequacy and predictability of support awards have been greatly alleviated by the use of realistic formulas or standardized support tables" (Glendon, 1987, p. 87), and are enhanced by more rigorous enforcement of payment as well as by supplemental payments by the government, which are forthcoming without individuals feeling shamed or inadequate. These are built into the social welfare system. Furstenberg and Cherlin noted in reviewing Glendon's work with reference to divorce in the United States:

> In granting a divorce to parents, we are liberal; in assisting their children we are illiberal. Until recently, we did less than any other country to ensure that absent fathers support their children; yet we offer their children less public support. The result

is that American children face the worst of both worlds: more so than children anywhere else, they cannot rely on either their parents or their government to support them. (1991, p. 97)

The Family Support Act of 1988 required "all states to provide for immediate wage withholding for all support orders by 1994" (Veum, 1993, p. 229). In October 1992, Congress passed the Child Support Recovery Act of 1992 (Public Law 102-521). Under this law, "willful nonpayment of support for a child residing in another state became a federal crime. Support arrearages must be greater than $5,000 or unpaid for more than a year" for the federal government to intervene (*Child Support Report*, 1994a, p. 6). In both this country and others, however, men (and sometimes women) disappear to evade support orders, and, in some cases, no one really expects them to pay support.

In Australia, the advisory committee that recommended a child support formula held "that children are entitled to receive a portion of their parents' income whether high or low. This places emphasis on horizontal equity that children in divorced families should be treated similarly to those from intact families that share in both parents' income" (Stuart, 1991, pp. 145–146).

This proposal strongly resembles one made by Garfinkel and Uhr (1984) under which all parents living apart from their children would be liable to a child-support tax, based on their gross income, collected through paycheck withholding, and proportional according to the number of children to be supported. In addition to reducing welfare costs and caseloads, Garfinkel and Uhr asserted that a legislated social child-support program of this nature "should also avoid burdening taxpayers, overtaxing absent parents, and worsening the economic predicament of AFDC beneficiaries" (1984, p. 115). They wrote that every child in a single-parent household should receive at least a minimum benefit from the absent parent and/or public subsidy. To critics who attacked their idea as an intrusion on the absent parent's privacy and power to decide how to spend his or her income, Garfinkel and Uhr responded that "there appears to be a consensus that, in the case of child support, the public interest and the interests of children outweigh the rights of their parents to economic freedom and privacy" (1984, p. 118). Given the huge amounts of child support funds that are not paid nor collectable, the great burden on AFDC that exists as a result, and the 40 percent or more of children living below the poverty line, it would be interesting to see if this proposal could be enacted and enforced "in the public interest" as well as the children's. A related proposal is to add a Child Support Assurance (CSA) element to existing Social Security programs, with support funds deducted from the noncustodial parent's earnings:

> An assured child support benefit is a government guarantee of a minimum amount of child support to those legally entitled to receive private support. For example, if the assured benefit were $200 per month and the noncustodial parent paid only $150, the government would make up the difference. . . . An assured child support benefit would increase economic security, reduce dependence on welfare, and increase paternity establishment. (Garfinkel, Melli, & Robertson, 1994, p. 95)

The likelihood of such a proposal being enacted into law, however, is remote in the mid- to late 1990s, given the antiwelfare stance of the majority in Congress.

In some cases, a parent is obliged, under more than one court order, to pay child support to more than one family. If he or she does not have enough funds to satisfy these obligations, "States must honor orders for current support before past-due support or paybacks, and each current order should receive something from the amount collected" (*Child Support Report*, 1994b, p. 5). Making this ruling effective should be easier because the Family Support Act of 1988 mandates that all states have "operational, automated statewide child support enforcement systems" in place as of September 30, 1995 (Marr, 1993, p. 1). Interstate clearinghouses also enhance the collection of support orders when the parent under order moves to a state other than where the original order was issued. However, court staffs in enforcement units are often shorthanded, and may not move rapidly to implement collection or see that some penalty is imposed for violation of the agreement and/or court order.

"Advocates of joint custody claim that by increasing fathers' formal attachment to children through legal recognition of paternal rights, joint custody will increase the amount of child support that fathers pay" (Seltzer, 1991, p. 899). Nonetheless, a case on appeal before the New Jersey Supreme Court argues that if a father cares for his children part of every week, then his child support payments to their mother should be reduced somewhat to allow him more flexibility in spending money on the children directly (Sullivan, 1995). There certainly is some logic and merit in the position as there is in a father's view that if the children are with him for a month in the summer, his child support amount should be decreased for that period of time since his expenses will increase. Fairness should be reciprocal.

As Seltzer (1991) points out, the truth of the father's position may vary with his income. In addition, joint legal custody does not ensure cooperation between the parents. Conflict between the former partners may result in support payments being withheld as a weapon in the war against the ex-spouse. Analysis of data from the National Longitudinal Survey of Youth does not support allegations that positive changes in visitation access have positive effects on child support and vice versa (Veum, 1993).

It is often convenient to divide child support into two parts: Type A expenses that are regular, recurring, and often paid by the nonresidential parent, and Type B expenses that are nonrecurring or irregular, and of which the nonresidential and residential parents both pay a share. Abel and Neumann (1994) suggest that Type A fixed expenses include:

- Rent or mortgage payments.
- Real estate taxes.
- Utilities.
- Automobile expenses.
- Food, including school lunch money.
- Clothing (basic).
- Personal care.
- Entertainment, eating out with children, family trips (with nonresidential parent).

All of these would be prorated with a portion attributable to expenses for the child's upkeep.

Type B expenses are those that change as the children grow older and are directly related to the children's needs:

Changeable Expenses

- Child care/babysitters/summer camp.
- Nursery school/private school expenses.
- Extracurricular activities including lessons, clubs, scouting, religious instruction.

- College (may be handled separately).
- Weekly allowance, if appropriate.

Occasional Expenses

- School supplies and uniforms.
- School trips.
- Gifts to children's friends.
- Sporting goods and hobbies.
- Toys and games.

Unpredictable Expenses

- Medical and dental insurance and fees for children.
- Psychotherapy and tutoring.
- Housekeeper (salary/taxes/etc.).

One adult child of divorce "remembers going back and forth between her parents' separate households as economically 'schizophrenic.' Her mother was awarded custody, and they lived at a subsistence level. Her father had penthouses, limousines, and airplanes" (Fassel, 1991, p. 105). This situation is all too frequently experienced, even if not quite at these extremes. Fassel asserts further, "It is a rare father who pays a child's college expenses" (1991, p. 105). If this is so, whether or not the father has remarried, why should his children be deprived because he could or would not stay married to their mother? Would he have paid college tuition had the marriage remained intact? If he would have, then why should his children be penalized because the marriage was dissolved? This is a major cause of anxiety for mid- and late adolescent children of divorce, as discussed in Chapter 10.

The issue of nonpayment of support orders, or attempts to evade/delay/reduce compliance with them, is a puzzling one. One researcher asked, "If fathers love their children, and if they have more money relative to needs after than before separation and divorce, how can they fail to pay child support? Yet fail they do. Why?" (Haskins, 1988, p. 306). In a study of 150 fathers subject to the Child Support Enforcement Program in North Carolina, albeit an atypical sample of divorced fathers, the major justifications they believed were adequate "for missing child support payments were that the father is unemployed and that the mother does not spend the money on the children"

(Haskins, 1988, p. 322). This group of largely black, low-income fathers "denied the importance of all other rationalizations— anger at the mother, having a new family, mothers not needing the money, having unpaid bills, and disagreeing with the mothers' child-rearing practices" (p. 322). In practice, if not in questionnaire responses, however, such rationalizations *are* often used as justification for not paying child support by thousands of absent fathers of all races and income levels. Notice that there is no mention of children's needs in these statements. Instead, retribution and punishment of the ex-wife appear to motivate the withholding of payments.

In some jurisdictions, a parent who is in arrears on child support may be ordered by the court to "pay up—or else," the "or else" being a jail sentence or, in some states (e.g., Indiana, Oklahoma, South Dakota, Texas), loss of the parent's driver's or professional license. Although the penalty may be appropriate for violating a court order, it hardly helps the dependent child, for an incarcerated parent not only cannot earn the money to pay support but may lose his or her job as a result of the enforced absence. Also, the child may be furious at Mom for "putting Daddy in jail." Other legal remedies, described in the following paragraphs, should be more effective means of enforcing support orders.

A number of laws have been passed to try to enforce child support orders, each of which has tried to close loopholes in earlier laws. The Aid to Families with Dependent Children (AFDC) program, enacted in 1935, "was primarily intended to assist children whose fathers had died. . . . By 1982, less than 1% of the recipient children were eligible due to the death of the father" (Lima & Harris, 1988, p. 21). Amendments to the Social Security Act over more than two decades, beginning in 1950, attempted to relieve the taxpayers of the burden of paying support to children whose fathers were absent rather than deceased. Finally, in 1975, the Child Support Enforcement (CSE) Program was established "to strengthen the law and improve state programs for establishing and collecting support" (Lima & Harris, 1988, p. 25). Additional amendments were passed in 1984 to provide incentives to the states to enforce the laws.

When a parent does not pay child support, it is now possible to attach the parent's salary in many states. When a parent has moved out-of-state to evade responsibility, there are now state laws to encourage interstate cooperation to enforce support orders. A model state law—the Uniform Interstate Family Support Act (UIFSA)—was approved by the National Conference of Commissioners on Uniform State Laws in 1992 and has been endorsed by the U.S. Commission on Interstate Child Support and the American Bar Association, adopted in 21 states plus the District of Columbia, and introduced in additional states (*Child Support Report*, 1995). Overall, the "core of UIFSA is that it limits control of an interstate child support case to a single state" (*Child Support Report*, 1994c, p. 3). It is hoped that this will reduce the jurisdictional delaying tactics that some absent parents have employed. In addition, the Child Support Recovery Act of 1992 "made it a federal crime to willfully fail to pay a past due support obligation with respect to a child who resides in another state (Elrod, 1994, p. 486).

Another technique used to collect delinquent child support is a deduction of the amount due from federal income tax refunds. In tax year 1994, more than $828 million in delinquent child support was collected in this way, benefiting more than 1.1 million families (*Child Support Report*, 1996):

> State child support enforcement agencies report names of parents who owe child support and the overdue amount to the Federal Office of Child Support Enforcement (OCSE). These persons are notified in writing of the amount which will be withheld to cover their child support debt and that amount is then deducted from their income tax refund. (p. 5)

Both AFDC and non-AFDC families benefited from this practice.

As noted earlier, medical insurance becomes very expensive if one is not part of a group plan. Under a 1993 tax code revision, Qualified Medical Child Support Orders ("Quamso") were established, enabling a custodial parent to "enroll the children in the noncustodial parent's health plan, submit claims, and receive payments without approval of the noncustodial parent. The noncustodial parent can be forced to pay the premiums through automatic payroll deductions" (Elrod, 1994, p. 486). Although this is important for any child's well-being, it is a more critical problem if the child is chronically ill or handicapped in some way, so that the custodial parent cannot go out to work.

DIVORCE IN THE "MEDICARE YEARS"

As already noted, those women who married 30 to 50 years ago, in a society that regarded homemaking and child rearing as a woman's principal if not only occupation, are at a marked disadvantage if divorced in today's society. As one attorney put it, "Seriously at risk are the heroines of the Betty Crocker culture, women who have already devoted their most career-productive years to homemaking and who, if forced into the labor market after divorce, suddenly will be viewed as modern dinosaurs" (Starnes, 1993, p. 70). Decades of homemaking represent substantial labor on her part, a meaningful contribution to the marriage that enabled her husband to focus on his job. Making this point, in litigation or mediation, is essential if the wife is not to be left a pauper. Unrealistic judicial perspectives, however, can leave the older divorcée in financially strained circumstances, and yet without the economic resources to appeal truly inequitable decisions, for if she loses an appeal, she still has to pay legal fees.

The current costs of medical insurance, in advance of or to supplement Medicare, and the probability of greater need for medical care with increasing age constitute an added source of anxiety for the displaced homemaker. Horbatt and Grosman make a strong argument for considering retiree health benefits as "a form of deferred compensation, earned by the employed spouse during the course of the marriage" (1994, p. 327) and therefore to be considered as part of marital property subject to equitable distribution. They further recommend, "She should receive her equitable distribution share of such retiree health benefits in a lump sum award at the time of the divorce based upon an actuarial valuation" (1994, p. 343). The problem for many of these women is that without such a distribution they may not have funds sufficient to pay health insurance premiums.

In a sense, women in domestic service occupations who have worked out of the home since adolescence may occasionally be in a better position to continue employment than the "Betty Crocker heroines" are to find jobs. True, they rarely have enjoyed the comparative luxury of the women who employ them, and they may not have had the security of insurance or material goods, but mentally they are (and have been) oriented to working as long as they are able to do so. If their employers have withheld and paid Social Security taxes for them over the years, they will have some personal postretirement income in addition to Medicare or Medicaid. On the other hand, the only marital asset to be divided may be their marital home, which means that it may have to be sold in order to obtain any liquid property to divide. Thus the low-income divorcée may "leave the marriage with limited income potential, few if any assets, and no home" (Starnes, 1993, p. 87). To a woman in her 50s or older, this is a bleak prospect.

ALTERNATIVES TO ECONOMIC DISASTER

After considering the economic plight of each of the parties from the several perspectives discussed in the foregoing pages, it becomes apparent that some alternatives must be developed so that each party may receive his or her fair distribution of the family's assets. Although neither of the parting spouses may be willing initially to compromise, this is the path that reality should dictate.

A premarital agreement is one way that has been proposed to avoid the unhappy economic consequences of divorce. In those states that have adopted the proposed Uniform Premarital Agreement Act, "what may be included in a formal antenuptial agreement is partially controlled by state law. Such agreements can specify a wide range of property rights and obligations . . ." (Kaslow, 1991, p. 379), and state law also spells out what kinds of agreements are invalid and may later be held unenforceable. Sometimes it is the parent of one party who insists that a prenuptial agreement be drawn up to protect assets, such as a family business or inherited wealth. As Kaslow has indicated, "This tends not to happen among lower and lower middle class families. They have little to protect and are too involved in daily survival tasks" (1991, p. 381). Where such an agreement is to be drawn, it is advisable for each party to have separate legal counsel before signing anything, if only to ensure that they are both fully informed as to what they are agreeing to.

Stake (1992) has suggested that couples should create antenuptial agreements on the division of their marital assets that would be enforceable in the courts. He avers that such an agreement "can provide a basis for jointly optimal division of duties by eliminating the fear of the consequences of differential investment in market and household skills if the parties later separate" (p. 416). Stake further asserts that the agreement would force couples to confront incompatibilities (and areas of fundamental disagreement) before marriage, and would reduce the pain experienced by children when their parents argue about financial settlements under the present arrangement. He proposes that legislation be passed in each state that would mandate the existence of a premarital agreement, possibly providing statutory options, before a marriage could occur. (As already noted, many states have passed legislation for voluntary agreements.) In his view, "A mandate may be the only effective way to remove the state from the role of deciding what is best for couples and to provide intending spouses a meaningful opportunity to make these important choices for themselves" (p. 446).

To be fair, he outlines as well a number of problems that could ensue from such a policy, not the least of which is imbalance in negotiating skills—which can exist not only before marriage but also at its end. There is little provision, for example, for changes in level of maturity during the marriage that might have resulted in different choices had the parties been more mature, and possibly more realistic, when they negotiated the agreement. Also to be considered is that often, when couples are young and very much in love, they are naive and idealistic. To them, the idea of a prenuptial agreement that provides for the eventuality of the demise of their marriage would be abhorrent and counter to their commitment to each other.

Although the contract would be designed at a time when the couple is cooperative and might avert bitter battles at the time of divorce, what might it do to the premarital expectation that marriage is "until death do us part"? Despite awareness that one in two marriages is likely to end in divorce, is it appropriate to enter marriage, or to encourage at that time, anticipation that it may not work? Does the reduction in financial squabbling and need for judicial intervention in the disposition of resources at the time of divorce justify the emotional stress engendered by mandating or even proposing premarital agreements for all marriages? Prenuptial agreements in the case of remarriage are fairly common, especially where one (or both) of the spouses-to-be has children. Even these, however, are recommended rather than mandated. Often one party is angry at being asked to enter into such an agreement because it seems to signify lack of commitment to the relationship as well as a lack of trust. The one pushing for it does not want to risk being taken advantage of, being married for his or her money, or having assets intended for his or her children depleted. The proposal of an agreement may pose an obstacle to getting the marriage off to a happy start.

Another possibility, proposed by Starnes (1993), is to view marriage as a partnership. From this point of view, the partners, during the marriage, invest to some degree in each one's human capital. Upon dissociation from the partnership (dissolution of the marriage), a "buyout" by one partner may be appropriate. Starnes presents a number of possibilities as to the ways in which this may be determined, as well as a formula for arriving at the financial cost.

Starnes's proposal suggests yet another alternative—the post-nuptial agreement. This "can ensure that a mate regains control of the assets he or she brought into the marriage and then comingled with the partner's funds. . . . Such contracts should also specify how any appreciated property will be handled" (Kaslow, 1991, p. 384).

While it may be true that, when married, two can live more cheaply than one, once the partners have divorced, the cost of maintaining two households may be more than double the cost of one.

CONCLUDING COMMENT

The division of existing marital assets as part of a divorce can be far more complicated than most separating spouses realize. Teaching young women to set aside, as wives, a portion of their weekly income from their husband or job so that they will have a nest egg in the event of a future divorce projects some of the same negative aura as the prenuptial agreement. Also, in some states, what they set aside is considered a divisible marital asset, as is the jewelry they receive. Perhaps their best insurance policy for the future is to acquire a good education and job-related skills as these are the only assets that are nondivisible. Finding ways to keep the division of marital assets honest for all parties while respecting the positive relationships of newlyweds warrants creative thought on the part of many professionals.

CHAPTER 7

Parenting and Child Custody Issues

THE CARE OF ANY MINOR CHILDREN of a marriage is a key issue to be resolved when the parents separate and divorce. As one element of the divorce settlement, the "children can be regarded as chattel or their needs seen as a challenge" (Schwartz, 1994a, p. 72). Crucial issues include: With whom will the children live primarily? Who will provide the bulk of their financial support? The usual answers have been "the mother" to the first question, and "the father" to the second. However, this is no longer invariably the case; some fathers (about 10%) are being awarded primary residential parent status and an increasing number of mothers are contributing to the financial cost of raising children. In many cases, the dilemma for the courts has been and continues to be: "What solution is in the best interest of the children and what is the most equitable custody arrangement for the parents?" (Magid & Oborn, 1986, p. 96). Is it possible to resolve this issue evenhandedly? Will both parents agree that the decision is fair and best?

Custody has four aspects:

1. *Physical.* The day-to-day living arrangements.
2. *Legal.* Major decisions such as religion and religious education, type of schooling (public or private), medical care, parental "rights."

3. *Economic.* What each parent is to contribute to the child's financial support and well-being—housing, food, medical and dental care, insurance, educational costs, clothing, vacations.
4. *Emotional.* The nurturance, guidance, love, and encouragement that is provided on a consistent basis, whether or not the child is "in residence" at a particular time.

Children should be allowed easy access to both parents by telephone, fax, videotapes, audiotapes, letters, e-mail, and so on, so that they can maintain regular contact with both parents. Swiss courts advise at least one visit per month between the nonresident parent and the children, although more frequent contact may occur where all parties are willing (Zollinger & Felder, 1991).

THE NATURE OF CHILD CUSTODY

Custody Criteria

Elrod and Walker (1994) identify seven custody criteria: (a) statutory guidelines, (b) children's wishes, (c) joint custody laws, (d) who is deemed the more cooperative parent, (e) history of domestic violence, (f) health (parents' or children's), and (g) attorney or guardian ad litem (GAL) recommendations for the child. Only 7 states employ all of these; 8 do not have joint custody laws; and 10 make no provision for the children's wishes (Elrod & Walker, 1994, p. 568). Another criterion in some states may be parental *skills* in addition to parental "fitness" (cited in a Mississippi case; Elrod & Walker, 1994, p. 578). The 1994 Supplement to Florida Statutes 1993, provided in Appendix B, is a good example of specific criteria and judicial language.

Section (3)(a) of the Florida document is particularly salient to the thesis being presented here that neither adult should engage in parental alienation (Palmer, 1988). This section states that the custody evaluator should consider "which parent is more likely to allow the child frequent and continuing contact with the nonresidential parent" (Dissolution of Marriage; Support; Custody, 1992 Revision, p. 27).

In many states, joint custody is the legislative mandate, with exceptions based on unfitness of one parent, or parental agreement for some other arrangement. This preference has replaced the earlier standard of the "more fit" parent; it is hard to prove one is unfit. Exceptions are cases where alcoholism, drug abuse, child or spouse abuse, and incest can be documented. Joint custody presumes that the parents can and will cooperate for the benefit of the children, but this is not always the case. However, there may also be a conflictual or a disengaged pattern of coparenting. As Maccoby found in the Stanford Child Custody Project, "The amount of hostility and legal conflict surrounding the divorce itself is implicated in the kind of coparenting pattern that a parental pair adopt" (1991, p. 1). Indeed, "Some parents who seek shared custody do so to manipulate or vent hostility toward an ex-spouse" (Rothman, 1991, p. 215).

Physical Custody

Physical custody may be *joint* and shared, equally or not depending on various circumstances such as the child's age and the parents' circumstances and availability for caretaking. Whether children move back and forth from one parent's home to the other with mutually agreed-upon or judicially prescribed frequency will depend on such factors as whether the parents live near each other or are in distant geographic locales. Other arrangements are possible, such as being *primarily with one parent,* but with varying visitation arrangements for the other; *sole custody,* with limited or no visitation with the noncustodial parent; and *split custody,* in which one or more children live with each parent, often with visitation arranged alternately so that contact is maintained with both parents and siblings in the same household at some times. Although there may be appropriate reasons for this last option in some families, it may also deprive the children of a mutually supportive sibling network as well as continuity and stability of relationships (Hyde, 1991; Kaplan, Ade-Ridder, & Hennon, 1991), and is generally not advisable unless the children cannot get along together or one is a special needs child requiring much attention. Children should not be divided evenly as the property may have been as they are *not* property, nor is the foremost consideration here what the parents want. The caretaking arrangement must be predicated on the best interest of the child:

> From the family systems perspective, split custody is seen as a problematic custody arrangement. Interference with how the family members interact with each other is inevitable. . . . [S]eparating siblings does not allow them to respond as a system. This would seem to exacerbate the existing conflict. In such arrangements, the family becomes unable to adapt as a system to the changes brought on by the divorce and custody arrangement. (Kaplan et al., 1991, p. 264)

"When it comes to visitation rights, many judges prefer not to spell out chapter and verse. They have learned through past experience that the specifics of visitation are difficult if not impossible to enforce if the parties are determined not to abide by the agreement" (Rothman, 1991, p. 202). American courts tend to encourage the couple to work out their own visitation agreements and to make the commitment in writing, which then may become part of the divorce document.

Some practitioners who specialize in custody work believe the *parenting plan* should be quite specific as children and their parents need predictability, stability, and the ability to plan their time. If specificity is combined with fluidity, when needed, everyone may benefit more than they do from ambiguity (Kaslow, 1995b). The term *parenting* is preferable to "custody" since parenting implies *responsibilities and rights*, that both parents continue to have since they are not divorced from their children. "Custody" implies ownership, which neither has been nor should be the case, as one does not ever have ownership of another person. The concept of parenting is more syntonic with the ideal of sharing in the children's lives.

Changes in a Parent's Status and Requests for Agreement Modification

If circumstances change radically, with one parent becoming abusive, addicted, or engaging in criminal behavior, for example, the other parent can ask the court to modify the agreement so that the child(ren) will not suffer from continuing unsupervised or turbulent visitation. Homosexuality of a parent is not perceived to be detrimental per se to a child and so should not interfere with that parent's right to visit with his or her child unless the child's best interests are at risk (Hyde, 1991). If it is the primary caretaker who "comes out" as a homosexual, however, and especially if that parent is living with his or her same-sexed partner, the other parent may seek a reversal of the custody agreement. Whether a judge grants that reversal will depend not only on expert testimony concerning the effects of such an arrangement on the child(ren), but also on the judge's attitude toward homosexuality. "In deciding on custody awards, the court may presume that homosexuality per se makes a parent unfit, presume that a child may be harmed by exposure to homosexual behavior, or require proof that the parent's homosexuality has or will have an adverse effect on the child before custody is denied" (Fowler, 1995, p. 363). Even in cases where the alternate caretaker is neglectful or abusive, some judges still rule against the otherwise "fit" homosexual parent (McCullough, 1996). Judicial discretion in cases involving a homosexual parent is the rule in Canada under the Canadian Charter of Rights and Freedoms (1982) and the Canadian Human Rights Act (1985), both of which recognize gay and lesbian rights (Casey, 1994).

As McIntyre (1994) points out, courts in the United States tend to be biased against homosexual relationships and therefore to negate primary custody by the homosexual parent or even overnight visitation if the noncustodial parent is cohabiting with a same-sexed partner. The typical reasons cited include the possibility of sexual abuse of the child, exposure of the child to homosexual behaviors, the development of homosexual preferences by the child, infection of the child with HIV, and/or the embarrassment or stigmatization of the child because of community prejudices. In large urban communities with a sizable homosexual population that includes couples with children, this is apt to be less of a problem than in a small city or rural area where living a gay lifestyle evokes censure and ostracism. When children are rejected by peers, and sometimes neighbors and teachers, because of a parent's sexual orientation, such social opprobrium can add markedly to the pain, bewilderment, and heart-wrenching the divorce causes the child(ren). A number of publications offer detailed discussions of the distinctive aspects of socialization experiences for children growing up with a gay or lesbian parent (see Gottman, 1990; Green & Bozett, 1991; Patterson, 1995). The approach taken shows commonalities and variations across homosexual couples and environments and the psychosocial complexities encountered.

McIntyre suggests that negative judicial decisions can be averted if the divorcing couple use mediation to develop a co-parenting agreement, possibly combined with a legal agreement by the gay couple regarding their rights and responsibilities as equal parents (1994, pp. 142–146). Provision may even be made for visitation by the partner if the gay couple ends their relationship. The mediator may also be able to help the child(ren) understand the homosexual parent's preference, in an effort to reduce the breakdown of the parent-child relationship. Mediating instead of litigating may be advisable particularly in states where prior decisions have been handed down that have declared "lesbians and gay men to be unfit as parents because of their sexual orientation" and where they have "been denied custody or visitation with their children following divorce" (Patterson, 1995, p. 264).

In many jurisdictions, a father may gain custody of children based on the fact that the mother is working outside the home or is involved in furthering her education, and is therefore not available to the children as a full-time homemaker mother. It is interesting to note that care by a nonparent (e.g., grandparent or day-care center) is perceived as satisfactory, however, when custody is awarded to the father (Clay, 1995).

Similarly, different moral standards may be applied to male and female parents concerning the nature of their sexual relationships with a third party. Sometimes such gender-based decisions have been reversed on appeal (Ellison, 1991), but the issues continue to be a factor, however subconscious, in many custody decisions, with women who have affairs being penalized more often than men are. She is still viewed in some quarters as an adulteress or "fallen woman" and therefore as an unfit mother.

Fathers and Custody

Despite legislative support for custody arrangements to be based primarily on the "best interests of the child," in actuality decisions may be made based more on the earlier "tender years' doctrine," in which it was assumed that children should normally be in the care of their mothers, at least until age 7 and preferably until age 14, since bonding with the Mom, as the main nurturing parent, should not be disrupted. In recent years, thousands of divorced fathers have formed organizations that serve as advocates for them in visitation conflicts and in their efforts to be the primary caretakers. Frequently, their ex-wives have denied them visitation despite their having fulfilled support obligations regularly, or the ex-wife may have moved out of the court's jurisdiction without permission to avoid paternal visits (Durkin, 1994). The fathers' rights groups then act both as support teams for the distraught father and as advocates in the ensuing litigation. Many of these groups have joined together under the umbrella of the Children's Rights Council (formerly the National Council for Children's Rights) to secure a more balanced response from the courts as well as to influence legislation affecting fathers and their children.

Data cited by Facchino and Aron (1990) indicate that the number of divorced fathers gaining custody of their children more than tripled in the period from 1970 to 1985. The father may have gained custody because (a) he had an equal or major role in child care during the marriage, (b) the mother abandoned this role at the time of separation, or (c) he could afford a tougher, more skilled attorney and won the battle for custody—sometimes to punish his wife and much to her consternation and humiliation. In some cases, these fathers now receive child support from the noncustodial mothers (Greif & DeMaris, 1991). This is most likely to occur "when the mother has a high income, is white and college educated, and is visiting frequently. Over time," it is noted, "the chances of getting support decline" (Greif & DeMaris, 1991, p. 169). Actually, as time passes, support may diminish whether the father or the mother has primary caretaking responsibilities. Also, according to the Greif and DeMaris study, *"Fathers raising older children exclusively are the least apt to receive child support"* [italics in original] (1991, pp. 173–174).

A second cadre of fathers with respect to custody are those who, in effect, abandon their children after the divorce and do not see them for years, or only on a very occasional basis such as once every year or two (Lewin, 1990). Usually these fathers default on paying child support. Their children wonder what they did wrong, why their father has disappeared from their lives, and—often encouraged by their mothers—may turn what was once love for their fathers into hate because of his abandonment. Ultimately, someone should help them to realize that it was not a flaw in them that led to Dad's desertion, but rather something in his personality. This is often a task for a therapist.

The third group of fathers includes those who remain actively involved in some form of reasonably amicable shared parenting—caring about their children and not denigrating their former spouses. This is the optimal arrangement and will be discussed more fully later in this chapter.

Legal Custody

Legal custody, too, can be joint, or may be granted solely to the primary physical caretaker. In joint, or shared, legal custody, both parents have the right to be informed of their child's progress (or problems) in school, to attend teacher conferences and special school events, to have a voice in the selection of the school or college the child will attend, to review medical and dental records, and to decide what religious training the children will have and where they will worship (Maccoby & Mnookin, 1992; Rothman, 1991, p. 204). Sometimes the parents decide that each will take the major decision-making responsibility in different areas, thus avoiding having to make joint decisions about everything. Thus if the mother is a physician, she may be in charge of the health and medical care arena. If Dad is in the arts, he may be responsible for the child's exposure to various forms of cultural activities.

In cases where the parents practice different religions, an increasing phenomenon today, some posit it may be assumed that if the noncustodial parent "proposes exposing the child to a different religious system during periods of visitation . . . the child will be confused and thereby harmed from the exposure" (Wah, 1994, p. 273). This will vary with the age of the child as well as the degree of pressure exerted by each parent on the child to follow his or her religion. Mere exposure to other religions may be educational rather than a cause for further parental confrontation, while proselytization by one parent (as against the other) may become a cause for modifying a custody order.

If one of the parents joins and becomes engulfed in a pseudo-religious cult, such as Hare Krishna, Church of Scientology, or the Unification Church, the dilemma of the other parent about shared custody may be intensified when he or she does not want the child brainwashed or coerced into thinking all nonbelievers of the cult's extreme position are "of the devil" (Isser &

Schwartz, 1988; Kaslow & Schwartz, 1983). When cult member-
ship is a factor in a divorce or child custody action, it needs to
be handled with great sensitivity and the profound concerns
heard and attended to seriously.

CHILD CUSTODY EVALUATIONS

Divorce mediators and attorneys alike claim to direct their efforts, except in very adversarial divorce actions, to being "fair"
to each parent in the matter of custody. Where there is conflict
about child custody, including charges of parental unfitness,
mental health professionals may be asked by the court to evaluate the parents and children. Not only do these professionals
have to be attentive to professional guidelines for such evaluations (see APA, 1994, for widely used guidelines; Appendix C
of this volume), but they need to be aware that parents may bias
the information "they provide to an evaluator in a direction that
supports their position in the litigation" (Ash & Guyer, 1991,
p. 835).

Gindes (1995) points out that the guidelines are "aspirational"
rather than prescriptive or directive, and that terminology needs
to be clarified. With reference to evaluation of the parents, she
states:

> Parenting capacity needs to be assessed within the context of
> the parent's overall psychological status and functioning. An
> evaluation that just addresses parenting capacity would provide
> only a partial view of the parents. . . .
>
> The guidelines state that the values of the parents relative to
> parenting, as well as to other aspects of their behavior, are to be
> considered. The term "values" needs to be clarified or, prefer-
> ably, omitted. The Uniform Marriage and Divorce Act states that
> "[t]he court shall not consider conduct of a proposed custodian
> that does not affect his relationship to the child." (p. 43)

The Evaluation Study

The evaluation report should include a statement of the problems and issues that have led to the need for such a study in addition to such basic information as ages, health, employment
status, and family history of each parent, and age(s) of the
child(ren). The evaluator should interview both parents at

length, gaining insight into their views of themselves and their spouse as parents as well as their perspectives on how the custody and visitation issues should be resolved.

According to Stahl (1994):

> The parent's perceptions of his or her children and their needs should be described. In so doing, this section focuses more closely on the parenting issues in the evaluation and on the parent's ability to understand the child developmentally, respond to his child's emotional and structural needs, and understand issues of limit setting and discipline. (p. 83)

Psychological testing of each adult will reveal personality traits and potential behaviors that may indicate the parent's ability to understand and support the children or the presence of problems that could be harmful to the children. It is important to enumerate the strengths of each parent as well as any weaknesses that might surface.

The evaluator should interview the children and observe parent-child interaction, if possible, in the home setting. It must be ascertained whether the children understand why the evaluator is talking with them, and if not, this should be explained. They should be told that their responses will be held in confidence unless the child gives permission for quotation of some of their statements. (This is obviously not the case for infants and toddlers; confidentiality will depend on level of cognitive development and understanding.)

Additional information may be obtained as needed, and with the requisite permission of the parents, from extended family members, teachers, and others who have interacted with the family. These collateral sources may be able to provide information about the children's reactions to the stressful family situation that is neither apparent to the parents nor reported by the children themselves. It is the responsibility of the attorney(s) to make sure the mental health professional will have access "to all of the people the professional believes to be necessary to conduct the kind of evaluation required by the referral question" (Bricklin, 1995a, p. 9).

If a guardian ad litem has been appointed, his or her input should be appended to the report or filed separately, with the findings and considered in the total evaluation. This final report should assemble the data in an orderly fashion, tie it to the issues in question, and lead to recommendations for handling the issues.

As Clark (1995) suggests:

> An effective report should have a section which has a formulation of the expert's opinion in the case. This would include how the evaluator views the parents, the children, and the dispute, a descriptive statement about each party, as well as opinions about the parenting skills of each disputant, and the existence and extent of any psychopathy in any participant. This section should have direct reference to relevant law. (p. 36)

The summary should be focused on the children and their needs and the parents' ability to meet those needs so that the judge is provided with the information essential for making a decision. Most, but not all forensic psychologists engaged in doing custody evaluations adhere to the maxim, "We should not answer the ultimate question" (in this instance, "Who do you recommend be awarded primary custody or primary residence"), no matter how much pressure is placed on them by the attorney(s) or judges. They believe their role is to present the data, recommend how each parent might improve his or her parenting, and describe what the child needs—but not who should get primary custody. Only the judge is mandated to decide this when the parents can't agree.

One of us (FK) has evolved, with input from other experts in the field, a comprehensive protocol for child custody evaluations. It entails an extensive and expensive procedure, but it is posited that children of divorce whose parents are unable to agree on a viable, thoughtful shared parenting arrangement are entitled to a complete assessment, with all significant parenting figures involved, so that their best interests truly are considered paramount. The protocol appears as Appendix D in this book. When attorneys and judges refer children for custody evaluations, they are sent the protocol so that they will know what is involved in the lengthy procedure and that the evaluator believes determining the best interest of the child(ren) and making decisions about their present and future is so important that it warrants the investment of time, energy, and money. Other valuable protocols are presented and discussed in Ackerman (1995), Bricklin (1995b), Maccoby and Mnookin (1992), Schutz, Dixon, Lindenberger, and Ruther (1989), and Stahl (1994).

From the Child's Point of View

Allegedly, all parties, as required by law in most states, are to attend to the children's "best interests." However, "the children, especially preadolescents, are rarely consulted about *their* needs and relationships" [italics in original] (Schwartz, 1994a, p. 72). Consider, for example, the plight of an 8-year-old boy, "the object of a seven-year custody dispute [who] has been court-ordered to change houses every two days until the case is settled" (Smith, 1995). According to his mother, he is concerned about who will pick him up on a given day and whether he can come home (presumably to his mother). [Question: Why couldn't the youngster remain in one place and the parents move in and out?]

Attorneys rarely consider whether the children's views, if they are mature enough to have their views considered, and the parents' desires about what constitutes the best interests of the children are in harmony or in conflict. This does not mean that a youngster must state a preference for one parent or the other, but it does imply that the quality of their relationship with each parent, as they perceive it, as well as other needs and activities, should be given consideration in determining where they will live along with the parental positions. However, such questions should not be asked in a way that makes the children feel guilty of disloyalty to the parent for whom they do not express a preference.

Are children to be uprooted from their friends and neighborhood? Is their schooling to be interrupted by living alternate years with each parent in different communities? Does the decision that they are to spend weekends and vacations with the nonresident parent conflict with their need, especially as they move toward adolescence, to be with peers more than with parents, or interfere with major school activities? Even in this era of increasing sensitivity to child abuse by adults close to them, does the court hear their requests to be moved out of a situation that is physically or emotionally harmful to their mental health? In cases where one parent has primary physical parenting responsibility and the other has visitation "rights," the level of parental cooperation or conflict (and therefore degree of risk to the children) must be kept in mind, as well as the age and developmental level of the children in establishing a visitation schedule (Garrity & Baris, 1994).

"Young children and adolescents alike need to know where they will be living and with whom to reduce disabling anxiety and threats to self-esteem, and to maximize their emotional security" (Schwartz, 1994a, p. 79). This means, in essence, that the matter of substantial questions affecting the children should be handled expeditiously rather than being perceived as part of the comprehensive divorce settlement. Living arrangements and child support should be determined promptly after separation of the parents, based on the children's developmental level, with the possibility that these will be renegotiated periodically as the children's needs change. For example, babies and toddlers cannot form strong attachments and gain a sense of security if they are shifted back and forth frequently. The ease with which preschool children can move from one home to another fairly frequently, on the other hand, is quite different from that of the ease or desire of a preteen who has become involved with athletic teams, Scouts, or other interests. Over time, the preteen's schooling and social relationships differ from those of a mid-adolescent, and the amount and kind of contact each age group wants with parents will differ also.

Too many children's needs and desires are not heard. It is for this reason that many mental health and legal practitioners urge that a guardian ad litem or a child advocate be appointed by the court to give the child a voice in his or her present and future. The responsibilities of such an individual have not been clearly delineated as yet (Halikias, 1994) but might include being supportive to the child as well as being a spokesperson for the child. One would hope that this individual would be knowledgeable about child development and would therefore be able to educate the decision makers about the ramifications of proposed caretaking arrangements as well as the need to make such arrangements in a timely fashion to reduce turmoil for those least able to cope with it. Sometimes a therapist or mediator indicates that he or she will take the "voice of the child" with the parents to clarify and interpret their feelings, needs, and wishes, and to ensure that these do not get lost in the parental skirmish for power.

Children's preferences and the reasons behind them must be thoughtfully weighed. Is their choice based on wanting to be with the more lenient and permissive parent who will allow them to leave their room disheveled and their homework undone? Is it based on feeling sorry for a parent who is suffering from the divorce and perceived rejection and has become withdrawn, depressed, or alcoholic? If so, should we allow the child to be pulled into a long-term parentified or caretaker role? What if their expressed preference is based on wanting to be with the more affluent parent, who can provide much more because his or her income will keep growing? The overriding question remains, what will be best for them, and the answer may vary depending on who decides.

Another major factor in soliciting input from children is that the professional(s) involved should indicate they are being asked their thoughts, but the final decision rests with their parents and/or the judge. Parents should not abdicate their executive authority in the family (Minuchin, 1974) even though the family is becoming bi-nuclear (Ahrons & Rogers, 1987); when they do, children feel uncertain about their parents' ability to set limits and to care for them adequately and appropriately. They also acquire too much power and may then coerce a parent to give into them by threatening to select the other parent if they do not get what they want (Kaslow & Schwartz, 1987b). Also, to ask children to choose one parent over the other is to ask them to commit a sin of disloyalty (Boszormenyi-Nagy & Spark, 1973/1984), which will precipitate feelings of guilt and a sense of betrayal. Doing this should be avoided.

POSTDIVORCE

"After a custody settlement, children continue to be affected by the quality of their parents' relationship. Ex-spouses may argue over visitation schedules, important decisions about child rearing, and routine discipline" (Kitzmann & Emery, 1994, p. 150). There is a widespread assumption that mediation, geared as it is to cooperative problem solving, should persuade the ex-spouses to focus on joint child-rearing practices rather than on their marital conflicts, thus reducing the conflicts in this area compared with litigated divorces.

In a study comparing children (ages 2–17 years) of parents who had used mediation ($N = 32$) or litigation ($N = 26$) for their custody agreement, "children whose parents had gone through mediation 1 year earlier did not show fewer problems on average than did children whose parents had gone through litigation, nor did they show better parent-child relationships" (Kitzmann & Emery, 1994, p. 153). A more decisive factor seems to be revealed in the finding that "children whose parents reported a decrease in conflict over the first year had fewer behavior problems than did children whose parents maintained a high level of conflict" (Kitzmann & Emery, 1994, p. 156). Several tentative explanations for these findings are offered, which are related to the size of the sample, the expectations of the parents regarding divorce, or the amount of time spent in the mediation program; nonetheless neither these nor other interpretations of why they obtained these results seem to justify mandating mediation as the means of reducing the impact of parental divorce on the children. When chosen voluntarily, mediation may be more effective.

There are conflicting conclusions from studies of the effects of custody arrangements on children and their parents. In a rural North Carolina county, for example, joint custody was rarely awarded in the 1980s (Berger, Madakasira, & Roebuck, 1988). Relitigation of joint custody awards was not significantly different from the rate for exclusive (sole) custody awards, but perhaps more instructive, nonadjudicated custody cases had a very low rate of relitigation and "were also associated with a very low rate of postdivorce conflict when compared to exclusive and joint custody" (Berger et al., 1988, p. 607).

On the other hand, Nelson (1989) found that while joint custody led to more communication between the parents, "they also experience greater hostility and conflict in their relationship" (p. 155). This can have negative impact on the child(ren) who must continue to live in a tension-filled atmosphere after the divorce as well as prior to it. A third, and considerably smaller study than the two previously cited in numbers of subjects, found that sole custody arrangements were more stable than joint custody arrangements (Radanovic et al., 1994). Parents in this last study had little contact or communication with each other, although each parent apparently had "continuing concerns about their children's emotional well-being and the negative influence of the other parent's behavior on the child"

(p. 434). These few studies suggest that it is necessary to consider many factors before declaring that one custody arrangement is superior to another—length of time the arrangement has been in place, geographic factors, level of conflict and level of communication between the parents prior to the divorce, personality and character of parents and of children, and ages and number of children in the family unit.

Lessons may be learned from the experience of African American families:

> [These families] traditionally are centered around the children, creating a pedi-focal system. . . . [T]he family unit can be defined as including all those involved in the nurturance and support of an identified child, regardless of household membership. . . . It means putting the needs of children above adult's conjugal needs. (Crosbie-Burnett & Lewis, 1993, p. 244)

In practice, this means that legal as well as biological/adoptive family members, and caring nonfamily members are active in the care and nurturance of children when a parent is unavailable. The experience of African American families in learning to live within two cultures (their own and that of the larger society) could be applied to socializing children of divorce to function effectively in a society that assumes everyone lives in a nuclear family when their own reality is different. These families demonstrate the importance of the continuing involvement of extended family members, both kin and close friends.

PARENTING CLASSES AND COURSES

What might be more effective than mandating mediation is the growing movement to mandate parenting classes prior to the granting of a divorce. Predivorce parenting seminars do (or should) alert the parents to the negative effects of continuing conflicts on their children. One such program, in Franklin County (Columbus), Ohio, requires attendance at one 2½-hour session "in which parents are given an intensive dose of information to alter their cognitive framework and provide an emotional experience motivating them to approach the divorce process in a manner more constructive for their children"

(Petersen & Steinman, 1994, p. 30). They must attend the seminar within 45 days of filing for the divorce; this is an attempt to reduce the negative effects of conflict and litigation surrounding the divorce on the children. The seminar, using didactic lectures, videos, slides, and a handbook, focuses on four areas: the adult's experience in divorce, children's experiences in divorce, building a coparental relationship, and problem-solving. Among the encouraging results obtained from 600 initial seminar participants were (a) "Almost two thirds of the parents reported that the knowledge gained from the seminar may make a difference in how they interact with their former spouse around the children" and (b) 65 percent of the parents indicated a willingness "to consider mediation as an alternative to litigation in resolving conflicts over their children . . ." (Petersen & Steinman, 1994, p. 37).

In Connecticut, which has a seminar for parents involved in family division court cases (Public Act 93-319), an educational program was first developed for divorced (and separated) fathers, designed both to maintain their involvement with their children and to encourage child support payments (Devlin, Brown, Beebe, & Parulls, 1992). The Act, which went into full effect at the outset of 1994, requires that the course "shall include, but not be limited to, information on the developmental stages of children, adjustment of children to parental separation, dispute resolution and conflict management, guidelines for visitation, stress reduction in children and cooperative parenting." The presiding judge may order parents, with certain exceptions, to attend this parent education program whenever a minor child is involved in the case.

Similarly, a voluntary and confidential program called Peace (Parent Education and Custody Effectiveness) has been offered by the Westchester, New York, Family Court since 1992. "The purpose of the program is to teach parents how to settle their differences in ways that will not hurt their children" (Greene, 1995). The three 2-hour sessions are focused on (a) the legal system, (b) the effects of divorce and separation on the children, and (c) the effects of divorce and separation on the adults.

Common sense suggests that at least some parents will be positively affected by the information in such programs, reducing the impact of their separation and divorce on their children, and even on themselves perhaps. (An entire issue of *Family and Conciliation Courts Review* is focused on "Parent education in divorce and separation. The content of such programs is surveyed in an article by Braver, Salem, Pearson, and DeLusé, 1996; and an initial review of programs in progress across the United States is available in an article by Blaisure and Geasler, 1996.)

Another approach to reducing potential custody and access disputes is the London (Ontario) Custody and Access Project, which offers both family assessment and mediation services to parents in conflict on these issues. In the assessment process:

> Parents learn about their children's needs, hear reframed interpretations of their conflicts, experience reality testing with regard to their beliefs about what is best for the children as compared to the opinion of an independent assessor, face the difficulty of balancing their pursuit of their own wishes against the risks of a court trial, and experience some direct or indirect influence from the assessor's opinion. A settlement during an assessment can result from a three-way, rather than a two-way negotiation process of mediation. (Austin & Jaffe, 1990, p. 173)

A limited follow-up study at least one year after case final reports were prepared indicated that most parents in the sample reported less stress for themselves and perceived their children's adjustment as improved.

OTHER CUSTODY ISSUES

Particular difficulties arise when disputing parents live in different jurisdictions (states or countries). In the case of different states, the question of which state is the "home state" may be determined by where the divorce was granted, or where the parent with primary custody resides, or where the child has lived for an appreciable period of time. Where jurisdiction lies may be resolved by the Uniform Child Custody Jurisdiction Act (UCCJA) if it has been adopted by the state(s) involved. The judicial resolution of international child custody disputes may fall under the Hague Convention and, if appropriate, the International Child Abduction Remedies Act (Elrod & Walker, 1994).

Judicial rulings are not always carried out, resulting in prolonged turmoil for the child(ren).

During this phase of the legal divorce, which focuses on the coparenting/child custody and visitation issues (see Table 2.1, Stage IV), most children feel apprehensive and insecure. Their behavior may reflect their inner turmoil in a variety of symptomatic ways—ranging from becoming silent, sullen, and withdrawn to becoming boisterous, hostile, and aggressive. They may develop psychosomatic ailments or an eating disorder, such as anorexia or bulimia, or regress to less mature patterns of sleep and toileting behaviors. Or, they may adjust reasonably well, if their parents do, and if animosity is kept at a minimum (Wallerstein & Kelly, 1980).

For those children who are deeply troubled, a variety of treatments should be considered including individual therapy where they, and not their parents, are the center of attention (play therapy for younger children, activity and talk therapy for older ones, and perhaps art, music, and movement therapies with some); parent-child therapy in which they can disclose their fears and resentments in a safe sanctuary and not feel guilty or worry about being punished; sibling system therapy and/or "children of divorce" group therapy (Kessler & Bostwick, 1977; Roizblatt et al., 1990) where a problem-solving approach to this life transition process is taken and the peer group provides a sense of belonging and shared experience. Treatment can be supplemented by bibliotherapy using such books as Ricci's *Mom's House; Dad's House* (1980). The closer to the time of the divorce upheaval that children receive help in understanding the experience and gaining some sense of control over charting their own course in the present and future, the better the prognosis is for their present and future well-being. The effects of divorce on children are discussed further in Chapter 10.

CONCLUDING COMMENT

For the divorcing couple, and at times even for the professional helping them, the details to be resolved en route to the final parting are so numerous that some questions may be overlooked. Koopman, Hunt, and Favretto (1994) have developed and used two very helpful checklists, one for spousal agreements and the other for child-related agreements. For each item included on each checklist, there are five options: Nonapplicable; Not included; Precluded by nature of order/referral; Included in general terms; or Included in specific terms. Use of these checklists, or modified versions of them, is strongly recommended both to keep the issues in focus for the couple and to reduce the possibility of malpractice liability for the professional.

CHAPTER 8

Spiritual and Religious Aspects of Divorce

CEREMONIES AND RITUALS

In all societies, significant life events, both happy and sad, are marked by some kind of ceremony or ritual, often with religious overtones. Ceremonies and rituals are utilized throughout the personal, family, and community life cycles in recognition of special events and important transitions. They start when a baby is born with a naming, baptism, or bris ceremony. Rites of passage from childhood to adolescence seem to be universal and are observed in diverse ways by Native American tribes, South Sea Island cultures, and the Jewish religion through Bar and Bat Mitzvah ceremonies, to mention just a few. When a couple marries, the centerpiece of the wedding celebration is the ceremony—whether the occasion is large or small, formal or informal, held in church, on the beach, or at the office of a justice of the peace. When someone dies, there are prescribed patterns for the viewing, the wake, the funeral, the burial and aftermath, often derived from one's religion, and if not, from family, community, or tribal tradition.

Rituals are believed to help with healing, as they tend to "embody our feelings for us" (Blessum, 1988), and to enhance a sense of connectedness to others who participate in the same ritual, such as laying flowers at the grave of a loved one, either together or separately. Sometimes the same ritual, with perhaps slight variations, is conducted in many different places at the same time, such as Catholic Mass on Christmas Eve or Jewish high holy day services. Knowing that others are (or have been) participating in a similar service can bring great comfort, as this experience provides many people with the feeling of belonging to a larger world. For many, the familiarity of a repetitive church liturgy or of a traditional family holiday dinner provides a sense of security and predictability in a world in flux.

Rituals may involve music, dance, tears, trance states, prayers, chanting, fantasies—all of which serve to help people cope with the special event or trauma; they may incorporate highly rational behaviors or veer toward being quite irrational, though heavily endowed with personal meaning. Some individuals, including some humanistically oriented therapists (Gibson & Lathrop, 1988) and some clergy believe they can be transformative. Therapists who create or cocreate ceremonies tailored for their specific clients' needs, to help them overcome an impasse in their relationships or to deal with a particularly devastating event, report they find these rituals quite effective (see, e.g., Imber-Black, Roberts, & Whiting, 1988).

In this light, it may seem surprising that divorce ceremonies have been relatively rare, given the pain, grief, and mourning involved with this life cycle event and prolonged transition period. Until recently, any such ceremonies received scant attention in the therapy literature (Close, 1977; Kaslow, 1993b; Kaslow & Schwartz, 1987b). However, life cycle rituals are closely related to religious beliefs and practices; since the Catholic Church is opposed to divorce, as are many Protestant fundamentalist sects, and much of the Muslim world also prohibits divorce, ceremonies did not evolve to mark this splitting apart of the family unit.

Of the major religions in the world, the only one that we are aware of, from our own heritage and through our efforts to gather data, that has had a divorce ceremony for many centuries is Judaism. The husband traditionally has been permitted to obtain a divorce if his wife was unable to bear children or had committed adultery. When I (F.K.) became intrigued with the potential of a divorce ceremony for helping divorced couples neutralize their remaining animosity and hurt, as well as for offering their children an opportunity to describe their experience of divorce to the parents and to state what might help them complete their healing and "let go" of the anger and blame, I sought to collect whatever ceremonies I could acquire. I found that except for the "Get" ceremony conducted by a Rabbinic tribunal, little else existed (more on this later).

RELIGIOUS PROCEDURES AND REQUIREMENTS THAT AFFECT DIVORCE AND ITS SEQUELAE

Roman Catholic Church

Since the Roman Catholic Church has traditionally disapproved of divorce, and some married couples cannot or will not stay together, the annulment process evolved and has been used instead. One petitions the Church to declare the marriage null and void (i.e., to rule that it is canceled out as if it never happened). In some Latin American countries, like Chile, grounds for an annulment might include that someone lied about his or her age or address or was not mentally competent to make a commitment/contract to marry at the time it took place. This seems to pose an enormous dilemma for all, except perhaps the Church. If the couple have produced children, what does it mean to them to be told that their parents were married, but not really, since it is now nullified? The implication that either one or both lied when they got married, or are lying now to obtain an annulment, certainly is confusing to children and does not convince them that either the Church or their parents have integrity. They understand that somewhere there has been some duplicity or complicity to get an annulment; this is not a healthy model of candor for children. Another contradiction is that although the marriage really was not legitimate, the children were brought up as if it did exist and in recent decades have been considered to be legitimate, even if an annulment is granted. Such double-talk causes mystification.

The process of annulment in the United States tends to be lengthy and tedious. Sometimes therapists are asked to fill out a lengthy inquiry form if individuals seeking an annulment report that they have been or are in therapy (see Appendix E for form currently in use in some Florida archdioceses).

An annulment invalidates the prior marriage so that the parties can be permitted to remarry within the Church. Cadigan (1994) wrote about her experience with this when her ex-husband,

after 23 years of marriage, 4 children, and 15 years after their
no-fault divorce, notified her that he was seeking an annulment:

> [He sent her] articles from Catholic magazines defining annul-
> ment as a reconciling, benevolent and healing process that can
> "liberate" couples whose marriages, in spite of many years and
> the presence of children, were founded on "seriously inadequate
> abilities to love, relate and cohabit in a life of mutual concern
> and regard." (p. 22)

Cadigan found that she was unable to see herself as having been
an inadequate wife during the marriage, and wondered what a
nullification of that marriage would do to their children's status
in the eyes of the Church as well as their own self-image. Her reaction coincides with the dilemmas described earlier, in what
we have found to represent a fairly typical scenario.

Judaism

Just as Catholicism requires an annulment before someone can
(re)marry in the Church and have the marriage duly recognized,
Orthodox and Conservative Judaism require that the legally divorced individuals apply for and be granted a "Get." Unless the
individual has received such a "bill of divorcement," neither Orthodox nor most Conservative rabbis will officiate at a second
marriage. A Reform rabbi will, since in this more liberal wing of
Judaism, a Get is not a prerequisite for remarriage (see Appendix F for copy of the Ritual of Release).

    Only the husband can initiate this process, and if he does not,
his wife becomes an *agunah*—"a chained woman." This is attributable to the fact that in traditional Judaism, the husband is
the head of the family and has the right to seek and grant a divorce; the wife does not. As an agunah, the woman is unable to
remarry within the faith, although "if a wife obstinately refuses
to accept a d[ivorce] which her husband is entitled to give, the
husband can be granted permission to remarry without the dissolution of his former marriage" (Werblowsky & Wigoder, 1965,
p. 118; see also Cohen, 1996). Some grounds on which a divorce
may be sought include ill treatment, refusal of cohabitation, and
"well-founded suspicion" of adultery by the wife, but not the
husband. In Israel, where the Orthodox rabbinate controls
marriage and divorce laws, the evident discrimination of these

traditional rulings is cause for much protest, particularly by women who have been in the agunah status for many years. On the other hand, in Great Britain, the protests of agunot have prompted the Chief Rabbi and a *Beth Din* (a court of three rabbis) to take steps both to provide in a prenuptial agreement for a Get and to restrict contacts with a recalcitrant husband until he gives his wife a religious divorce (Leipziger, 1996). "In addition, legislation has been introduced in the British Parliament that would forbid Jewish men from remarrying under British law if they refuse to grant their wives a get" (Leipziger, 1996).

A Beth Din meets with the parties, often in separate sessions, and attests to the religious divorce. This cannot be obtained until the civil divorce decree has been granted. Acquiring the Get, however, is a cold, dispassionate procedure that does little to relieve the negative emotions felt at the dissolution of what had been anticipated as a "live happily ever after" marriage. Rabbis in the Reconstructionist movement, a more liberal branch of Conservative Judaism, have been developing a more egalitarian and less painful procedure for the Get, in which either party (or both) can initiate the process (Silverstein, 1994).

Case Example. A Religious Divorce

Edith L., formerly married for 27 years and now newly divorced, met with the Beth Din to finalize the religious divorce. The rabbis were located in an office bare except for their desk and the chairs needed for four people. Their questions were asked matter-of-factly, with no tone of sympathy for her pain in the divorce. As part of the ritual, they marched around her several times (almost as if to reverse the traditional seven circuits of the bridal couple at an Orthodox wedding), and then she was asked to sign the formal documents. Ten years later, asked to recall this event, Edith could only visualize the coldness of the situation and the added pain she had experienced at the time.

She added a comment that it had been such a difficult experience that she had repressed as much of it as she could. This was truly a "painful parting" for her, made more so by the unspoken implication that she had somehow failed her coreligionists. (case files of LLS)

Interestingly, the Get is mentioned in the Bible. There are three references to it, in Deuteronomy 24:1, Isaiah 50:1, and Jeremiah

3:8. The prophets refer to it in a figurative sense, but the law of presenting an actual bill of divorce is clearly delineated. The existence and acceptance of a procedure for divorce is reflected in that an entire tractate of the Talmud is devoted to the varying conditions of divorce and the legal response. It can be summarized in the essential formula of the Get: "Let this serve you as a bill of divorce from me, as a letter of dismissal and deed of liberation, that you may marry any man you wish" (Gittin 9:3).

According to Jewish law, the bill of divorce is handed by the husband to his wife with the formal declaration in the presence of witnesses (although this is not always the case). The court (Beth Din) consists of three men, usually rabbis, conversant with religious laws of marriage and divorce. There are also rules of delay that can offer opportunities for reconciliation. Specific regulations include a rule that the judges cannot be related to either party, nor can any witnesses or the scribe who writes the Get be so related.

Some areas of Jewish law voice opposition to groundless divorces: "If a man divorces his first wife, the very altar weeps. He who sends away his wife is a hateful person. When a divorced man marries a divorced woman, there are four minds in the bed" (Gittin 90b; Pesachim 112a). The implication is that divorce and remarriage should be avoided if at all possible. Even in the relatively rare cases where the wife seeks to leave an abusive marriage, she is encouraged—especially in some Orthodox communities—to stay rather than leave (Axelrod, 1996).

There is little question that the Get was instituted by and, essentially, protects the rights of the husband. Although there are impressive efforts at protecting the woman in the marriage contract (ketubah), the power of creating the divorce proceedings still is the husband's prerogative. In recent decades, the question of the wife's rights has become more and more of an issue. The egalitarian nature of relationships has led to a challenging of the husband's sole power to initiate the Get.

A controversial component has been the Lieberman Clause, which was proposed for inclusion in the ketubah in the Conservative Movement and has been used to a significant degree in weddings performed by Conservative rabbis. The clause was designed to circumvent a husband's refusal to issue a Get even though it is desired by the wife. This new provision, agreed to by husband and wife at the time of their nuptials, allows the appointing of a Beth Din that can issue the divorce in lieu of the husband's doing so.

The clause answers the problem of the agunah referred to earlier. This term is applied to a woman whose husband disappears—perhaps he was an unidentified war casualty; or he may have moved to another country and changed his name; or he refuses to issue a Get. The Lieberman Clause has been controversial because it is identified with the Conservative Movement and is not accepted by the Orthodox community. There also is no clear indication that it can be enforced by a secular court.

In Israel, matters of family law are delegated to religious courts. A bizarre example of this concordat recently was publicized when a man died in prison after more than two decades of incarceration. He had been imprisoned because he would not issue a Get to his wife. He decided he would rather spend a better part of his life in jail than issue this document. Meanwhile, he prevented his wife from remarrying by his recalcitrance.

There is little question that the conflict between women's rights and traditional privileges is a major issue in the entire question of issuing gittin. Since traditional Judaism accepts the divine origin of its Law, the question of basic changes becomes mired in more than the effectiveness of egalitarian rights. Authorities throughout the ages have tried to ameliorate the inequities that place power essentially in the husband's hands. Ingenious reinterpretations of the Law have been proposed to blunt his preferential status. However, the basic problem remains (i.e., the inability of the wife to institute her own proceedings). (The foregoing was excerpted and rephrased from personal correspondence with [Conservative] Rabbi Gerald Wolpe, Har Zion Temple, Merion, PA, June 1995.)

Islam

The perpetuation of male dominance regarding divorce is found in the Muslim religion also, where wives and children are often still regarded as chattel, with no rights. If an Arab Muslim woman wants a divorce, there is a legal and religious presumption that the children belong to the father and will reside with him and his family of origin. The mother may even be deprived of her ability to see the children. Rarely would she become the custodial or residential parent.

Such religious dicta serve to coerce women into remaining in marriages that leave them isolated or that may be emotionally cold and unsatisfying, physically or verbally abusive, or degrading. Rather than providing comfort and guidance, such traditions negate the heart, soul, and spirit of those trapped in horrible relationships.

Protestant Denominations

Author FK wrote to numerous clergy in different Protestant churches to ascertain current developments regarding their evaluation and utilization of divorce ceremonies. The following responses are representative of those received:

> The United Methodist Church does not have a divorce ceremony although I and many others have advocated the creation and inclusion of one in the Book of Worship. Such a ritual could be extremely helpful for certain couples going through a legal divorce. (Personal correspondence with William G. Brockman, D. Min., LMFT, Director, Samaritan Counseling Center, Fort Lauderdale, FL, September 1994)

A Methodist clergyman reported that divorce is accepted in the United Methodist Church and that this church expresses concern for the well-being of all members of the dissolving family.

An Episcopal clergyman who requested to remain anonymous, sent the following statement in August 1995:

> It is our conviction that since the Church has liturgies for every other life event, it should have one for divorce. The rationale that the Church should not be seen as endorsing divorce has, in my opinion, no validity; the Church does not "endorse" sin, yet has a rite of reconciliation. Without a public rite, neither the Church community nor the couple remarrying have any appropriate way to come to terms with the meaning of their remarriage in the community.

This excerpt highlights that the absence of a ceremony or ritual in a specific church conveys nonacceptance of divorce, and makes the healing process more amorphous and ambiguous. Self-acceptance and forgiveness of self and former partner are more difficult when the religious context denies or ignores the existence of the process or event.

We have been informed that the 1987 new book of worship of the United Church of Christ includes the Order for Recognition of the End of a Marriage. Thus at least some of the more liberal Protestant churches are seeking, like Reform Judaism, to recognize the psychosocial reality of the divorces sought by their congregants, and are working to facilitate the religious aspect of this process in a manner that will help heal wounds left by the schism. We believe this is a long overdue development.

PHILOSOPHIC UNDERPINNINGS OF A THERAPEUTIC DIVORCE CEREMONY

In many countries around the globe, people have both civil *and* religious marriage ceremonies. Couples either choose and/or are required to be married in a church, synagogue, or mosque before the eyes of God (and their relatives and friends). For many, the religious service supersedes the civil/legal service in import; it is this ritual that consecrates the marriage and marks the specialness and sacredness of the event. Usually, it signifies not only the joy and wish for fulfillment of the shared dream of the couple, but also the hopes of the new couple's respective families of origin. For all, it promises the possible perpetuation of the family into the next generation.

All too often, the dream of the couple to "live happily ever after" does not reach fruition. They are disappointed in a marriage that does not fulfill their expectations. Disillusionment and despair replace optimism and love. No matter how hard they may try, distrust and chronic discontent surface. Efforts to "communicate better," repair power imbalances, and restore affection and intimacy are ineffective. Ultimately, the emotional estrangement is accompanied by physical estrangement. They may or may not seek assistance in marital, and later, divorce therapy. No matter whether the couple enters the adversarial system directly by contacting two separate attorneys, or whether they decide to mediate their divorce (Folberg & Milne, 1988), the process ends up in court and they receive a judicial decree that legally grants the divorce. Generally, the legal process is cold, lonely, and characterized by anger and hostility. What had begun in happiness and at a mass celebration formally ends with each former partner in a dreary courtroom alone except for his or her sole attendant, the attorney—who is paid to be there and is rarely an emotionally supportive friend.

Hundreds of patients have described to me (FK) the forlorn sense of isolation they experienced at the time of the legal ending of their marriage. Many expressed the desire to have their marital dissolution recognized and accepted by their church, as their wedding had been. I encourage patients to approach their clergyperson and request that such a ceremony be developed and performed on their behalf. Occasionally, a minister assents; patients who undergo this process report a new sense of closure. But for others, a deep void is experienced.

Several years were spent experimenting with the creation and modification of a ceremony, which was used with patient families and as part of training workshops with therapists engaged in divorce therapy. Based on these experiences and the positive feedback received from patients and from therapists in many countries about the immediacy and profound nature of their responses, and the lingering benefits derived, a model ceremony was written up around 1982 that is quasi-therapeutic and spiritual, and adaptable also for religious purposes. This particular ceremony deals with sadness and loss. It contains a beacon of optimism, however, in that this different way of parting permits "letting go" and the freeing up of bound energy to begin a new phase of one's individual and family life cycles.

This divorce ritual, modified over time, has its rationale in elements of several theoretical schools. From the psychodynamics/object relations school comes the utilization of life cycle and stage theory concepts and the emphasis on the reassurance children need of object constancy from and with their parents. Derived from contextual/relational theory is the premise that it is detrimental to children to be placed in a position of being expected or pushed to betray their loyalty to either parent. The structuring of continuing generational boundaries and mutual responsibilities flows from both relational and structural conceptualizations. The ceremony, as a strategic intervention, reflects the integrative, diaclectic approach described in this book and elsewhere (Kaslow, 1981b).

Therapeutic/Healing Divorce Ceremony (Short Version)

The adult participants stand facing each other and the children stand facing me. We are in a square or rectangle, depending on the number of participants.

FK: Mr. Green, please thank your wife for the good years and happy times you remember.

MR. G: *(Usually puzzled—pauses—chokes and responds—surprised at the positive memories this question evokes)* I really had forgotten—amidst my anger—how much I once loved you. You were so lovely, talented . . .

FK: Mrs. Green, can you tell your husband about the good things you will always cherish about your marriage?

MRS. G: *(Often teary and barely audible, affirms the sharing, fun, and early realization of her dream and how wonderful she thought he was.)*

FK: *(To each of the friends separately)* Please tell Mr. or Mrs. Green how you are prepared to be available to them during this difficult transition time and what their friendship means to you.

FRIENDS: You can call me at any time to talk, cry, go somewhere with you. . . . I'm here for you in any way that you need me because you're a super person and a wonderful friend.

FK: *(To children)* Can each of you tell your parents what the divorce means to you and what you want from your parents subsequent to the divorce?

EACH CHILD: *(Something like . . .)* I am so sad that this happened, but I know you tried your best. I need to know that you will each continue to love me, take care of me, let me love and care about each of you, and see you as much as possible. Please do not ask me to take sides or interfere with my relationship to Mom [Dad]. *(This is usually said with great sadness, wistfulness, and through tears.)*

FK: *(To each parent)* Can you tell your children how they were conceived (or adopted) in love, born at a time when you cared very much for each other, and were delighted to be having a family? Also, let them know what your thoughts are about your future relationship to them.

EACH PARENT: *(Tells in his/her own words what each child has meant to them, and affirms that their parental feelings and role will continue.)*

FK: *(To anyone else at the ceremony)* Please tell Mr. and Mrs. Green what is in your hearts as you help them to feel some inner peace and some healing.

When everyone has said what they feel compelled to communicate, depending on the feeling tone being conveyed, I may ask if they all care to hug each other as a more amicable goodbye to the original family. (Kaslow, 1993b, pp. 341–344, ©1987 Florence Kaslow)

Such a ceremony, when warranted, should be held any time after the first crucial two years have elapsed after the physical separation. Prior to that people are still struggling with too much anger, remorse, and bitterness to be able to integrate the positive aspects of the marriage with the negative aspects and perceive it as a hologram. Unless such a rapprochement occurs, either with or without a ceremony, there can be no true acceptance and forgiveness. Therefore, before utilizing such a ceremony, it is important to ascertain that the couple wishes to bring psychic closure to their marriage. Sometimes this does not occur until 5 to 10 years after the legal divorce is concluded. In some cases, a history of physical or emotional spousal abuse may be contraindicative for such a rapprochement.

All of the families with whom I have used this therapeutic strategy have expressed appreciation for the release from the remaining unwanted emotional shackles. In acknowledging what was valuable in their relationship, they counter the feelings of failure carried for too long. In openly communicating deep feelings and memories with their children and finally listening attentively to what they have to say, a new bonding begins. Amid tears of relief, this parting occurs minus anger and the desire for further recriminations and retribution.

CONCLUDING COMMENT

To close this chapter, we return to the case of Luigi and Sylvia Royale to illustrate how the religious aspect of their divorce was expressed and dealt with, as it inevitably must be by anyone seeking church approval and/or spiritual peace around their divorce.

Involvement in Church and Religion

Luigi had turned to his priest and had not gotten very satisfactory help from him. When he began socializing and became sexually active with other women before the final legal decree was issued, and continued "making up for lost time" the first few years after the legal divorce had occurred, he decided he could no longer abide by the teachings and dictum of his former church. Yet he believed in God and wanted to "be at peace with his Maker." He decided to join a liberal Unity Church and found himself welcome there, and not judged. He later met Leona at a church function and was delighted that "I found the woman I've been yearning for in God's presence." When they decided to live together, he felt comfortable and happy with his choice. He knew that in the event they chose to get married, his adopted church would not expect him to go through what he considered "the charade of annulment," and he was grateful that his behavior and feelings were finally consistent with his beliefs.

Sylvia found some succor and many friendships within her own Methodist Church and was glad she had never converted to Catholicism, despite how fiercely Luigi had urged her to do so. Proudly she told her therapist, "I now realize this was one part of me I was not willing to give up for him; how odd that this was my area of strength. It's so nice not to have arguments over which church to go to anymore."

PART III

Consequences of Divorce: The Community and Social Divorce

ALTHOUGH THE MARRIAGE MAY have ended in a painful parting, life does go on. The ramifications of divorce affect the parties' social relationships and their functioning within the community.

Of primary concern are the ways in which the divorce affects any children of the marriage. They live in a single-parent home for at least some period of time, unless both parents remarry hurriedly, and possibly in a blended family in some of the postdivorce years; their relationships with extended family members, including grandparents on both sides of the family, are altered; and their academic and social lives are affected.

A second concern is the postdivorce adjustment of the two adults as individuals, whether they function as single parents or subsequently remarry. Their interactions with family and friends, as well as the view of them in their new roles, are altered. These and related issues are the bases for the forthcoming chapters.

CHAPTER 9

An Overview of
the Aftermath

THERE ARE SEVERAL OBVIOUS problems that occur and adjustments
that have to be made by the parting disputants. They must resolve
economic and legal issues as well as deal with the effects on emotional and physical health and social life. These effects vary by
gender, age, length of marriage, presence or absence of children,
ethnicity, religion, stage in the life cycle, existence of social supports and networks, and relationship postdivorce with the ex-
spouse. The numerous variables make research and statistical
analysis of the effects of divorce difficult, as Kitson and Morgan
(1990) have stated, but as they have also pointed out, such research is important because of the implications of divorce for society in general as well as for social policy and planning. In this
chapter, we will indicate some of the variability in effects, with
elaboration to follow in the next few chapters.

CHILDLESS MARRIAGES

When a childless marriage dissolves, a major element of potential controversy—child custody—is not present. If it has been a
short marriage and the partners were quite young, they may recuperate rapidly and eventually see the marriage as a brief in-
terlude. Whatever the length of marriage, the issues to be dealt
with are clearly affected by the variables just identified and by

157

the depth of their conflict or their positive feelings toward each other. Compared with divorcing couples who have children, childless couples have the advantage of being much more mobile. They can relocate anywhere without judicial restraints imposed because of child caretaking and visitation. They need never have contact with each other again if that is their desire. Nevertheless, not having children does not negate the possibility of being depressed or of developing other health problems as a result of the anger or grief of one or both partners. Sometimes the sorrow emanates from the continuing great affection one feels for the other even after experiencing much rejection.

For the ex-spouse who experiences severe physical and/or emotional sequelae to the separation/divorce, appropriate therapy is as warranted as in any other emotionally troubling situation. Telling the individual to "put it in the past . . . it was an unfortunate mistake . . . it's over" does not heal the hurt of the spouse who may have been rejected, or who feels like a failure in the "game" of life, or of either partner who now questions his or her ability to make a good choice, trust another person fully, or relate to other people. Therapy is certainly needed if divorce occurred because one spouse was an abuser of the other and if, even in the face of the reality of rejection, the abuser jealously feels, "If I can't have her (or him), no one else will." Spousal abuse, whether it serves as grounds for the divorce in court or not, may be related to jealousy and real or imagined feelings of being betrayed by a spouse in extramarital affairs. In some of the worst cases during and after divorce, the abuser may stalk the ex-spouse and at some point attempt to murder that individual (and possibly others). Should the situation be this dangerous, it would be appropriate for the therapist to advise the client to seek a protective restraining order from the court and possibly also to inform and seek protection by the local police. Therapy also seems vital when someone feels abandoned and totally disrupted because a marriage of several decades has been torn asunder.

More and more frequently, we see virtual newlyweds, usually in their 20s, splitting apart after a year or two of marriage, or even less. One analogy describes such brief marriages in this way: "While couples in these marriages do not wed with the intention of divorcing, their temporary stay in marriage is much like the starter [first] home of a generation ago, shed as the family outgrew it" (Schupack, 1994, p. C1). If they are young adults, one or both may remarry with few of the complications faced by those who have children.

Depending on the length of the marriage, there may be issues relevant to health insurance and the distribution of marital assets (including Social Security payments) to resolve. Most young people, married less than four or five years, will have fewer concerns in these areas than couples in mid- and later life, who have been married 20 or more years, or who are dissolving a remarriage. Nevertheless, these can be major issues if the parting is not only painful but rancorous, or if one member of the pair does not have separate access to health insurance.

In any divorce, the psychological aftermath is partially contingent on a number of factors within the marriage. If one spouse perceives him- or herself to have been rejected by the other, there may be lasting damage to the rejectee's self-esteem and self-image—a feeling of failure—that precludes becoming involved with a new partner, at least for many years to come. Where adultery has occurred, the other spouse may not only be wary of trusting others of the opposite sex in a dating or more serious relationship, but may also fear trusting anyone else in any capacity. Conversely, a newly divorced spouse of whatever age may move quickly to another intimate relationship, even a new marriage, in an effort to reassume the role of a dependent/ protective/cared-for (choose one) individual, or as a defense against aloneness or loneliness. If any of these behaviors interferes with effective functioning, therapy may provide an effective mode of dealing with the underlying problems. Here individual therapy from a systems perspective with a clinician well steeped in the dynamics of divorce is likely to constitute the treatment of choice.

MARRIAGES WITH CHILDREN

In keeping with both the family systems approach and external reality, it is necessary to consider what happens to the younger members of the family when a marriage dissolves. It is readily apparent to almost everyone that the percentage of children under age 16 living in single-parent homes has risen substantially in this century, especially in the past 20 to 30 years. Although some of these situations are due to death of a parent, and others to births to unmarried mothers, the highest proportion results from marital "disruption." Bumpass and Sweet (1989), using data from the 1987–1988 National Survey of Families and Households, found that 4 percent of children born prior to 1930 did not live with both parents continuously because of marital disruption while 14 percent were in single-parent households because of one parent's death. Only a few decades later, for children born in 1960–1968, the percentages were sharply reversed: 19 percent of children in single-parent homes were due to marital disruption and 5 percent were due to parental death (see Figure 9.1).

"Approximately 40 percent of all children born in the late 1970s and early 1980s will experience the divorce of their parents and the often significant interparental hostility and discord that can accompany divorce" (Cummings & Davies, 1994, p. 1). Estimates by the early 1990s were that fully 50 percent of children under 16 years of age would live in single-parent homes at some point, whether because of marital disruption or death, or because of unwed childbearing (Furstenberg & Cherlin, 1991). Indeed, Bumpass and Sweet found, "For the majority of children—white and black—who live in single-parent families,

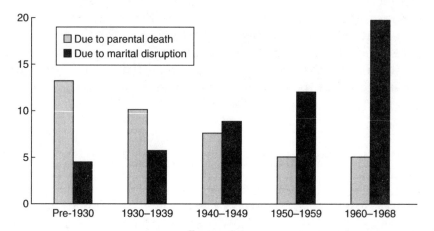

FIGURE 9.1

PERCENTAGE OF CHILDREN UNDER 16, BY BIRTH COHORT, LIVING IN SINGLE-PARENT HOMES, PRE-1930 TO 1960–1968 (*Source:* Chart developed (by LLS) from federal survey data in Bumpass and Sweet 1989.)

this situation is likely to persist for the remainder of childhood" (1989, p. 259).

Major questions arise about the role of each parent subsequent to the divorce. It would truly be in "the best interests of the children" if the parents could maintain warm and stable relationships with them that would help the youngsters to enjoy life and to mature in a healthy fashion. Frequent visits between father and child(ren) have been found to have positive effects on the quality of their relationship (Arditti & Keith, 1993). Too often, however, the parents' continuing disagreements produce a fallout that affects the children negatively, emotionally, and/or financially. In addition, relationships between the children and the nonprimary caretaker may take on an artificial quality. On weekend visits, many fathers (usually the nonresident parent) seem to feel obliged to entertain the children in a way that would not occur in an intact family, spending more hours (and more money) with them than most at-home fathers do in a month. They are often called "Disneyland Dads."

Moreover, children soon learn to manipulate their parents, playing one against the other to gain privileges or material things that again would not be as readily available in the intact functional family. In other cases, where a parent has become involved in a new romantic association, the children may feel like barely welcome intruders and possibly impediments to the parent's new relationship. On television and in films such as *Irreconcilable Differences* and *Kramer vs. Kramer*, these complications are dramatized, with the anguish and anger of the children readily apparent. Sometimes a parent may take flight from the marital strife and disappear, desperately needing time alone to recoup his or her perspective, but it is difficult for children to understand and accept such a total negation of their need for loving contact.

With older children, other questions may arise that may not even have occurred to the adults involved, as the following case note shows.

Case Example. Questions of Identity and Locale

When James suddenly walked out on Roberta, his wife of some 25 years, their children anxiously asked whether she was going to resume using her maiden name, presumably because of her anger with him. She thought about the question and what implications might arise from her response. For example, if she said "yes," would the children feel that she was also rejecting them, or would they be embarrassed by her using a different name? If she said "no," she would continue to bear a name that brought on painful memories. Since she was an artist, she felt that it would be more appropriate to keep her current last name, which is how she was known professionally.

The next question that her children put to Roberta was whether she was going to move to her native city since, other than the children, she had no family in her present location. This was easier to answer "no," as she wanted to be where her children were, as well as her friends and her professional connections.

These issues were important to her adolescent and young adult children, for they were basically asking whether their mother was, in a sense, going to "walk out" on them as their father had. In her eyes, she saw no need to inflict further distress on them than the separation and divorce had already caused. (Case notes of LLS)

Each of the separating spouses should spend some time reflecting on how to relate to the former partner, if only in terms of the effects of their postdivorce interactions on their children. Granted, this does not happen in enough families. However, unless one parent walks away completely from the children (or is ordered to do so by the court because of abusive behavior or some similar problem), there will inevitably be some direct contact between the ex-couple as coparents. With school-age children, there are parent-teacher conferences, recitals, sports activities, religious events, and graduations at which both parents should be present. If the adults can focus on the *importance to the children* of these events and their desire for both parents to attend without dissension or tensions surfacing, the children will be both appreciative and better off. If the child is having learning problems, the appropriate parental efforts should be directed toward evaluating and resolving the problem, not on blaming the other parent for the child's difficulties. If, on the other hand, the child is the "star" of an occasion, they might want to take a modicum of joint credit and feel proud that they had done something "right" even if they could not continue living together in a warm familial way.

Similarly, even when dealing with grown children, there are still many occasions when the children are the central figures and the parents play a minor, if perhaps supportive, role, like college graduations, engagements, marriages, births of the next generation. Again, the divorced parents should focus on sharing the joys, not taking away from them by ostentatiously refusing even to greet each other civilly or behaving in even more negative ways (Kaslow & Schwartz, 1987a). Perhaps one parent, who may be a narcissist, feels no regrets or remorse for the ending of the marriage, while the other is only too cognizant of the causes of the divorce. The latter should, even if silently gritting teeth, be able to comment on what a happy occasion this is for their child and remain focused on that point for the time in which they are all together. The grown child should not have to add anxiety about temperamental parental behavior to what may be an already emotion-laden day.

CHILDREN OF DIVORCE IN ADULTHOOD

The events of childhood, often internalized, have a cumulative impact on children as they develop, whether these have been positive experiences, physical illnesses, or emotional traumas. The timing of a divorce in terms of the child's age and stage of development, and the events in the child's life subsequent to the divorce will obviously affect that child's relationships with parents in adulthood. What role has each parent had in the child's life over the years? Was the child brought up in a single-parent home or in a blended family? Has one of the parents, or both, remained embittered over the years, providing a distorted emotional perspective for the children as they matured, or have the parents taken new paths after recovering from the initial trauma, providing a healthier model of growth and learning from experience? Did either parent engage in disparaging the other (parental alienation syndrome) thus conveying that one parent was mean, evil, or despicable—thereby creating self-doubts in the children (Gardner, 1992; Palmer, 1988)?

If the parents' divorce occurred when the children were minors, interaction between children and each of their parents is dictated in part by the terms of the custody agreement and in part by the actions of each parent. Visitation is affected by the grievances, real or exaggerated, of each parent, and to some degree by the parent's choice to be an integral part of the child's life or to be an absent parent. There is leeway in how they interpret and implement the marital settlement agreement.

On the other hand, if the divorce took place when the children were in late adolescence or early adulthood, then the youngsters may have had a much larger role in determining the nature of their ongoing relationship with each parent. If the father has remarried, however, and possibly acquired more children, either as parent or stepparent, his relationships with his adult biological children may be affected in ways that may be difficult to predict because of the variable influence of factors such as his education, physical distance from children, and time elapsed since divorce (Cooney & Uhlenberg, 1990). (It is not clear why this study was limited to biological children. Presumably, children adopted in infancy would have similar voices in their relationships with their parents.) The personality of the stepmother is another variable that influences the post remarriage relationship. Even without remarriage, Cooney and Uhlenberg assert that unequivocally "divorce has pronounced negative effects on men's contacts with their adult offspring and on their perceptions of adult children as potential sources of support in times of need" (1990, p. 685). This may not be invariably the case. We have seen relationships that improve when the mother is not an intermediary or because Dad mellows and comes to cherish his children more.

If the mother has remarried, whether a man with his own children or a childless one, her attention is likely to be drawn to creating a happier new relationship for herself in her midlife (or later) and she is less likely to focus as completely on her children, at least for a while. To some of her grown children, this may be a relief, as too much maternal involvement in their adult lives may not have been particularly welcome, even when understandable from their mother's point of view. Other adult children may resent the stepfather's preeminence in their mother's life, particularly if her babysitting services are curtailed as she begins spending more money and time on her own pleasures. This, however, is the children's problem primarily, and they may need therapy about how to deal with their resentment.

The relations between adult children, sometimes themselves married, and their divorced parents may become contentious around holiday times, with each parent (if in the same geographic area) expecting the children to celebrate at his or her home and resenting it if the children join with the other parent.

Again, this is a problem that can be resolved peacefully if all parties are willing to consider a variety of possible options. The continuum of solutions can range from a simple alternation of Thanksgiving Day dinners (your house this year; mine next year) to a joint dinner if the parents, and their spouses if any, are sufficiently amicable. On the other hand, if the divorce was based on spouse or child abuse, and the grown children fear that violence might erupt again, or the issues were never really resolved, it is unlikely that they will care to spend a holiday with the abusive parent, obviating the need to deal with a potential conflict at all.

In terms of marriage of the children of divorce themselves, a news magazine article published in 1992—labeled "The Legacy of Divorce" on the cover—presented a rather bleak picture:

> Compared with people who have grown up in intact families, adult children of divorce are more likely to have troubled relationships and broken marriages. A desire for stability sends some down the aisle at too young an age, and they wind up in divorce court not long afterward. Others fear commitment because they learned too well the lessons of their childhood—don't trust anyone, not even Mom or Dad. Even when divorce releases children from their parents' violent or emotionally abusive marriage, they worry that they don't know how to be half of a happy couple because they've never seen one close up at home. (Kantrowitz, Wingert, Rosenberg, Quade, & Foote, 1992, p. 49)

This is likely to be an outcome, a sad one, not foreseen (or even thought of) by the parents. Most children of divorce, no matter what their age when the divorce occurred, learn some bitter lessons. If one parent is a spouse abuser, the grown children may batter their boy- or girlfriends or spouses since this is the behavior they saw and internalized in their own homes. If one parent committed adultery that contributed to the divorce, the same-sexed child may construe this as appropriate behavior while the opposite-sexed child cannot trust a member of the opposite sex to remain faithful. If the parents kept their feelings inside themselves, rarely communicating, the children may not be able to express their feelings, whether positive or negative. Parents are powerful models for their children, from infancy onward, although many parents, particularly during crises, tend to forget this.

RIPPLE EFFECTS OF DIVORCE

*The Social, Community, and Extended
Family Aspects*

Like the proverbial pebble thrown into a pond, separation and divorce have substantial ripple effects on relationships with many others significant to the parting pair. If divorce is an anathema to other family members, the couple's split may create a divisive wedge within the extended family. If there is a child custody battle, grandparents on the side of the noncustodial parent may find themselves almost shut out of their grandchildren's lives. Friends, for reasons of their own, may take sides with one party and abruptly terminate contact with the other. Playmates of the children may be restricted from visiting at their home or having them come to visit; it is as if their parents fear that divorce is a contagious disease. We have had cases like one in which the custodial father of a little girl found that her pals from nursery school could not play, much less sleep over, at her house because their mothers didn't trust a single dad with their young daughters. He was shocked by others' fears that he might be incompetent at parenting and/or a child molester. In reality, he was a fine, nurturing parent. Each of these relationships veers off on a unique path.

Relationships with the Extended Family

The extended family, composed of the couple's siblings, parents, and other relatives, may or may not take sides during the separation and after the divorce. Where the marriage was relatively brief and there were no children, contact with the former in-law family may simply evaporate. In rare cases, a former son- or daughter-in-law may continue to interact with the ex-spouse's family because there is genuine positive feeling in the relationship and/or because there are children for whom the relationship should be maintained. Sometimes in-laws have become involved in a family business and it is mutually advantageous to have this aspect of the connectedness continue. [*Note.* If such a relationship is to be maintained, both "sides" will need to avoid reference to the causes underlying the divorce while they focus on the common effort to make the business successful.]

At the other extreme, one spouse's family may decide that "blood is thicker than water" and cut off the former in-law son or daughter as if he or she were dead, no matter what the circumstances of the separation and the strength of a prior attachment. Where there are children old enough to comprehend what is transpiring, such behavior on the part of relatives may have a negative impact because of the unfairness with which the one parent has been treated. Such internecine family warfare is almost always destructive to children who come to see relationships as ephemeral and to lack a sense of intergenerational harmony or continuity.

With the exception of cases involving spousal or substance abuse, it is advisable for parents of the parting couple to be supportive emotionally, to try to defuse the conflict to a point where the principal parties can deal with their problems rationally (perhaps even recommending mediation), and to refrain from assuming that their child is 100 percent in the right and the child-in-law totally wrong. Siblings, too, would better serve the couple and themselves by similar attitudes and actions. These reactions may be colored, however, by religious or cultural backgrounds. For example, in comparison with divorced Anglo mothers, divorced Mexican American mothers "reported about double the frequency of nonsupportive reactions such as parental blame, parental concern about the morality of divorce, and strong emotional upset" on the part of their parents (Wagner, 1988, p. 76).

Interaction of the children of divorce with aunts, uncles, and cousins on both sides of the family will depend on how close they were before the marital dissolution, as well as the reaction of these relatives to the separation and divorce. Some aunts or uncles may function in a highly supportive role for the children, and cousins may continue to interact despite their elders' negative relationships. These roles will vary to some extent with physical proximity and the ages of the children involved, as obviously mature children of divorce have a mobility and independence that younger children and adolescents lack. There is very little research extant on postdivorce relationships with extended family members other than grandparents, although occasionally anecdotal material sheds some light on this question.

Participants in a conference entitled "Family Law in the Next Century" recognized the need to consider extended family members and their roles in divorce as well as other family relationships (Levy, 1993). Among the issues discussed were the award of custody to a stepparent rather than a biological one under certain circumstances, grandparental visitation and custody petitions, and stepparent child support during marriage to the child's biological or adopted parent. On each of these issues, cases supporting the role of extended family individual(s), as well as opposing them, could be found.

Rights of Grandparents

Looking at the parents of divorcing couples from the perspective that they have grandchildren who are also involved in the marital dissolution, a number of situations may emerge. First, the grandparents may serve as caretakers of the youngsters during or after the parents' separation, while the parent with primary caretaking responsibility is at work. For some, this may be an unmitigated joy. At the very least, in this positive role, they may serve as emotional supports for their grandchildren of any age, helping members of the younger generation to cope with the trauma of the family breakup. For other grandparents, much as they might like to help in this way, their own health, work schedules, and/or financial needs may make providing direct child care difficult. In addition, most of them have developed their own cadre of friends and activities from which they should not be separated for any prolonged period. Grandparents, like parents, need respite time and support from others (Schwartz, 1994c).

Some may find themselves assuming major financial responsibility for their grandchildren's needs, including education. In such instances, the spirit may be more willing than the purse, with the grandparents denying themselves of things they need or pleasures they want in order to provide for the younger generation. If this is the case, the grandparents may have to substitute giving their emotional support to the children, possibly a shoulder to cry on or an objective listening ear, rather than funds they cannot furnish without depriving themselves of necessities (or desired things or experiences).

A second possibility is that the grandparents may become involved in the custody dispute, legally seeking to retain access to their grandchildren, despite the divorce, if the primary care-taking parent denies them visiting time. The success of their efforts tends to vary by state, with visitation rights often more difficult to obtain than custody of their grandchildren (Wilks & Melville, 1990). Every state has passed legislation that affects grandparent visitation (Elrod, 1993; Thompson, Tinsley, Scalora, & Parke, 1989), although judicial rulings in specific cases tend to be governed by what is in the child's best interest rather than in the grandparents' interest (Blau, 1984). For example, if a child has lived with a grandparent for a year and they had a well-established relationship, a court might decide that unless there was a compelling reason against it, provision should be made for grandparent visitation (Allen, 1985). On the other hand, if a visit with the grandchild(ren) at the home of the child's parent has a negative impact on that parent's physical or mental health, that could be a compelling reason not to award the grandparents visitation rights (Elrod, 1993). Perhaps the children could visit the grandparents with their other parent, or on their own if they are old enough (and if no court order has been issued banning any such contacts). A fourth possibility is that, despite a court ruling granting grandparent visitation, a hostile child-in-law may simply refuse to allow them any contact with the grandchildren, whether or not the elders had any role in the marital conflict or had acted in a manner detrimental to the youngsters.

Grandparents in New Jersey who have been denied visitation with their grandchildren, in practice or by judicial mandate, have formed a support and advocacy group called "Grandparents Count" (Nazareno, 1995). One of their particular concerns is lack of access to grandchildren because the custodial parent (usually the ex-child-in-law) has moved to another state, thus making contact more difficult. Gifts, cards, and letters sent to the grandchildren may be returned unopened, making the rift even more painful. One can sympathize with grandparents who are treated as outcasts; this is a great tragedy for them. Furthermore, the lack of inter-generational interaction often is not in the grandchildren's best interests because they lose the benefits of contact with and love from their grandparents.

A study with college students from intact and divorced families, however, presents a somewhat different view, possibly because of different ages of the subjects as well as more variable geographic proximity within the family. Creasey's work with grandchild-grandparent relationships (1993) found that gender as well as whether the grandparents were on the mother's side or the father's affected the late adolescents' view of closeness to their grandparents. Granddaughters from divorced families "perceived less optimal relationships with paternal grandparents than granddaughters within intact families, and in general, than grandsons from divorced families" (1993, p. 525). At the same time, their relationships with maternal grandmothers were closer than was true for grandsons. Frequency of contact between the generations, whether by phone or in person, and strength of the relationship influence each other, but which is the primary factor depends in individual cases on such variables as the quality of the predivorce relationship, the respective geographic locations of each party, and postdivorce animosities.

A Canadian study, focused on court-referred subjects, paid special attention to the role of grandparents in the divorce suit and in the family structure. Wilks and Melville (1990) found, "Despite the anguish that grandparents may feel about the disruption in their children's lives; despite their sometimes conflicted relationships with these children; and despite the frequent presence of new partners in their children's lives, grandparents appear to assume an interested and responsible role toward their grandchildren" (p. 12). In addition to the daily services they provide to their children and grandchildren, they provide a sense of security, continuity, and belonging that is essential to the youngsters' well-being.

Today, many who are grandparents are still gainfully employed, while others have retired, often to a warm weather site distant from their children and grandchildren. Their relations with a former child-in-law and their actions subsequent to the separation certainly influence whether this distance becomes an excuse for reduced contact with their grandchildren, or whether they are denied visitation outright. Those who live in the same community may or may not be able to see their grandchildren, as indicated earlier, depending on the nature of their interaction with the custodial parent. "To the extent that grandparents are denied access to grandchildren as a result of divorce, they may experience difficulty in resolving their own developmental issues, feel a sense of dissatisfaction with their lives, or feel that some part of themselves is missing or incomplete" (Myers & Perrin, 1993, p. 64). We agree, and believe, in addition, that being excluded from the lives of grandchildren whom they love and cherish is detrimental to the grandparents' well-being. Causing such exclusion out of spite or other malevolent intent results in a great loss to all deprived of this relationship.

From the grandchildren's point of view, if they lack access to their grandparents, they may envy their peers' visits with grandparents at holiday times or feel the loss of the affection and mentoring that grandparents can provide. They may, as they grow older, feel deprived of the part of themselves that emanates from the family roots, legends, and traditions most often transmitted by grandparents. This ties in with the view of many grandparents who see themselves as "purveyors of family traditions" (Kruk, 1994, p. 42).

If grandparent-grandchild contact is, or is likely to be, disrupted due to divorce, Kruk (1994) suggests that alternative dispute resolution techniques be used to restore the relationship. He proposes that if the divorcing couple is working with a mediator to resolve their disputes, the mediator should ask about relations between their children and the grandparents. If there is a positive relationship, the mediator might try to include the oldest generation in planning postdivorce parenting arrangements. On the other hand, "If there is any indication of potential future difficulties in regard to grandparent access or parental disagreement in this regard, it may be necessary to include grandparent visitation as an issue for negotiation" (Kruk, 1994, p. 47). If the grandparents lose access after the divorce, in the absence of predivorce mediation, he believes the mediator might be able to ameliorate the situation by working with all parties at one or two specially called sessions.

Old Friends and New

People often say that they know who their real friends are when trouble comes. How true this is in the case of divorce! When word gets out that a couple has separated, some friends disappear from both parties' lives, almost as if they feared contamination; some remain friendly with one party and ignore the other ever after; a few may try to maintain relationships with both; and one or two may create an active support network for one of the spouses. When old friends no longer call, it is painful. The few who rally round are welcome indeed, for they save the individual from feeling like a pariah as well as helping to maintain a semblance of normal social interaction for the one left alone.

What may be most difficult for the individual abandoned by old friends is to refrain from harboring anger and resentment against them. He or she needs to be aware that the divorce may evoke the friends' anxiety and uncertainty about their own marriage. In other cases, the friendship was based on a close tie with the ex-spouse rather than on rapport with the couple as separate individuals. It may take a few years after the separation or divorce, but eventually the divorced person needs to be able to acknowledge the former friends with civility, if not warmth, if only to be perceived as doing well in his or her postdivorce life. Actually, this helps the divorced individual to maintain a positive self-image, based in part on the reflection of positive perception by others who see someone who is self-confident rather than distraught, self-pitying, or hostile.

If films, soap operas, and case histories are to be believed, the male divorcé is typically welcomed as a guest at friends' homes and eagerly sought after to accompany single female friends, whereas his female counterpart is perceived as a threat to intact marriages. For both parties, there is often a feeling of being a fifth wheel with married friends; thus a need to make new friends becomes imperative. If a divorced person relocates, friends may be found in the new community. Developing new interests, perhaps initially to fill empty hours, frequently leads to new companions. Sometimes the person alone finds other formerly married persons and they form their own support network, engaging in activities together as well as listening to each other's tales of woe when necessary, perhaps even being able to offer a different perspective on how to deal with a difficult situation.

Individual therapy can be helpful as they strive to improve their postdivorce adjustment and achieve psychic resolution of those traumatic events that occurred. Becoming involved in a group such as Parents Without Partners can provide entrée to new friendships, activities, and a forum in which to talk with others who share a similar situation about the reality issues they are dealing with during this phase of their lives.

The following chapters expand these ideas with respect to the children of divorce, relationships with families of origin as well as the in-law family, friendships, and other issues faced by the now dissolved couple as they move forward in their lives.

CHAPTER 10

Effects of Divorce
on the Children

*One out of two American children lives in something other than what the
Census Bureau defines as the "traditional family": a married couple living
with their biological children and no one else. . . . Of the nearly 64 million
American children under 18 years of age, 15 percent of all children live in
blended families, defined as homes that include at least one stepparent, stepsibling or half-sibling, according to the report, based on 1991 data. (Vobejda, 1994)*

IN DISCUSSING THE EFFECTS OF separation and divorce on children, their stage in the developmental life cycle at the time these
events occur is of primary concern, for the aftermath is contingent on such variables as age; emotional, cognitive, and moral
levels; their unique personality; and their own experiences
within the family. Accordingly, this chapter is divided by age
groups. Some issues affect children of all ages; these areas will
be discussed first.

An interesting historical note on the effects of divorce comes
from the Terman study of geniuses begun in 1921 and still in
progress. Investigators have found that "those children whose
parents divorced faced a 33 percent greater risk of an earlier
death than those whose parents remained married until the
children reached age 21" (Goleman, 1995, pp. C1, C9). One of
the researchers in this longitudinal study, reflecting on the rar-
ity of divorce 60 to 80 years ago and the stigma attached to it,

believes "that it was the stress and anxiety caused by their parents' strife that took its toll in later life" on these gifted individuals (Goleman, 1995, p. C9).

Also to be considered here is the individual child's style of coping with stress and distress. "Three basic styles of coping with exposure to background anger have been identified: concerned, angry/ambivalent, and unresponsive" (Cummings & Davies, 1994, p. 52). The child who exhibits concern when others exhibit anger but does not become actively involved in the situation is regarded as adaptive. Those characterized as angry/ambivalent are not only more demonstrative of their feelings, but also report more "out-of-control" feelings, such as crying, and frequently experience an increase in aggressive behavior. The child who does not express distress or anger, much rarer, is perceived as being unresponsive, and it is difficult to determine how much emotion is being suppressed or internalized. Each of these patterns reflects the unique character of the child's personality and experience.

FACTORS THAT MATTER

A key factor in short- and long-term effects has to be the nature of the divorce, as perceived by the children (and perhaps by one of the parents). Fassel (1991) has suggested several contributory factors: "the disappearing parent, the surprise divorce, the always-fighting divorce, the let's-keep-this-from-the-kids divorce, and the late-in-life divorce" (p. 7). Other variables in the formula that determines children's reactions to divorce include gender, resiliency, only child or one with siblings, parental interaction postdivorce, and changes in lifestyle resulting from the divorce, as was seen in Figure 2.1.

Following the initial responses to the crisis period in their parents' divorce and remarriage, some children exhibit remarkable resiliency and in the long term may actually be enhanced by coping with these transitions; others suffer sustained developmental delays or disruptions; still others appear to adapt well in the early stages of family reorganization but show delayed effects that emerge at a later time, especially adolescence. (Hetherington, Stanley-Hagan, & Anderson, 1989, p. 304)

There are also significant differences between children whose parents separated 10 years earlier and who are now adolescents or young adults, those who are adolescent children of newly divorced parents, those who were adolescents at the time of the divorce and are now young adults, and those who are young adults when their parents part. Children of separating parents perceive the split differently depending on their age, cognitive level, and other factors alluded to earlier that were operative at the time. The work of Jean Piaget helps us to understand the role of cognitive development in such perceptions (1951, 1981). Clues to children's understanding of divorce may be found in their verbal responses, in their drawings (Oppawsky, 1991), and in their behavior. Ten years later, their needs have changed, the relationship between their divorced parents may have changed, and the effects of the marital dissolution will vary to some extent, depending on what has transpired in the postdivorce family over the decade. Studies of the impact of divorce on the children that assess their adjustment at only one point in time, often within the first year after separation, tend to ignore not only comparisons with children in intact marriages, but also the effects of changes in the standard of living for the children. There is an overuse of clinical samples as well (Kurz, 1995).

At least four other variables must be considered in assessing the sequelae of separation and divorce for children, and these factors are often overlooked. One variable is whether the children have been either victims of or witnesses to incest or other forms of abuse within the family. If they have, then the parting of their parents may be at least in part a welcome, long overdue relief to them, since presumably the abusive adult will no longer be in the home or possibly even an active participant in their lives. The remaining parent then becomes their protector, and the relationship between them may grow stronger and become imbued with new respect. Sometimes, however, as Fassel (1991) found, some resident parents verbally and/or physically abused their children because they did not know any other ways to express their anger, frustration, and other negative feelings. The "united front" that parents have often been enjoined to present in child rearing (Minuchin, 1974) does not necessarily work in positive ways where incest, physical, or emotional abuse are present.

Conversely, if the children are placed in the primary custody of the violent, abusive, or intrusive parent, or are ordered by the judge to have unsupervised visits at that parent's home, their fears may escalate and their behavior problems become intensified. Although some allegations of abuse are false, mental health professionals, attorneys, and judges need to listen attentively to such complaints and have such charges thoroughly investigated. When the accusations are true, it is incumbent on the legal and judicial systems to join the nonabusive parent and the mental health professionals in protecting the children from further harm and continuing fear. The court may decide to permit visitation with the abusive parent only in a supervised setting, or, at the extreme, may issue a protective order that prohibits any contact between the abusive parent and the child(ren).

A second factor, similar to but sufficiently different from the first to warrant separate mention, is a parent who is a substance abuser. Children of alcoholic and/or drug-addicted parents (or live-in parent surrogates) often are exposed to scenes of violence, loud arguments, and phone calls in the middle of the night to retrieve a drunken adult from a bar or to pick up the adult at the police station; to parties at their home or nearby that end up as drunken brawls; to seeing a parent so inebriated that he or she is irrational and totally unreliable. Often money that is sorely needed for food or to pay the rent is squandered instead on drugs, alcohol, or gambling. Being reared in such a dysfunctional environment feels unsafe, chaotic, and unpredictable. If the separation and subsequent divorce end the exposure to these noxious influences and their accompanying turbulence, the child(ren) may react positively to a saner and more predictable environment.

Despite a parent's abusive and/or addictive behavior, children need to know their parent cares about them and has not abandoned them. Sometimes children retain a strong attachment to the positive aspects of the parent and persist in the desire to see him or her when the person is not "under the influence" or acting out violently. It is important for therapists, lawyers, mediators, and judges to recognize this. Further, they should recognize that if one parent is portrayed as so bad that he or she cannot be seen, the child is likely to feel damaged also since half of his or her genetic makeup and social and emotional heritage derives from this parent. In addition, supervised visitation or nonvisitation can be time limited or contingent; if the person goes into a recovery program and does well, as a profession committed to growth and change, therapists have a responsibility to urge that visitation be increased later. Conversely, if a person escalates addictive behavior or further decompensates, then visitation should be curtailed. Visitation plans should not be concretized; they must be flexible enough to accommodate children's changing developmental needs and parents' altered competencies (Kaslow, 1995b).

A third variable that may play a role in the aftermath for children is pertinent in adoptive families. It might be supposed that adopted children, who are often thought to be especially vulnerable to rejection or loss, would experience poorer adjustment in family dissolution than would biological children. Nonetheless, "how they respond to life events will depend on their personality structure, the status of their existing relationships, and their developmental stage" (Rosenberg, 1992, p. 111). Greater difficulty in adjusting to divorce has not been found to be the case for those children adopted as infants or toddlers, whose parents subsequently were divorced, and who were of elementary school age at the time of a study by Brodzinsky and associates (Brodzinsky, Hitt, & Smith, 1993).

On the other hand, greater vulnerability to any familial stress, not only divorce, might well be expected in children who had previously experienced multiple foster home placements, or who were adopted at an older age. Few of the studies on the mental health of adopted children differentiate adequately between children adopted as healthy infants and those adopted at later ages, possibly with negative past experiences or genetic background about which the adoptive parents may or may not have been informed prior to placement (Schwartz, 1996).

The fourth consideration, which applies to some but not all children of divorce, is the effect of relocation subsequent to the separation or divorce. In some cases, relocation is necessary because the primary caretaker no longer may live in the family residence, either as a result of the distribution of marital assets or because of reduced economic resources. In other cases, relocation may occur because of parental remarriage or a new job. New York State's law has been regarded as the strictest with respect to relocation of the custodial parent and the child, permitting it only under "exceptional circumstances":

The exceptional circumstances test has been interpreted to require economic necessity on the part of the custodial parent, and mere economic betterment, remarriage, or even an actual offer of promotion and salary increase will not suffice to grant permission to remove the child. (Grayson, 1994, p. 532)

However, in a ruling by New York State's highest court two years later, the judges moderated this position and averred that decisions in cases involving relocation "should be governed by one central concern: the best interest of the child" (Hernandez, 1996, p. A1). Some lower court judges were troubled by this ruling, feeling that would place them in the difficult position that confronted Solomon in biblical times (Hoffman, 1996).

"Relocation of the custodial parent and the child hampers, and in some cases, may even destroy the noncustodial parent's visitation rights" (Hyde, 1991, p. 9). Florida courts, however, include consideration of whether the relocation is designed to subvert visitation rights of the noncustodial parent as one of six "tests" in resolving relocation requests (Hyde, 1991).

From a psychological perspective, geographic distance may result in several different types of outcome:

(a) positive, that is, reducing frequency of transfers and other opportunities for chronically conflicted and discordant parents to ensnare and/or abuse children; (b) negative, that is, by secondarily stressing child(ren) already rendered vulnerable by divorce and its aftermath and further depriving them of ongoing parental and other attachments and resources; (c) neutral, that is, when cooperating and reasonably well-functioning parties seek not to alienate their reasonably well-functioning child(ren) from respective parents who affirmatively promote opportunities for quality visitation. (Weissman, 1994, p. 178)

Change is particularly stressful for children, and is increased when the move is tied to remarriage of the primary caretaking parent. The courts, seeking to determine what is in the child(ren)'s best interests, are likely to ask in what ways relocation will serve those interests and how it might be inimical to them.

In an era of multinational corporations and easy overseas travel, the possibility of a custodial parent moving to another country adds to the relocation dilemma. Should overseas relocation occur, "courts have a greater concern about jurisdictional conflicts. Further, noncustodial parents' visitation rights are heightened due to the added difficulties of international travel. Finally, courts must consider children's rights not to be compelled to leave the United States" (Grayson, 1994, p. 539).

In general, courts have not favored relocation as it deprives the noncustodial parent of access to the child. However, if the move is in the child's and the custodian's best interests, it may be approved. In one case, for example, a custodial parent's request for permission to move out of state was successful when she "claimed that relocation would promote her well-being and self-fulfillment, which would in turn positively affect the child's best interests" (Ellison, 1991, p. 623). As of early 1996, "high courts in at least 20 states have upheld the right of a custodial parent to relocate, even if the move made it harder for the other parent to see his or her child" (Hernandez, 1996, p. A1). What is taken for granted by most people as a "right," such as the freedom to travel or to relocate for personal reasons, comes under judicial scrutiny when child custody is involved.

> When children move they need to adapt to a new home, neighborhood, school, peers, and community. The children are separated from familiar persons and places, and are confronting new and often confusing experiences. This displacement can be stressful, but the extent to which the stress affects the emotional and social functioning is unclear. (Cornille, 1993, p. 282)

By contrast, relocation by an intact family may be presented as a family adventure and is generally tied to a change in work assignment (military or civilian) or something else perceived as a positive event. While stressful because of the loss of the familiar, the stress can be ameliorated by the family's mutual support. When the relocation follows changes in the family unit, as in divorce and possibly remarriage, it is less likely to be viewed positively and may generate strong feelings of anxiety as well as anger toward the caretaking parent who may be seen both as impotent to prevent the change and as an uncaring activator of it.

The effects of relocation will vary with age of the children, the precipitating circumstances, and the preparation for the move. If the resident parent repeatedly links it to the other parent, now ex-spouse, in a disparaging way, the children will tend to have negative reactions. Even in this situation, however, it is helpful to the children to visit the new community and its schools prior to the move. If this is impractical, then Cornille (1993) suggests obtaining photographs of the community, information from the schools, and perhaps materials from the local Chamber of Commerce. For many children, the most critical problems are the leaving of friends and being accepted by peers in the new school; thus every effort should be made to ease this transition, particularly if it occurs during the school year.

Even older children of divorce, who no longer live at home, may experience anxiety and distress about a parent moving out of the familial home, perhaps to a smaller house or to an apartment. Such a relocation is perceived as additional painful confirmation of what they already know—their family (and its environment) has been dissolved. If they are involved in their own lives as young adults, this reaction tends to be shorter-lived, although nostalgia for the setting in which they grew up and their (mythical) happy family may continue for years.

At all ages, children's adjustments to the marital dissolution and other stressors are very much affected by their parents' reactions to the situation (e.g., depression) and their parents' ability to meet the children's needs. Summarizing several research studies, Portes and colleagues suggest, "It is the level of conflict rather than the divorce per se that affects the adjustment level of these children" (Portes, Howell, Brown, Eichenberger, & Mas, 1992, p. 614).

A helpful "Conflict Assessment Scale" is found in Garrity and Baris (1994, p. 43), which provides descriptors of conflict level ranging from Minimal to Severe. Those couples who accept that their lives are no longer mutually compatible but recognize that their parental responsibilities continue are more likely to be at the "Minimal" end of the continuum and the effects of their divorce on their children also tend to be minimally negative. At the "Moderate" level, however, the children find themselves the prizes in an ongoing power struggle between their parents, and they are caught in a painful loyalty bind that often is displayed in maladaptive behavior and long-lasting pain. Those children living with "Moderately Severe" conflict between their parents are perceived by Garrity and Baris as being in an environment that is psychologically abusive, while those living with "Severe" conflict are in an environment "that is an immediate and direct threat to children's emotional and physical safety" (1994, p. 49).

Camara and Resnick (1989) had found earlier that what was important for children's well-being postdivorce was not so much how the parents resolved their differences between themselves but rather how they resolved their differences as coparents. Or, as Maccoby and associates stated, the effects of conflict "depended on how conflict was managed vis-à-vis the child—and the extent to which the child felt caught between parents as a result of the conflict" (Maccoby, Buchanan, Mnookin, & Dornbusch, 1993, p. 36). Where conflict over custody and visitation continued for extended periods postdivorce, Johnston and associates found "consistent evidence" that children who have more frequent access to both parents, usually as a result of mandated joint custody,

> are more emotionally troubled and behaviorally disturbed. . . .
> Specifically, children who share more days each month with both parents are perceived by their parents as significantly more depressed, withdrawn, and uncommunicative, as having more somatic symptoms, and as tending to be more aggressive. (Johnston, Kline, & Tschann, 1989, p. 588)

This appeared to be more evident in girls than boys. They concluded that, "in cases where the parents continue litigation, recommending or ordering joint custody or frequent visitation . . . is contraindicated" (p. 590).

It goes without saying that the economic impact of divorce falls heavily on the children. "Specifically, the chances of a White child's being poor were almost five times higher if living with a single mother than if living with two parents, whereas the chances of a Hispanic or Black child's being poor were only about three times higher if living with a single mother than if living with two parents" (Laosa, 1988, p. 43). These estimates reflect the differences in income among the groups, and from all reports, have not improved since the 1980 Census.

YOUNG CHILDREN

Infants may be unaware of their parents' separation and divorce on a cognitive level, but they are responsive to the stresses in their environment and are certainly affected by their primary caretaker's distress. Even babies *in utero* are alleged to be negatively affected by the mother's distress if the separation or divorce occurs during pregnancy (Mussen, Conger, & Kagan, 1979). The quality of the care infants receive may be reduced; they may be neglected; they may suffer separation anxiety; they may bear the brunt of one parent's frustration and anger, becoming victims; or, conceivably, they may be virtually "smothered" by becoming the center of a parent's universe.

Toddlers and preschoolers, on the other hand, are much more aware of the tensions in the family and the persisting absence of one parent. Lacking comprehension of the dynamics of the situation and being in what Piaget calls the preoperational stage of cognitive development (Piaget, 1951), however, they may believe that their behavior has caused the problem. In addition, during the predivorce period, "they may have been more aware of and frightened than anyone thought true by loud and angry voices, slammed doors, maternal tears, and spousal or child abuse" (Schwartz, 1992, p. 326). Apart from the promises they make, silent or aloud, to behave better so that the absent parent will reappear, their anxiety and distress may result in regressive behavior, such as bedwetting, babified speech, temper tantrums, or increased clinging to the resident parent.

Prior to the adoption of no-fault divorce in California in 1970 and subsequently in the other states, children of divorce were rarities in school. If their status was known, many teachers and school counselors had pessimistic expectations about their performance and behavior. Very often, since these children of "broken homes" were also perceived by their peers as being "different," such negative prophecies were self-fulfilling. While a few teachers may have made an effort to be supportive of these youngsters, there were no support groups as there are today, in which the children could gain a greater understanding of their situation and realize that they are not unique or misfits.

Early childhood teachers need to be alert to changes in the behavior of children in both preschool and primary school—either to disruptive acting out or to withdrawal—and to recognize that the changes are frequently due to the traumatic event of potential separation or divorce. Frieman (1993) asserts that the "children believe that they will do better work in school if their teachers understand what is going on in their lives. Youngsters hope that their teachers, knowing about the pressures they are experiencing, will be more tolerant of occasional lapses in their school performance" (p. 59). They also hope that the teachers will provide the extra emotional support that may not be available at home. In addition to listening to the children's concerns, teachers of these youngsters may be able to provide outlets for the children's feelings through puppetry, painting, or other expressive classroom activities.

Young schoolchildren may respond to divorce in a variety of ways. Some may deny its reality because it threatens their sense of well-being and security. They can remember happy times the family enjoyed together, and these conflict with the current reality. Some may "indulge in magical thinking in order to reunite the family; they may feel that they have failed to keep the family together and experience guilt over their own inadequacy; or they may even 'wish away' a stepparent or an aggressive/abusive parent" (Schwartz, 1992, p. 326). An additional difficulty for many children in the elementary school years is spending less time with their mothers postdivorce because mother is employed and she had not been before (Buehler & Legg, 1992).

Visitation schedules need to consider the age and developmental needs of the child. Overnight visits are rarely appropriate for infants and toddlers, even when the parents are cooperative, as the children tend to suffer anxiety when being away from the primary caretaker for any length of time. Daily visits by the nonresident parent when possible, however, help to maintain bonds between that parent and the child. Preschoolers can gradually adapt to an overnight visit, plus perhaps an evening during the week, depending on the parent's work schedule. By the early elementary school years, some children can cope developmentally with multiple overnights or even alternative weeks with each parent if the parents live in close proximity and are highly cooperative regarding parenting, but this may pose other practical problems.

Case Example. Long Distance Parenting

In the case of the Youngs, one parent lives in the Midwest and the other in a mid-Atlantic state. Divorced when their daughter Katie was an infant, they had alternated custody every three months throughout her preschool years, with the child flying from one parent to the other on that schedule. When Katie was interviewed just before her sixth birthday as part of a contemplated change in custody arrangements so that her schooling would be uninterrupted, she had neatly compartmentalized her life with each parent into clearly separate "boxes." She responded to questions about her life in each home with a maturity unusual for her age, occasionally expressing some distress about leaving friends or kindergarten activities that she was enjoying because it was time to be with her other parent. Despite the recommendations of psychologists consulted by each parent, her elementary school years were, by parental agreement, going to be divided as Grades 1, 2, and 4 with one parent, and Grades 3 and 5 with the other. This may have satisfied the parental needs for joint custody, but hardly portended an optimal schooling experience even for this bright child. (case files of LLS)

For some adults who had experienced their parents' divorce in the preschool years, their reports indicate that the initial abandonment surfaces in continuing feelings of rejection, fear of intimacy, anxiety about the stability of their own marriages, and the need to "overcare" about others in order to earn acceptance by them. "A major issue for them is lack of communication with their dads. . . . They struggle with low self-worth, resentment, and lack of assertiveness" (Fassel, 1991, p. 49).

OLDER CHILDREN AND ADOLESCENTS

As children move into their preteens and adolescent years, they begin to realize that the parental separation is not their fault and that they can do little to modify the situation. This realization does not reduce their distress very much, nor does it change their desire to have a reunited family. They are, however, more often helped today by in-school support groups that have been formed as more administrators and counselors have become aware of the growing number of children of divorce in their student population. This is in marked contrast to the picture before the advent of no-fault (and therefore an increase in) divorce. Children of divorce groups, run in schools, in churches, or by private practitioners, are usually short term in nature, reality-oriented, and focused on problem solving. Various clinical (Kessler & Bostwick, 1977; Kaslow, 1995b) and research reports (Roizblatt et al., 1990) indicate that these groups are effective in helping children to cope better, to feel less isolated, and to acquire some understanding and perspective about their situation. More on this later in the chapter.

The sensitivity of school personnel to the by-products of divorce that affect their students needs to be increased. Nielsen (1993) presented a number of suggestions ranging from offering after-school programs for "latchkey" children to providing both parents (and possibly stepparents) with copies of all information relevant to the child's school progress and events to modifying class assignments that might be appropriate for intact families but not dissolved ones. She also suggests that counselors share information with single and remarried parents that deals with research findings on children's coping with divorce.

Adjusting to the Change

As noted, younger children tend to think that the parental separation is their fault. This suggests an inner locus of control, but is more likely reflective of what Piaget (1981) saw as the children's egocentrism. As children move through the elementary school years, however, they begin to perceive that they have little control over their parents' behavior and a more external locus of control evolves.

> Because most divorce-related events are both beyond a child's control and involve important domains of the child's environment, the experience of many negative divorce events may cause children to reevaluate their degree of control over the world. Diminished perceptions of control may cause psychological adjustment problems by creating feelings of anxiety or helplessness. Alternatively, diminished perceptions of [personal] control may affect adjustment more indirectly by interfering with the selection of appropriate coping strategies. (Fogas et al., 1992, p. 590)

Apart from the cognitive shift as children move into Piaget's "concrete operational stage," youngsters in the elementary and middle school years have more memories of family outings and activities that they would like to see continue. Their greatest wish, sometimes despite a parent's remarriage, is that their family should be reunited (Kaslow & Schwartz, 1987b).

Since an external locus of control view is appropriate in the separation/divorce situation, the need is to keep it from disabling the children emotionally and behaviorally. This can be accomplished by teaching them positive or active problem-solving strategies with which to cope with the negative events occurring in their family. "As children disengage from problems over which they have little control, they should experience less frustration as well as gain time and energy to develop age-appropriate competencies and skills" (Fogas et al., 1992, p. 596). Further, if they have nonconflictual visitation with the noncustodial parent, they appear to adapt better to the divorce, having less anxiety about being abandoned and developing more self-esteem as their lives proceed more smoothly (Kurta, 1994).

An often overlooked consideration in research and in caretaking arrangements has been that the children of divorce frequently have siblings; they are not necessarily only children. Siblings are usually supportive to one another as the family changes, especially if they continue to live together, which we believe is preferable, absent compelling reasons to separate them.

In one study focused specifically on 133 sibling pairs (58 mixed-sex pairs, 35 sister pairs, and 40 brother pairs) aged 10 to 18 years, of which 99 pairs had shared residence for the 4 years or more since the parental separation, the emphasis was on the similarity or difference in adjustment made by each member of the pair (Monahan, Buchanan, Maccoby, & Donenbusch, 1993). It was found that "siblings who lived apart were more different than pairs who lived together" (p. 164). However, even siblings who lived together "differed in their perceptions of their home and reported different adjustment" (p. 164). The fact that sibling pairs who lived together experienced the same environment in different ways, although to a lesser extent than those living apart, is no surprise as such differences would be found even in an intact family with variability stemming from factors such as age, temperament, and other individual characteristics.

While the Monahan et al. (1993), study looked at this middle group 4 years postdivorce, they had no comparable data on the sibling pairs from the immediate postseparation period on which to base changes or persistence of effects of the parental split. One example of such persistence of effect is seen in a

10-year follow-up of girls who had been preadolescent at the time of their parents' divorce (then ages 9–13). Wallerstein and Corbin (1989) found that less than a third of their 27 subjects were doing well:

> Whereas close to 60% were doing poorly. . . . More than one-half (56%) of these young women seemed especially anxious about making commitments and were consciously preoccupied with fears of betrayal, which intruded into their relationships. . . . The discrepancy between their dreams of enduring love and commitment and their fears of betrayal and abandonment generated severe tensions. . . . (p. 597)

In another follow-up study, done with Finnish students first queried when they were 16 and studied again 6 years later, girls from divorced families ($N = 208$) had significantly more somatic complaints, lower self-esteem, and reported more negative life-events and interpersonal problems than did their peers from intact families ($N = 633$) at the follow-up time (Aro & Palosaari, 1992). Males from divorced families ($N = 145$) differed significantly from their peers in nondivorced families ($N = 568$) only in the area of somatic complaints.

Interestingly, "In terms of family background, greater differences in depression were found between daughters of divorced and nondivorced parents of white-collar families (18% vs. 9%) than in those of blue-collar families (16% vs. 14%)" (Aro & Palosaari, 1992, p. 424). Among the problems confronting young adult female children of divorced parents, compared with daughters of nondivorced parents, were higher rates of divorce, separation, and abortion. In addition, even after adjusting for social class differences, fewer children of divorced parents had completed high school or were studying at the university level. To Aro and Palosaari,

> Lower school performance, less education, more risky health behavior, earlier transition to working life, earlier transition to parenthood, and more abundant negative life events suggest that the life trajectories of children from divorced families differ in many cases from those of children from nondivorced families. The results also suggest that the life trajectories of children from divorced families more frequently contain stressful paths and more distress. (p. 427)

They point out, however, that most of the young adults from divorced families "showed good psychosocial adaptation as young adults" (p. 428).

Fassel (1991), on the other hand, found that many adults who were children of divorce in this age range have had difficulty achieving intimacy, trusting others, and asking for help. Also, they have retained the polarized thinking of the preadolescent period. Those who had reached their teens when the divorce occurred may feel "familyless" and therefore work diligently to ensure the stability of their own marriages. Some "who took mediator roles as teens tend to continue these roles in adulthood . . . [and] appear to have a more realistic view of the strengths and weaknesses of their parents" (p. 53).

Effects on Schooling

For young elementary-school-age children of both genders, the anxiety, distress, and fantasizing following parental separation and divorce occur at critical stages in both cognitive and psychosocial development. They tend "to seek emotional support in different ways during this period of disequilibrium, with boys becoming more actively aggressive and girls more withdrawn. This also affects their learning patterns and the ways in which they are perceived by teachers and peers, among others" (Schwartz, 1992, p. 327). In a study of midwestern fifth and sixth graders from divorced and intact families, for example, Beer (1989) found that children from divorced homes had lower self-concept and self-esteem scores, and lower GPAs, as well as higher depression scores than their peers from intact homes. Although older elementary school children have both greater understanding of the marital dissolution and of alternative ways of coping with it, they, too, may suffer lapses in school performance during the most stressful periods of family problems.

Many teachers and counselors still perceive divorce as automatically a cause of many children's lower grades and adjustment problems when, in fact, this may not be the case. As Atwood (1993) noted, much research on the effects of divorce on children relies on teacher ratings. "As might be expected, because some teachers have internalized the socially created negative definitions of children of divorce, the findings in these studies support the traditional assumption that divorce is bad" (1993, p. 15). An earlier study by Guttmann, Geva, and Geffen (1988) found that such negative stereotypes on the part of teachers (and peers) "would have an adverse effect on evaluations of that child's academic, emotional, and social functioning" (p. 566). As noted previously, divorce is in fact sometimes a relief when the marriage has been continually embattled, and some youngsters actually become more self-reliant and emotionally mature as a result of having to assume more responsibility at home because the resident single parent needs their assistance with daily matters:

> A number of factors, other than the divorce itself, have an impact on students' grades and behavior after their parents separate. The most important are the family's income, the frequency of contact between fathers and children, the conflict between parents both before and after the divorce, whether or not the mother remarries, and the student's personality and academic skills prior to the divorce. (Nielsen, 1993, p. 179)

Some of the preceding factors are interrelated, particularly family income, frequency of contact with each parent, and parental conflict. These may vary with whether or not the father (usually) pays child support on time so that the mother and offspring do not suffer a sharp reduction in standard of living or have to pursue the father in court for funds due. The student's resiliency in the face of difficulties prior to the divorce is likely to reduce vulnerability to this crisis, and indeed may turn the student to academic effort as a means of coping with it. On the other hand, distress at the family's dissolution and anxiety about a parent's pain and/or anger can certainly contribute to emotional maladjustment and lower grades, at least for the first several months after the parents separate. In both cases, the child's unique personality and academic performance are going to be affected by parental conflict both before and after the separation.

Some older children may be obliged to serve as surrogate parents for younger siblings if the residential parent is dysfunctional or absent at work. This may force them to mature more rapidly and to learn to assume responsibility, but at the same time these chores take time away from their schoolwork, their social development, and peer group activities. Is this in the youth's best interests? If not, where can the less available parent acquire the assistance needed? Absent financial and extended family resources, this poses a huge dilemma.

Support Groups

There was a time, as noted, when the child of divorce was a unique figure in the schools. This is no longer true. School personnel have had to adapt to the needs of many children troubled by their parents' separation, as well as the complications of communicating with parents who may not communicate with each other. Although the schools can do little about the parents' lack of positive communication, many make an effort to help the children. Support groups for latency-age children started to emerge as the divorce rate began to climb in the 1970s, and have increased as the need has continued over the past two decades. More recently, according to Farmer and Galaris (1993), groups for preschoolers and adolescents have also been developed.

For most children, support groups under the leadership of a trained group facilitator may help them to cope with the changes in their lives as they interact with peers who have had similar experiences. The groups may continue for several weeks or several months, and may or may not have parallel parent groups running concurrently. Crosbie-Burnett and Newcomer (1990) recommend a minimum of 6 sessions with the children, with 8 to 10 sessions preferable, running 50 minutes or more each, as a practical program. They point out that the "emotional potency of the topic can leave children feeling vulnerable and emotionally abandoned if the group is only long enough to help them identify feelings, but not resolve them or gain new skills" (p. 76). Although the support group is therapeutic, it is not a substitute for individual psychotherapy where that is needed, and indeed may supplement such psychotherapy. As in any therapeutic situation, what is said in the group is held confidential, although group leaders may make suggestions in an indirect way to parents based on what is expressed by children in the group. Before giving more direct input to parents, leaders should obtain permission from the children.

Fernandes, Humphreys, and Fincham (1991) established parallel parent and child groups that met over an 8-week period, using a variety of information in the screening process to establish groups that would be compatible on the basis of age and recency of divorce (in this case no more than two years). Their experience

> suggests that groups should not span more than three grade levels. By restricting the age range, we were able to ensure discussion of similar feelings and issues related to divorce and receptivity to age-appropriate group activities. Also, similarly-aged group participants foster age-appropriate modeling and learning. (p. 27)

Intervention activities need to be varied and selected with an eye to the children's ages. In the project described by Fernandes et al. (1991), group discussion of divorce-related feelings, reading age-appropriate books on children's reactions to divorce and what it means, teaching problem-solving steps, and games related to these were all included.

In designing the parents' group, which ran concurrently with the children's group, there were three major goals:

> (a) to enhance parents' understanding of children's needs as they go through the different stages of divorce and to help them work out ways to meet their child's needs; (b) to help them become more effective in child management; and (c) to provide a supportive environment in which to address their personal needs. (Humphreys, Fernandes, & Fincham, 1992, p. 19)

The parents are asked to focus on their children's reactions to the divorce, on how much time they spend with the child each day, and in exchanging views of events in the respective support groups with their children to foster a sense of togetherness and cooperation. The group's facilitators provide information on child development and what the authors call some of the "psychological traps of divorce," such as becoming overinvolved with work or a hobby at the expense of spending time with their children or, conversely, becoming so overinvolved with their children that they neglect their own needs for adult companionship.

The Marriage Council of Philadelphia, on the other hand, ran its groups for about four months, and had parents attend at least one children's session as a participant, the better to share feelings and divorce-related concerns (Farmer & Galaris, 1993). Here, the children's groups are more heterogeneous than those in the previous example, including all the children in a family aged 4 to 13 years of age. Therapists, who act as group leaders, work to create mutual respect among the children, while acknowledging the difficulties with which all of them are confronted. In addition to treating the comments of the younger children as valuable, they encourage the older children to help the younger ones by suggesting age-appropriate effective coping skills to them. Parents are encouraged to share with the group leaders specific problems or changes affecting their children, and are asked to approve contacts between the group leaders and others who may be working with the children in a therapeutic mode.

When a youngster brings up a problem in the group, often his or her peers make suggestions for a remedy, asking at subsequent sessions whether the remedy has been tried and whether it has been successful. Children can learn from each other's experiences and may adopt peers' suggestions more quickly than those of an adult. Other aspects of the children's sessions include a variety of group activities that point up the positive aspects of change, alternative techniques of dealing with feelings, discussions of events in their lives since the previous session, and clearing up of misperceptions about the family situation. Farmer and Galaris (1993) found that the children had some common concerns that arose throughout the series of sessions:

- Fear that the custodial parent will leave the child.
- Fear that if they express anger at the noncustodial parent, that parent may decide never to see them again.
- Preference for parents to get mad at the child's offensive *behavior* rather than at the fact that the child is angry with the parent.
- A need for adults to realize it is more upsetting to have a stepparent angry with them than it is to have a parent angry with them.
- Awareness of how they try to help their parents cope with the emotional upheaval caused by the separation and divorce. It appears that the children are also cognizant of the things they do to thwart their parents. . . . (p. 47).

While satisfactory legal agreements are being sought between divorcing parents about financial and custody matters, the experience can be wrenching for both parents and children, and often results in a substantial decrease in the amount and quality of attention a child receives (Farmer & Galaris, 1993, pp. 47–48).

Overall, the Marriage Council leaders found that the support group sessions increased understanding and interaction between parents and children. They concluded, on the basis of their experience and that of other researchers "that such outside-the-home supports can facilitate the child's adjustment to changes by increasing the child's understanding and acceptance of the events and by increasing the quantity and quality of discussion and interaction among the child, family members and others with whom he or she interacts outside the home" (Farmer & Galaris, 1993, p. 49). Presumably, some of the "others" are the child's teachers and peers.

Although support groups for children of divorce are becoming more available in schools and other settings scattered throughout the United States, this is rarely the case in other countries (particularly those where divorce is not legal, although other forms of marital dissolution, such as annulment, may exist). However, one such effort was made in Chile, directed toward seventh-grade boys (Roizblatt et al., 1990). This eight-session workshop (seven with the children and one with the parents) was designed to provide the children with an opportunity to explore and share their feelings while providing them with some understanding of the changeable nature of human relationships. The "tool" was a series of stories about a 12-year-old named "Valentine," whose parents separated, which led to many changes in his life and his feelings. At each session, the boys discussed Valentine's problems and their own similar experiences. At the final session, they wrote letters to their parents expressing a key feeling or thought. These were given to the parents (9 mothers and one father) at their session, along with specific suggestions for managing the involvement of their children in the divorce. A blind follow-up several months indicated positive effects for workshop participants compared with children who had not attended the workshop. The authors themselves concluded that the intervention program worked well for this group of 10 middle-class, psychologically healthy sons of divorced parents.

Several of the boys in the Chilean workshop had been children of divorce since infancy or early childhood. We would hope that a similar workshop could be introduced earlier in the divorce process in the future, to prevent the feelings of guilt, anger, and anxiety that so often plague elementary-school-age children of divorce.

Visitation Schedule

Preteens and young adolescents usually can handle regular visits with the nonresident parent quite well, whether these occur a few times each week, they are in alternating homes on a weekly or biweekly basis, or they visit the nonresidential parent for an extended period of several weeks during summer vacation. Much depends on whether the parents live in close enough proximity to enable the children to continue their schooling without undue commuting stress, or whether the children have their own age-related commitments that mitigate against frequent changes in residence. They should certainly be consulted about vacation plans or extended visits in another community if one parent has moved away. The relationship between children and the nonresident parent, especially if there has been a remarriage, should also have a bearing on the length of any extended visit. So should the needs of the residential parent for time alone or on a vacation that is not child-centered.

Midadolescent and older teenagers should be consulted about their visitation schedules. It is normal for teenagers to be separating themselves from their family in favor of involvement with peers, and the contact schedule with each parent must take this into consideration. In addition, some may have part-time jobs during the school year and full-time jobs during the summer that limit the time they can spend away from home. The nonresident parent must respect these needs, and not create or exacerbate a negative relationship with the children or the ex-spouse over the teenager's priorities. What the nonresident parent *can* do is to discuss (negotiate) with the adolescent times or periods of the year that might be mutually convenient for a visit or a trip together. Successful resolution ultimately entails balancing everyone's needs and priorities.

OLDER CHILDREN OF DIVORCE

Much of the research regarding children of divorce is appropriately concerned with the effects of divorce upon those ranging in age from infancy through adolescence. Yet, as indicated earlier, the effects of divorce continue to be felt into adulthood, whether the separation occurred before or after the individual reached the age of majority. Although the effects may vary as to positive or negative valence, they can persist throughout the adult child's life.

Some of the critical issues for adult children of divorce that Fassel (1991) found in her research included questions of trust, how to deal with feelings, and the realization that relationships can be painful. In later-life divorces, the parents may even state that they remained together only "for the sake of the children," thus foisting onto their children a sense of guilt for a prolonged unhappy marriage.

As clinicians, we must be concerned with how divorce has affected the young adult's sense of responsibility, capacity for trust and intimacy, techniques of conflict resolution, and relationships with family members of different generations. To what extent is the older adolescent or young adult able to accomplish the individuation process of the late teen years and early adulthood? College counselors as well as school personnel working with younger students need to recognize that each individual is affected differently by divorce and that they need to have information about the family's divorce experience if they are to help the student whose adjustment to the situation (and to college) is maladaptive (Lopez, 1987). Conversely, Allen and her associates found that among college freshmen, those who had separated from their divorced families tended "to adjust to this situation in a manner that does not limit their academic functioning, self-esteem, or sense of adequacy" (Allen, Stoltenberg, & Rosko, 1990, p. 60). As pointed out earlier, it is essential to know at what point in the subjects' lives the divorce occurred, as well as the quality of the parental interaction afterward, before accepting any study as definitive for any group of children of divorce.

Although living arrangements and legal custody may no longer be the paramount issues that they are for the younger child of divorce, adults in their 20s, 30s, and even later years are still often torn between their parents at holidays, at birthdays, at weddings, and at more pedestrian points of contact. Issues of concern to the child include: Do the parents have amicable or civil contact or are they in continuing conflict, and in what ways does their relationship affect their adult child(ren)? Does the young adult spend a Christmas or Chanukah with the non-remarried parent or the remarried one—or celebrate twice for every major holiday? If neither parent has remarried, how does the grown child relate to each? Can the parents be in the same room and not cause turmoil and dissension? If not, can their children celebrate events separately with each or will their chance to enjoy special occasions be shrouded in clouds of impending doom?

Has the parental divorce, which may occur today after 20, 30, or more years of marriage, soured the young adult on marriage for him- or herself? In what ways does this adult child of divorce view marital commitment? If one or both parents had extramarital affairs before the divorce, does this make the opposite-sexed offspring distrust all members of the offending parent's gender? All of these concerns and questions affect the young adult's persona and relationships in familial and career settings.

As Cooney and associates wrote, little research has been done with those who were late adolescents or young adults when parental divorce occurred (Cooney, Smyer, Hagestad, & Klock, 1986). In their study of thirty-nine 18- to 23-year-olds whose parents had been married an average of just over 20 years, they found that these college students experienced considerable stress as a result of the divorce. This exacerbated the stress they were already experiencing as they moved from home and high school to a residential college and to decision making that would affect their adult lives. Relationships with their parents changed, partly due to the subjects' developmental stage and partly due to the divorce. Typically, relationships with the mother improved, while they were more likely to decline with the father. Among the respondents, 64 percent had had initial concerns about loyalty conflicts, with holidays "a source of great concern for 85 percent of the group" (p. 474). Anger at one or both parents, and concern for their parents' future were reported by as many as three-fourths of the group, especially early in the divorce situation. The impact of these emotions and changing relationships on the subjects' lives in ensuing decades is unknown.

Emotional Issues

Studies of the effects of divorce on the emotional maturity of older adolescents and young adults provide somewhat varying data depending on the subject populations, the research questions asked and the instruments used. For some of these young people, the divorce may actually come as a relief from long-standing tensions within the family, while for others it may be a numbing shock because there had been no overt acrimony between the parents. Those who seek therapeutic help at their college counseling centers have reported a variety of symptoms such as anxiety, distress, feelings of insecurity and abandonment, and inability to concentrate (Kaslow & Schwartz, 1987b, pp. 180–181). Anger at one or both parents may also be present, as may distress caused by continuing parental conflict. However, our study of older children of divorce suggests that for this age group, "their own involvement with college, work, and/or marriage reduced the direct emotional impact of the separation and divorce" (p. 195). It may be that for some this was a healthy way of moving forward with their own lives; for others, such involvement may have been a form of denial of their distress. This age group does not, however, feel responsible for the parents' divorce as much as younger children do, has no expectations of parental reunification, and is more likely to find a support network among siblings, friends, and dates.

According to Garber (1990), divorce in and of itself does not account for feelings of high or low self-esteem. There was evidence, however, in his sample of college students ($N = 324$) that high interparental conflict, whether in intact or divorced families, was more closely associated with lowered general and social self-esteem. Such a finding suggests that popular perceptions about the effects of divorce on the children as they mature may be inappropriate preconceptions without support in reality.

Heyer and Nelson (1993) were concerned with possible differences in self-confidence, sexual identity, and emotional autonomy among college students that might stem from differences in family status. Their subjects included upper-class students from three categories: intact families, divorced but not remarried families, and divorced and remarried families. The children of divorce scored well on all three measures compared with those from intact families, with the authors attributing success to being given more responsibility where there is a single parent, to parental modeling in the case of sexual identity sophistication, and to their using independence and self-reliance as coping mechanisms in the divorce situation. What was not indicated, and might have influenced the results, was the subjects' ages at the time of parental separation. The role of socioeconomic status in easing adjustment also was not a variable.

In a study of college students whose parents had divorced while they were in high school or in college, Swartzman-Schatman and Schinke (1993) found that there were significant differences in attitudes toward the father and in general contentment with life between these subjects and a control group whose parents were not divorced:

> The group whose parents divorced while they were in college seemed to have an additional problem. Perhaps because they were older their parents felt, mistakenly, that they would adjust more easily. They did not take the time to tell them about the divorce together. In addition they seemed to play on their loyalties more and make them feel somewhat more responsible than they did to the high school subjects. (pp. 213–214)

The loyalty problems and parental manipulation of children's decisions about with which parent to spend holidays and vacations, specifically mentioned in this study, cause considerable distress, at least initially, to these late adolescents/young adults at a time when they should be focusing their time and energy on college, work, and peer relationships. These life events may alter the nature of their reality and life-space.

Issues of concern to older children of divorce, even in their adult years, include the continuing relationship between their parents as it affects them on a daily basis; the impact of divorce on the children's view of marital commitment, especially if extramarital affairs played a part in the parental separation; and the ways in which the children relate to the new family of a remarried parent. There is also the possibility, raised in Judith Wallerstein and Sandra Blakeslee's controversial *Second Chances* (1989), that as they become adults, the children of divorce may experience an eruption of long-denied feelings.

The key issue of parental relationships postdivorce continues to affect young adults. Are the parents civil when they meet, or in a state of continuing conflict, resentment, and rage? Any of the more negative contacts can make what should be happy occasions highly stressful. More mature and emotionally healthy adults, even if still harboring hostility toward the ex-spouse, set aside their feelings, at least in public, in the interests of their children when they must meet. Those parents who are cordial, if not amicable, can still provide strong support for their children as they move on to a new life stage.

On a more positive note, Fassel (1991) found that many children of divorce—as adults—had "developed independence, flexibility, and self-reliance" (p. 8). While some carry the fear of abandonment or closeness in relationships for a lifetime, others may have learned that they do not have to remain in dysfunctional situations. Similarly, Gately and Schwebel (1992), in their review of literature on the children of divorce, concluded that many of these children gave evidence of greater maturity, self-esteem, and empathy than their peers from intact families, as well as more androgynous thinking and behavior. These shifts appeared to result from shouldering increased responsibilities in the home postdivorce and from having parents who modeled nontraditional gender attitudes and behaviors or encouraged them to do so.

Educational and Career Aspirations

Among African American college freshmen, Phillips and Asbury (1993) found no differences in academic motivation and educational aspirations between those from intact families and those whose parents were divorced or separated. No indication was given by the students on how long their parents had been apart, which may have affected the results in this study, but the authors did indicate that these young people "could in some respects be considered already select and successful, as evidenced by their college matriculation" (p. 209).

On the other hand, Elliot (1990) found her sample of 14 college students who experienced parental divorce during their college/graduate school years to have feelings of anger and sometimes shock, relief if there had been marked marital tension at home, and a sense of loss. Concern about their parents' and younger siblings' well-being intruded on the thinking of many of these young adult students, but their ability to cope with the situation was enhanced by their maturity and nurturing behaviors toward family members.

Financial Concerns

Another source of anxiety in older children of divorce related to higher education aspirations may be more difficult for them to articulate. Even before an older child of divorce worries about his or her potential inheritance if a remarried parent dies (Kaslow, 1990b; 1995b), there may be very real concerns about college or graduate school tuition that might have been assumed in an intact family but are not as readily apparent in a divorced one, or about parental help in starting a business or professional career. In the longer term, there may also be concerns about who will support and care for an aging parent, typically the mother, if she has not remarried, or for an alcoholic or infirm elderly father.

In the matter of higher education tuition support, several states, including Alabama, Tennessee, and Utah are requiring that children of divorce be supported for a college education through age 21, or possibly longer (Elrod, 1994, p. 506). This policy reflects the belief that lack of a college education handicaps an individual in gaining meaningful employment in today's increasingly technological world. One judge in Pennsylvania ruled, however, that parents have no obligation to provide such support, contending that the state does not tell married couples that they have to pay tuition (*Blue v. Blue*, 1989). While this is true, in families where children have had a reasonable expectation that their parents would pay their college expenses, it appears that the youths are the losers if the economically able parent declines to do so and the children are achievement-oriented, good students.

In other situations, where the primary breadwinner would normally have provided the tuition funds, he (or she) may demand that the other parent share the expenses equally, even if unable to do so, or there will be no funds at all. Although there are two households to support postdivorce, which de facto has an impact on the amount of discretionary funds each parent has available, the children should not be penalized deliberately. Although the young adult can be expected to work to defray some expenses, at the cost of college tuition today they can rarely assume the entire burden, even if they can obtain scholarships and/or loans. Without postsecondary education, many will be inadequately prepared for an economy that has little need for unskilled and semiskilled workers. Recognizing this situation, Pennsylvania passed legislation (subsequent to the *Blue v. Blue* decision), effective in mid-1993, regarding postsecondary educational costs that allowed a court to order "either or both parents who are separated, divorced, unmarried or otherwise subject to an existing support obligation, to provide equitably for educational costs of their child. . . . The responsibility to provide for postsecondary educational expenses is a shared responsibility between both parents" (Penn. Cons. Stat. Ann., Title 23, 1993). This Act was overturned in *Curtis v. Kline* (1995) by the Supreme Court of Pennsylvania, returning the situation to that in *Blue v. Blue* (1989). Other states have passed similar laws. We would urge that the sharing be done on a basis proportional to income and assets and not that of "half and half."

There are other situations that require modification of the usual child support guidelines. Postmajority support may be an issue when a child is so mentally or physically handicapped that he or she will never be able to become self-supporting. On the other hand, if a minor child becomes emancipated through marriage or by moving out of a parent's home, support can be terminated (Elrod & Walker, 1994). In addition, if an adult child unilaterally severs the parent-child relationship, the child forfeits any right to support from that parent (*DeWalt v. DeWalt*, 1987).

Issues That Continue

The relationships between adult children of divorce and their parents may change over the years as the pain of the initial separation wanes and the children, as well as the parents, develop new roles and relationships. From one angle, the impact of the divorce on the adult child's views toward his or her own marriage, together with their attitudes regarding trust, commitment, responsibility, and parenting, must be considered. From another point of view, the effects of remarriage of one or both parents and the impact of this expanded family on the adult children emotionally, socially, and financially needs further examination through research. An extension of this last factor leads to the blurring of generational boundaries if the remarried parent has a second family and/or marries someone younger than the children of the first marriage, and if this represents a marked change in actual versus anticipated grandparental roles of the original couple, at least in the eyes of their children.

CONCLUDING COMMENT

After reviewing dozens of studies of the effects of divorce on children, Wallerstein (1991) concluded that "from the child's perspective, divorce represents an ongoing condition of family life that gives rise to a series of particular experiences and multiple life changes throughout childhood, adolescence, and often extending into adulthood" (p. 358). She further asserted that "the multiple economic, social, and psychological life stresses of being a single or a visiting or a remarried parent, together with the unanticipated psychic reverberations of the broken marriage contract, have combined to weaken the family in its child-rearing and child protective functions" (p. 359). Although we find her view to be overly pessimistic, there is no doubt that the effects of divorce in most cases are long-lasting, affecting both the parent-child relationship and other subsequent relationships. Some may become more wary of intimacy, while others seek intimacy as balm for the deep wounds experienced. Even where the adult has created a happier new life, the changes he or she has made in cognitive thinking and in personal behavior affect interpersonal interactions, presumably in positive ways.

Further substantiation of the long-term impact of divorce on the children involved is found in a longitudinal study of 240 children born from 1965 to 1970, whose parents were divorced before the children were aged 16. This study indicates:

> Even after controlling for variations across groups in parent education, race, and other child and family factors, 18- to 22-year-olds from disrupted families were twice as likely as other youths

to have poor relationships with their fathers and mothers, to show high levels of emotional distress or problem behavior, to have received psychological help, and to have dropped out of high school at some point. (Zill, Morrison, & Coiro, 1993, p. 96)

We do not find, as those cited above seem to, that receiving psychological help is necessarily a negative factor. To the contrary, it is often a means to develop ways in which to deal with the pain of a disrupted family. Therapy need not represent treatment for problem behavior, but rather may be an attempt to deal proactively and more effectively with the problems emanating from the family dissolution, to keep from getting fixated at the time of the divorce, and to enhance one's growth.

As parents themselves, most children of divorce are acutely conscious of the need children have for close ties between parents and their children, and try to provide the kind of support and attention that many of them did not receive in their families of origin. They are also aware of the costs to the children of a dysfunctional nuclear family or of an adversarial divorce, and strive to avoid inflicting such pain on their own children. In summarizing the responses of more than 250 children of divorce who were now parents, Berner found that they tended to characterize themselves as being overprotective, "as exhibiting a strong desire to shelter their children rather than make them independent. It was as if they were compensating for a missed childhood" (1992, p. 108). They tried to provide "fair, non-abusive, and consistent" discipline, often in contrast to their own experiences.

On the basis of his subjects' responses, Berner concluded:

> The childhood experience of divorce hangs over the child of divorce forever, although some struggle to put it behind them. In fact, this may be the single most important thing I have learned: The impact of divorce is everlasting. That does not mean children of divorce go through life flawed, but it does mean that a piece of them is still trying to resolve the trauma of their parents' divorce. Each has his own way of resolution. (1992, p. 118)

CHAPTER 11

Getting on with Life

As the trauma of separation lessens with the passage of time, the two parties face the need to reorganize their lives in terms of a new reality. There are the basics of living to confront: Where to live? How large is the budget? What about children's care? familial ties? social relationships? If one spouse sought to dissolve the marriage because of a new romantic relationship, many of these questions are resolved superficially and quickly for that individual in terms of feeling loved, cherished, and desired. If the new relationship results in remarriage, this brings new challenges, especially if the new spouse has children and possibly a living former spouse plus his or her extended family. For the individual who remains unattached, there are many new situations with which to deal.

For couples married in the 1950s, parting in the 1980s and 1990s has produced a number of challenges that are not present for those leaving shorter or more recent marriages:

[Women in their middle years] are rarely prepared to be the "seekers" rather than the "sought." . . . Even if they do meet a man, they wonder about how to behave, what to do if he makes physical advances, whether it's OK to have sex with him on a second or third date, whether to consider remarriage, or—Heaven help them!—what to do if the man rejects them. Men, similarly, find it difficult to date, are not sure of what the woman expects or wants of them (either physically or in terms of gender-oriented attitudes), and are equally fearful of rejection. In addition, today there is a very real concern about

contracting the human immunodeficiency virus (HIV)/ac-
quired immuno-deficiency syndrome (AIDS) virus or another
sexually transmitted disease, which may not be apparent until
several years after infection by a casual or a frequent partner in
either individual's past. (Schwartz, 1994b, p. 91)

EX-SPOUSAL CONTACTS

If, at the time of divorce, there are minor children, there will
inevitably be contact between the ex-spouses unless one parent has chosen to step out of the children's lives completely or
has been ordered to do so. Will these contacts be amicable or
hostile? If there has not been a history of abuse, can the parents
contain their anger at each other in the interest of minimizing
stress for their children as well as providing an example of mature behavior?

Ahrons (1989) interviewed 98 divorced couples and their
new mates one, three, and five years after their legal divorce,
and found that their relationships with former spouses fell
along a wide continuum. She has developed a typology of former spousal relationships and describes this continuum in accordance with it. The "perfect pals" not only continued a long
friendship, but also shared the parental roles and maintained
relationships with each other's extended families. More typical, she found, were the "cooperative colleagues." "Though
not good friends, they work very well together on issues concerning their children. They can also talk amiably about other
family members. . . . They do have conflict, but manage it well,
and can separate their conflicts as spouses from their responsibilities as parents" (p. 38). In contrast, there are the "angry
associates," whose anger persists at a slightly mellowed level,
and whose communication is "distant" if no longer as bitter
as it had been. The final group she identified were the "furious foes":

[They] have virtually no capacity whatsoever for cooperating.
Their divorces tend to be highly litigious, with legal fights continuing many years after the decree is signed. . . . for these
spouses, the other parent is the enemy. Like couples in conflict-
habituated marriages, they are still very much attached to each
other, although they would deny it. (pp. 40–41)

Even without continuing litigation, one or both parents may devalue the other to the children, creating major problems for them. A fifth group, the "dissolved duos," have no contact with each other because one spouse leaves the geographic area and totally withdraws from the former family.

As the years pass, as has been noted, for those who have children, there are many occasions when the ex-spouses must be at the same place at the same time—graduations, religious occasions, weddings, and the arrival of grandchildren. As Ahrons stated, "We haven't always celebrated our children's accomplishments amicably together, but over the years, with practice, we learned to tolerate our differences in order to reap some of the rewards of our parenting" (1989, p. 31).

With the aid of a family therapist or a mediator, the parents might be helped to develop a more mature perspective focused on the parental roles rather than the marital ones. If they can learn to be as concerned for their children in practice as they profess to be, they might work out a contract in which they agree on doing things that benefit them, but apply some tangible penalty if one does something to the other that hurts the children.

ALTERED LIFESTYLES

There are basically three possible changes in lifestyle after separation and divorce: heading a single-parent family, remarrying, or remaining single and not "head-of-family." Each brings its own challenges and even benefits.

Single-Parent Families

Single-parent families result from a number of causes, only one of which is divorce. Children may also live with only one parent because one parent has died and the survivor has not remarried, because there never was a spouse, or in the rarer instances where a single woman chose to have a child through artificial insemination or adoption. To bring some perspective to this situation, Laosa (1988) examined data from the 1980 Census regarding children in single-parent families. These data do not distinguish among the causes for single-parenting, but do reveal substantial differences among ethnic and racial categories. Among white families, for example, 14.4 percent of children lived with only one parent. In marked contrast, 45.8 percent of black children, 28.6 percent of American Indian children, and 23.5 percent of Hispanic children lived with only one parent. However, "only 11.5% of Asian families with own children were single-parent families . . ." (Laosa, 1988, p. 26). Laosa indicates there may be substantial differences within these groups, depending on which sub-group is examined (e.g., Hispanic: Mexican American, mainland Puerto Rican, Cuban, island Puerto Rican, Central or South American). All of these figures may well have changed, probably showing increases in the 1990 Census as changes in the divorce laws had greater impact; the data were not available at the time of writing this.

Marital dissolution where minor children are present brings, for a time at least, the existence of what Sager calls the double single-parent family (Sager et al., 1983) since there are two single parents and not one, which was the case in 40.4 percent of the children in the 1980 census. Another 27.8 percent were living with their mothers only because of parental separation (Laosa, 1988, p. 28). The arrangements for taking care of the children vary from one parent being the sole legal and physical caretaker to fairly equal joint custody by both parents. What is life like, however, for the parents in these variations of the postdivorce binuclear family (Ahrons & Rodgers, 1987)?

In the initial stage of being a single parent, the individual is confronted with many choices and decisions. Women especially "may first need to develop some financial and legal competencies to relieve their personal stress" (Brown, 1988, p. 379). Therapists can suggest resource people and adult education courses to help women acquire the necessary knowledge and skills to manage such financial affairs as a stock portfolio. These women may also need to reassure themselves about their competence as mothers, so that they can function in that role effectively when doing solo parenting.

Once the initial trauma has begun to lose its force, the reasonably healthy and capable single parent is able to stabilize the reduced family unit's functioning and begin to move forward with new goals and plans to reach them.

As Guttmann (1993) points out, social institutions (and politicians) view single-parent families as "abnormal" and temporary while at the same time expecting them to fulfill the same functions as two-parent families. As he further asserts, "Because many families are treated as 'nonfamilies' or are stigmatized as deviant, and a social distance is erected between 'normal' and 'abnormal' families, a self-fulfilling prophecy is put into effect" (1993, p. 87). The noncustodial parent has even less public and social support. The popular assumption that all single-parent families are dysfunctional is not supported in the available research. Rather, "results suggest that it is the psychosocial characteristics of the family unit, independent of the number of parents that affect the individuals in the family" (Guttmann, 1993, p. 95).

For the sole caretaker, there is total responsibility for all decisions with respect to the children. In some cases, a divorced parent moves to his or her parental home with the children, thus gaining some relief from a basically 24-hour-a-day job. If working, the parent may also be relieved of some cooking and other obligations of daily life. Of course, the parent may be placed in an undesirable position with his or her parents, being again perceived as a dependent (and perhaps not always grateful) child. For the grandparents, the upheaval and resulting extra demands, if the stay becomes prolonged, can be terribly taxing. In either case, it behooves the single parent to work toward making alternative living arrangements as soon as possible. Perhaps sometimes the grandparents will come to the their child's home and offer child care, or they might take the grandchildren to visit at or for day care at their home, but not reside together.

Two major concerns of the employed single parent are time management and child care. Which household tasks can be deemphasized or transferred to one of the children, without unduly parentifying the child, to save energy and time? Is a well-run day-care facility available for preschoolers at an affordable cost? Is there a supervised after-school program available for the school-age children? What resources are available if a child becomes ill? Can the parent develop a set of guidelines and consequences for the children and apply them consistently? Where in the schedule is there time for the single parent to enjoy the children and socialize with other adults?

In the single-parent family living independently, the parent, who is typically employed, may feel overwhelmed with the combination of work- and parenting-related responsibilities and tasks, leading to a major time-management problem. Although desirous of showing attention and affection to the children, resentment at the "overload" (and at the former spouse for making it necessary) may affect the parent-child relationship. In many cases, depending on the children's ages, this changed level of interaction results in a new and different type of bonding with the parent, perhaps with some of the children recognizing the need for them to take on more responsibilities. There are possible difficulties if the single parent depends on the oldest child to share too many of the activities in caring for the younger child(ren). At some point, that oldest child, in turn, may resent the burden as an interference with his or her own schoolwork and activities, social life, or college plans. The parent-child relationship may also be tested anew if the parent begins to date or to participate in activities to compensate for the decline in social life following divorce, or if offered a promotion at work that may entail occasional traveling. Juggling and finding a balance in the I, Thou (Buber, 1937), and We gestalt can be a formidable task.

Overall, families headed by a single mother seem to experience more difficulties than those headed by a single father, sometimes because the mother has fewer marketable skills or other resources with which to help herself and her family. When a problem arises, ecosystemically oriented practitioners look at the situation "in terms of the interconnectedness of social, psychological, physical, and cultural factors. The internal experience of the individual, as well as that person's material well-being, is greatly affected by the quality of connectedness between the family and the outside world" (Kissman & Allen, 1993, p. 41).

Where one parent is primarily responsible for the children and the other has visitation on weekends or for part of school vacations, the second parent may feel obliged to entertain the child(ren) throughout the visitation period. This is contrary to the experience during marriage, where both parents care for, teach, entertain, and otherwise interact with the children in spurts of time rather than full-time from morning through bedtime. It is an artificial situation that is difficult for everyone. As noted earlier, this seems to place more stress on divorced fathers (Umberson & Williams, 1993). Conversely, the children may enjoy the weekend and vacation parent who spends "fun time" with them rather than supervising homework, practice for activities, and assigning household chores, and may eventually request a change of primary residence to the more permissive or affluent parent.

Currently, there is strong sentiment for the involvement of noncustodial fathers with their children postdivorce. In a study of such fathers several years after divorce, they "indicate that [while] their parenting relationship with their children diminishes after divorce and that the divorce adversely affects their child's adjustment, they also report their post-divorce parenting makes a positive difference for their child" (Hoffman, 1995, p. 14). The fathers also recognize that "their ex-wives' support for and cooperation with their parenting role following divorce was also a significant variable contributing" to their assessment of their children's postdivorce adjustment (p. 14).

On the other hand, noncustodial mothers suffer more stigmatization, isolation, and depression because of their unusual status (Arditti & Madden-Derdich, 1993; Greif & Pabst, 1988). They may have voluntarily chosen to relinquish the caretaking role for self- or child-oriented reasons, or may have done so involuntarily because of a court order or financial or other coercion by the father.

The Greif and Pabst study (1988) of more than 500 noncustodial mothers from varied geographic, socioeconomic, and religious backgrounds, revealed that their subjects were almost evenly divided among three groups: those who were comfortable as noncustodial mothers, those who were uncomfortable in the role, and those who had "mixed" feelings. Those in the first group tended to have marriages that ended on "fairly good terms" (p. 163), have come over time to feel that they have made good decisions, are pleased with their child(ren)'s development over the years, and have created an identity for themselves that goes beyond the role of mother. On the other hand, those who are uncomfortable with their status were found to have had a more hostile divorce, and may have lost custody unwillingly. They have less social support, appear to have more continuing problems, and have not adjusted to a less-active parental role—with poorer relationships with their children. "They have not been able to mourn the loss of their parenting role effectively, and they remain bitter, often feeling victimized and out of control" (Greif & Pabst, 1988, p. 163). Those in the middle group quite literally have mixed feelings about themselves, some positive and some negative relationships with their children, and mixed experiences with regard to social support and their status.

In a small study of noncustodial mothers, Arditti and Madden-Derdich found that their subjects were moderately dissatisfied and relatively uncomfortable with the custody arrangements, perceived a lack of support from others, reported being less "close" to their children, and "felt guilty about not having custody of their children" (p. 309). They felt that they had had little choice in the resolution of the custody issue and did not perceive themselves as uncaring or unfit (although other people may stereotype them in this way). Visitation was seen as too infrequent and too short, often confounded with interference from their ex-spouse and relatively little discussion between them regarding the children. In this small sample:

> Limited choices, support, and financial resources all point to the oppression that these mothers experience. As a result of their marginalized status and oppression, these women remain largely invisible and outside the legal and mental health systems. (Arditti & Madden-Dredich, 1993, p. 312)

In a larger longitudinal, though regional, study, Braver and colleagues (1993) found that noncustodial parents vary among themselves with respect to relations with their children. A critical factor appears to be their perception of how much control or influence they have on their children now and for the future. Those who feel more "in control" tend to maintain more frequent contact and financial support. Those who feel they have lost their parental influence, however, tend to "withdraw from the obligations of parenthood, financial support, and an emotional relationship with the child . . ." (Braver et al., 1993, p. 20). This suggested, to this team, that joint legal custody and mandatory mediation of divorce disagreements to reduce the adults' disputes might increase compliance with child support decisions as well as improve relations between noncustodial parents and their children.

Life is a bit more "normal" for the parents when caretaking is shared on a regular basis, as when the children move from one home to the other on some regular and predictable schedule. (The effects on the children of frequent shuttling back and forth, however, vary greatly in such arrangements.) Typically the parents in these instances live nearby to eliminate or minimize problems related to disruption of schooling and accessibility to continuing peer relationships.

Blended Families and New Ties

Although remarriage is not a major subject of this book, a brief perusal of what is likely to be ahead if and when a remarriage occurs is included to provide an important aspect of the postdivorce situation and of what often happens to and for the children in a blended family.

In past generations, remarriage, blended families, and stepparents were common phenomena as people died at younger ages than they do today (Fisher, 1992). The surviving spouse, with or without children, typically remarried and frequently began a new family. What is different today is that remarriages more often follow divorce, not widowhood, so that the nonresident parent is still present somewhere in the family constellation (Kaslow, 1993c).

> Stepfamilies are a curious example of an organizational merger; they join two family cultures into a single household. Of course, first marriages amalgamate family sub-cultures as well, but there is a difference. Couples in first marriages generally have a chance to work out their differences before children come along. And when children do arrive, they are usually eagerly anticipated by both parents. Stepfamilies, on the other hand, are not afforded the same amount of time to build a family identity; rather, it is frequently imposed upon them. Stepfamilies must blend sub-cultures that have been established for years. (Furstenberg & Cherlin, 1991, p. 83)

Whether based on death or divorce, however, the children often have to deal with the myths (and resulting stereotypes) they have read and heard about "wicked stepparents" (Bray, 1995). One study that compared parent-child relationships among college students from stepfamilies and intact families suggested that "relationships in stepmother families are more likely to be dysfunctional than are those in stepfather and intact families" (Sauer & Fine, 1988, p. 448).

When one or both parties remarries, new family constellations are established that expand the relationships of all parties. If each party chooses a new spouse, some contact is almost inevitable among the four people.

> Among other things, parenting and stepparenting is unlike nuclear family parenting. Discipline issues are different, loyalty issues are prominent, constant changes in family composition may be occurring, and negotiation of different values and ways of doing things involves the children as well as the adults. All have lived in other households, and all have definite ideas about family life. (Visher & Visher, 1995, p. 26)

Unmarried men who become "instant fathers" through marriage to a divorced (or widowed) woman with minor children "have few places to turn for information and lack personal experience both as a father or as a husband" (Roberts & Price, 1987, p. 75). Consequently, they must learn these roles by trial and error, and with the patient support of their partner. On the other hand, they do not bring an ex-wife or children to the marriage as complicating or competing factors, which, according to Roberts and Price (1987), makes them more desirable as potential husbands.

If the new partner has children from a previous marriage, they too are affected by the advent of a new parent and his or her children, and there is an impact on all of these offspring if the new marriage produces children. Life can become very complicated for everyone. As Ahrons describes her own experience:

> My husband and I had more or less come to terms with our ex-spouses. Even though he lived a thousand miles away, my children saw their father regularly and we made parental decisions amicably together. He had remarried, fathered two more children, and his wife and I got along quite well. At the other extreme, my husband's relationship with his ex-wife had deteriorated into a sullen, non-speaking standoff, and although we lived in the same city, his children rarely spent time with us. This breach remained a painful void in our lives. (1989, p. 34)

What happens to the children in remarriage? Much depends on their ages at the time of the divorce and the remarriage, whether there are stepsiblings, and whether half-siblings are born into the new family. These circumstances are described at some length in Schwartz's (1993) paper, "What *Is* a Family?" Relations with stepsiblings may be anticipated positively, with the children involved looking forward to having a sibling (if an only child) or more "in-house" playmates, or negatively, as increased competition for parents' time and resources loom. Differences in ages, abilities, interests, preferences, family traditions, roles, loyalties, and privacy may be perceived as challenges or as the basis for mutual hostility (Rosenberg & Hajal, 1985). How do the children perceive this new family? What role do they see for each family member? How do they introduce the stepparent or stepsiblings to others? What do they call the stepparent— "Mom," "Jane," "Mr. X," "My mom's husband"?

Moving toward a perception of the new family as a nuclear family would seem to be easier if the child is very young, perhaps below school age, for the new stepparent will be an important factor in the child's life presumably for more than a dozen years. Such a perception will be less appropriate if the child is older, or if the child is involved frequently with the nonresidential parent.

For adolescents, there may be greater vulnerability to distress because this is the stage when they are seeking to establish their own identity, individuating from their family of origin, and consequently they have greater difficulty relating to the new stepparent as well. As Pasley and Healow found, the decision to invest energy into the new family may be inhibited by the desire for independence from the family in general and particularly from the stepfamily to which they feel little or no allegiance (1988, p. 265). The matter of setting rules for teenagers is difficult enough in intact first families, but even more so in remarried families:

> When the rules are imposed or enforced by an "outsider," such as a stepparent, the likelihood of resentment or disobedient responses increases. In a stepfamily, adolescents can compare stepparental disciplinary behavior with an idealized memory of "how it used to be" (during the single-parent stage), and/or to the more lenient atmosphere that may exist on visits with the nonresidential parent. (Pasley & Dollahite, 1995, p. 93)

There is often more embarrassment for adolescents because of demonstrations of affection and implications of sexuality between the parent and stepparent. This may be exacerbated if a pregnancy occurs, just as it is for some adolescents even between the original set of parents.

Bray's (1995) longitudinal Developmental Issues in Stepfamilies (DIS) Research Project, which studies children from nonclinical families, has found that children's adjustment, or lack of it, in stepfamilies varies with their age and the length of the remarriage:

> Children, ages 6–8, in stepfamilies remarried for 6 months and adolescents, ages 11–14, in stepfamilies together for 5–7 years had more behavior problems and lower social competency than comparably aged children in first-marriage families. There were no differences in behavior problems for children in first-marriage families and children, ages 8.5–10.5, in stepfamilies remarried for 2.5 years. The behavior problems with the youngest children were related to the early stressful transition into a stepfamily, whereas the behavior problems of the 11- to 14-year-olds were related to the transition into adolescence, parenting problems, and unresolved issues from the initial divorce. (p. 61)

When children in remarried families do act out, it is as important not to assume that the reason is solely that they are reacting to their parents' divorce and remarriage as it is to recognize that the changes in their lives may be contributing to their behavior problems. Life becomes immeasurably more complex when each of the newly paired parents has nonresidential children who appear alternate weekends or at vacation times, while the residential children are also moving in and out according to *their* visitation schedules. In addition, there are new as well as original extended families to which all of the parties must relate and who must integrate the newcomers. Constructing a genogram may help the therapist as well as the family members to comprehend these relationships and how they are all connected (Bray, 1995; Kaslow, 1995b).

Jacobson (1995), on the other hand, perceives the new family structure as a "linked family system," with the child as the link between the custodial (live-in) household and the noncustodial (visited) household. This perspective would appear to be valid whether there is a primary caretaker as is suggested by her description, or, perhaps more so, where the child moves from one household to the other on a weekly or biweekly basis.

Case Example. Interfamilial Cooperation

John and Jeanne were divorced after a dozen years of marriage and the arrival of two children, then aged 8 and 10 years. They agreed to live in proximity so that the children could move from one parent's home to the other's on a weekly basis. Two years later, John married Penny, a divorced mother with two children. She was primary caretaker for her children, who visited their father on alternate weekends. All three adults worked for the same company which produced some tense moments for the two women, but also facilitated their working out scheduling conflicts on a cooperative basis. One afternoon several years into John's remarriage, I witnessed the three amicably trying to juggle one child's dental appointment which that week's caretaker could not handle, while also finding a trade-off to compensate for the favor. (Case Notes of LLS)

There are less amicable situations, however, to which all parties in the linked family system need to be alert. Jacobson (1995) gave an example of a 9-year-old girl who lived with her remarried father and visited her mother. The stepmother, newly pregnant, felt overwhelmed by trying to handle the girl's school problems and resented being given so much responsibility for her; the father, working two jobs, was angry at his wife for not being willing to "take over" for him; and the girl's mother said she could not be the primary caretaker because of lack of funds and a poor relationship with the girl. How do such negative adult attitudes and behaviors impact on a child? In essence, she is being told that no one really wants to care for her unless she poses no problems at all. A family therapist needs to bring all of the adults together and make them aware of the effects of their attitudes and actions on the girl, and what some of the likely outcomes might be in terms of her future behavior.

A summary of several studies of remarried families indicates that in general:

Families in which the custodial father remarries and a step-mother enters the family experience more resistance and poorer adjustment for children than do families in which the custodial mother remarries and a stepfather enters the family. . . . Moreover, families in which both parents bring children from a previous marriage are associated with the highest levels of behavior problems. (Hetherington, Stanley-Hagan, & Anderson, 1989, p. 309)

A study of adolescents in remarried families, from both joint custody and sole custody arrangements, revealed significant differences in adolescent-parent relationships depending on the quality of the coparent relationships. The remarriage "had a more positive effect . . . when the co-parents had a friendly relationship," while adolescents "whose co-parents were hostile were reported to show an increase in psychosomatic and psychosocial problems around the time of the remarriage" (Crosbie-Burnett, 1991, p. 445). Girls in sole custody and boys in joint custody situations also reported higher levels of anxiety and more negative effects of remarriage on their relationships with their biological parents after remarriage. (p. 446)

Adaptability, flexibility, and time are required to build a positive and satisfying stepfamily relationship and to reduce the negative effects that might emerge from continuing friction among former partners. Concurrently, preexisting parent-child relationships have to be maintained, visitation schedules may intrude on or at least complicate the new family's activities, and there may be a good deal of "testing of the limits" by children vis-à-vis their new stepparents. Moving toward a new family integration is not easy, and the adults may find some clues to a successful path either through therapy or in a positively oriented support group of newly remarried couples. Therapy may assist each parent (and stepparent) to understand the challenges faced by the other in developing a balanced role in the new parent-child relationship system. Where the children involved are quite young, they need not be included in the therapy sessions, but older children may profit from as well as contribute to progress in sessions designed to make the new family more harmonious (Visher & Visher, 1995). As is the case in nuclear families, knowledge of how to parent does not come packaged with the arrival of children.

Earlier in this book (Chapter 6), there was discussion of the financial pressures on fathers who pay child support for the offspring of their first marriage and must also provide economically for their second (or third) family. What is not apparent in much of the literature is the role of the stepparent in supporting stepchildren, or what his or her responsibilities and obligations are to these children. State laws, where they exist, vary considerably (Mason & Simon, 1995). Discussion of the financial and other issues confronting blended families ought to take place before remarriage rather than becoming a source of friction that may propel the couple toward marital/family conflict and perhaps another divorce.

Remaining Single

The divorced person who remains single, but who is not functioning in an active parental role with minor children, may have nonresident adult children or may not have children at all. Several options are open to this individual. Assuming the role of helpless dependent, unwilling to take on any responsibility for self-support is one that some women play. By contrast, some former spouses, male and female, develop new interests, move to a new location, and may exhibit strengths that were latent during the marriage. Over time, they may surprise even themselves with their resilience and new, more affirmative, outlook on life.

Events of singles' clubs, such as dances or even low-key "coffees" or book reviews, provide social activity for many who choose to remain single. These are not the appropriate or most comfortable venue for everyone, but often meet needs during the early years of single life, until the individual has developed a new network of friends. The "personals" columns of newspapers and magazines, and singles' lists on e-mail or the Word Wide Web, are other sources for meeting new people. In the era of AIDS, however, many singles have become wary of physical involvement with new partners whose sexual history is unknown, no matter how they originally met them. Either frustration in this area of one's life caused by abstinence or avoidance of frustration by reckless sexual activity may prove problematic, but pervasive preoccupation with this issue is contraindicative for healthy being in the world.

One of the positive outcomes of remaining single, at least in the eyes of some people, is that there is no need to report to anyone. There is an absence of conflict and worry about another's needs and reactions. Others may feel isolated or detached if there is no one to consult with or with whom to make decisions.

This factor varies with the individual, and possibly even with chronological age.

RESTABILIZATION: REDUCING THE PAIN

As a traumatic event that changes a person's relationships and lifestyle, the pain of marital dissolution can take one to five years to lose its acute and totally-engulfing nature. The support of family, friends, colleagues, therapists, and groups established for this purpose is immeasurably helpful in this process.

Although separated and divorced people have long been suspected of having emotional problems that either contributed to their divorce or were the result of it, Nelson (1994) found, in a small six-year follow-up study, that female single parents did not differ significantly in emotional well-being from married women. He attributed this in part to the development of growth-activated coping skills to deal with economic changes and life strains resulting from separation. Some of these skills were acquired through additional education, while others drew on inner resources to promote autonomy and self-confidence in handling the new lifestyle.

For the adult children of divorce, however, there may not have been opportunities to express feelings of which they may have been unaware throughout their earlier years (Fassel, 1991). They may find a series of sessions with a mental health professional therapeutic. If concerned about ambivalent feelings toward their parents, these emotions can be examined, clarified, and many times reduced. If afraid to commit themselves to marriage because of what they have witnessed with their parents, they can be taught skills that will make them less defensive in a close relationship as well as more willing to perceive and understand their partner's point of view.

For many people, restabilization is attainable only if they learn how to ask for help when they need it. This may be difficult for those who have been accustomed to handling life's problems in conjunction with the former spouse. Initially, the need may be for help in coping with the affective impact of the separation and divorce. The single ex-spouse with little experience in money management needs to find trustworthy advisers who can help set up current budgets and long-term retirement plans;

who can teach the individual to deal with insurance needs and taxes; and who can offer sound advice on whether to stay in the family residence or to make other arrangements. On another level, as much as the single parent wants to be an effective parent, that individual has to recognize that both he or she and the children will benefit from respite care support, enabling the parent to enjoy a few hours or days of relief from juggling multiple responsibilities. The source of such support may be found within the family, from a close friend, or from paid help.

In central Indiana, a program called Expanding Horizons consists of support groups for newly separated or divorced women over age 50. The initial six-week program has a specific topic for each session:

Session I: Getting acquainted.
Session II: Goal setting and grief stage identification.
Session III: Self-esteem building.
Session IV: Coping with stress.
Session V: Small group sharing options.
Session VI: Goal setting recheck. (Blatter & Jacobsen, 1993)

At the fifth session, relationships with adult children and extended family members are one area of discussion, for example, and experts such as career planners and financial managers may be asked to speak. Alumni of the six-week program meet monthly both for support and for further growth in their planning for the future.

Although most people seek therapy initially around the time of separation and may continue until the divorce is granted and even beyond, therapists also see clients in the postdivorce period. In some cases, the client (usually female) develops a highly dependent relationship with the therapist that she finds difficult, or is unwilling, to break. Her transference to a caring, perhaps parental, figure offers her something that is missing from her new life as a divorcée. Therapy may also provide an oasis of calm during turbulence and a steadfast relationship while all others are in flux. This is a situation to which every therapist must be alert, and from which the therapist must be prepared to wean the client eventually.

Another issue with which the therapist may be confronted is the client whose spouse had had adulterous relationships during the marriage, who therefore felt rejected by the spouse, and who consequently is reluctant to trust anyone. At the extreme, such an individual may appear paranoid for a time. The person's reluctance to trust anyone, or perhaps especially someone of the opposite sex, reduces the effectiveness of the therapist's efforts to help the client on to new paths. Cognitive behavior therapy, and other interventions geared to working through the distrust so that it isn't overgeneralized, and gradually demonstrating the possibilities of trusting others, may help to overcome, or at least to reduce, this problem.

Often the cases therapists see at this later time involve remarried parties and the children of one of them. As Kompass (1989) indicates:

> The relationships within a family are generally not destroyed by divorce but merely rearranged. Years after the breakup, the original family members may remain interdependent and emotionally reactive to each other. The therapist who uncritically focuses only on the custodial parent, stepparent, and problem child as the unit of treatment could be failing to see how the child's behavior may be an indication of tension between the natural parents within the larger system. (p. 62)

Too often, the parental hostility continues indefinitely, with the children used as both battlefield and weapons, whether or not either parent has remarried. The probability of maladaptive behavior on the child's part, not to mention inappropriate behavior on the parents' parts, certainly evokes a need for postdivorce therapy. All of the parties will need to ventilate what is still troubling them and then learn more constructive ways to deal with issues, feelings, and relationships. If parental alienation has been engaged in, therapy for both the alienator and the children caught up in this situation may be essential.

It is easy to recognize that the child's behavior may indicate difficulties in the primary family, but it should be remembered that some cases may be due to problems in the new marriage rather than the old one. Consider that the stepparent, for whatever reason, has been unable to establish a positive relationship with a youngster, or that the difficulties lie in relationships among the stepsiblings in a blended family. Perhaps the second marriage is itself unstable and the child is reacting to the possibility of being uprooted physically and emotionally a second time. Or perhaps the child enjoys the attention he or she receives when acting out, or consciously wishes to sabotage the new family and recreate the former one, or is punishing the parent for upsetting his or her world.

Once more, the case of Luigi and Sylvia will illustrate the impact of divorce on children and extended family, the rapidity with which circumstances and behavior may change and the vicissitudes of entering into life beyond divorce.

Case Example. The Royales Return

Luigi decided that if his ex-wife predeceased him, the children would become the three equal beneficiaries to his life insurance policy. Since his fantasy for the future included a "beautiful, sexy young woman," he came to see that his children's concerns were rooted in a likely forthcoming reality. Thus, he decided to start giving each of them an annual tax-exempt monetary gift, and told them this would be forthcoming as long as his finances warranted it. They were pleased and relieved.

Luigi also reached a point where he was able to discuss with Sylvia and the children, in an extended family therapy session, that he wanted each of them to be able to relate to their children and grandchildren separately without drawing them into any kind of continuing war, and volunteered that he would discontinue blaming his ex-wife for driving him away. Initially, Sylvia, who felt every inch the spurned party, refused to promise not to criticize Luigi to their children. When Lauren and Margo pleaded with her to let them see and love both parents and not have to continue to "take sides," Sylvia reluctantly agreed to "think about it."

One night, her son Philippe invited her out to dinner and explained that they all loved and sympathized with her, but they also wanted to have their father in their lives, and if she continued to impede that, she would alienate them. Shocked and crushed, Sylvia sobbed. Later she told the therapist, "I heard his warning and decided to take it seriously." The next part of her recovery process probably began that evening. After this, she made more rapid progress in therapy. She was finally willing to accept a referral for a psychopharmacology evaluation and in about three months on an antidepressant, combined with continued individual therapy, her spirits had lifted and she was able to "look forward."

Extended Family and Community Aspects

Sylvia enrolled her mother in a senior day-care program, and this gave her some relief so that she could have "time out." With encouragement from the therapist and some internal motivation to expand her own horizons, Sylvia accepted a neighbor's invitation to take a continuing education course on Current Events at a nearby junior college. She found it different, interesting, and stimulating to go outside the family for some of her activities. When she learned that her church had a group for divorced single adults aged 50 to 65 years, she decided to "give it a try." She rapidly got involved on its program committee, attended many of its diverse functions, and became an active participant in its problem-solving discussions. From a self-styled "mouse and martyr," she began to change into a more assertive, well-rounded, and gregarious woman. She realized how much she had colluded in being Luigi's shadow and servant.

When Easter was approaching, the children and grandchildren assumed that Grandma was planning her customary Easter dinner, and Margo called to ask what time they should come. She was shocked when her mom replied gently but firmly, "My group is going on a retreat for that weekend and I thought I'd enjoy doing something different. I knew you would all understand since you have been telling me to 'get a life.' Perhaps Dad and his girlfriend would like to have you at their house. And I wonder, could one of you take Grandmom for the weekend in return for all of the times I've babysat for you all?" When Margo relayed this conversation to Lauren and Philippe, they were astonished, and were not so sure they liked their mother's use of her new-found freedom. They had anticipated changes from Dad, but not rock-solid, predictable Mom.

Terminating Therapy

A year following Luigi's announcement that he wanted a divorce and the family's entry into therapy, with usually one or several members of the family being seen weekly, in whatever combination seemed most compelling at the moment, the legal divorce was final, Luigi was living in his own new ocean-view condominium, and Sylvia was beginning to contemplate selling the family home and buying a smaller, newer townhouse. The property settlement had been completed and the monthly alimony checks were being sent on time. The Royale's adult children had found ways to relate to their parents as two separate individuals.

During the second year, Luigi decided to come to therapy on a once-a-month basis to "keep myself grounded." He was pleased with his children's growing acceptance of his decision, and that they were slowly building a relationship with Leona. Sylvia reported therapy had really altered her view of herself and the world, and decided she wanted to continue "growing emotionally" and so would come for sessions biweekly, as well as take one or two courses at the college each semester and stay involved in church activities as long as she found them satisfying. She blossomed, was toning up through walking and aerobics, was wearing makeup, and dressing more fashionably. One day Luigi said wistfully in his therapy session, "If only she could have done this years ago, maybe we could have stayed together." We discussed whether he could have tolerated her becoming so self-sufficient and attractive at that time. In retrospect, he wasn't sure.

By the end of the second postdivorce year, both had arrived at good psychic closure and were enjoying life beyond divorce. Both were able to agree to be at their grandson's high school graduation party and no one anticipated any hostility or conflict. Therapy was terminated by mutual agreement.

CONCLUDING COMMENT

"Getting on with life" is not easily accomplished at first and may require steps on a variety of paths until the newly divorced person finds the one that is most comfortable. False starts need not be totally devastating; they can be valuable learning experiences. It is important to be able to deal with the ex-spouse in a rational manner, without becoming tied up in matters best left in the past. It is important to develop time-management skills, as almost everyone has discovered in the complex lifestyles of the 1990s. And it is important to focus on the now and the future, as the past cannot be undone or rescripted.

PART IV

The Psychic Divorce: Healing and Closure

THE PARTING HAS BEEN PAINFUL but is now an established fact. The divorce is a legal reality, and adjustments to it emotionally, socially, and financially are gradually also taking shape. Each accommodation and transition may lead some to less pleasant circumstances, others simply to unanticipated changes in lifestyle. Those who have taken advantage of therapy or support groups are more likely to be able to move toward a mentally healthy outcome than those who have wallowed in their grief, self pity, and anger. Maintaining such negative feelings requires a great deal of psychic energy, depleting that available for daily functioning.

For most divorced individuals, particularly those who have not remarried, psychic healing begins (and may continue) with simply putting one foot in front of the other and moving forward. The path these steps follow may be a new one, perhaps even a more exciting one, and each step forward helps to bring closure to the pain of the marital parting. For some, adults and children alike, divorce presents opportunities to become stronger and more adventuresome; to break out of noxious or abusive situations; and to become happier, more fulfilled individuals.

CHAPTER 12

Toward Integration
and Wholeness

DIVORCE NEED NOT BE THE end-state of one's life, psychologically speaking. We have tried to show alternatives to the prototypical spouse-bashing litigation that leaves no one truly whole and too many in a downward spiral. Within a solution-focused orientation, having analyzed what went wrong and what the current picture is, we urge divorcing individuals to reassemble the pieces in a new and different way—creating a viable, appealing synthesis of their lives. The first attempt at synthesis may be evaluated as lacking in some way, so additional attempts should be made until the individual finds a resolution that is conducive to integration and wholeness.

THE PSYCHIC DIVORCE

It tends to take two to five years for the psychic healing and reequilibration to be completed for reasonably healthy individuals. During this period of time the coparenting and visitation arrangements should get worked out, be stabilized, and no longer be disruptive; both will have settled into their living quarters; relocations that need to occur will have happened; and the hostility should have abated. They have usually gotten beyond the feeling that "I will never trust another man [woman]" and may have begun to date again or reached a decision that they would prefer not to do so for a time. The decision is no longer based on anger and hurt, but rather on a preference for being single and not being obligated and accountable to a partner. Those who have "come out of the closet" will have faced the major issues that devolve from their identity.

Their conversation will have become less focused on the divorce and the past as the critical life event that permeates all of their thinking, and they will be talking and thinking instead about the present and the future. Optimism will have replaced pessimism and they will be feeling more confident, more capable, and proud of their ability to put their life together and to move forward.

Conversely, individuals who had severe personal pathology prior to the divorce or who have become deeply distressed during the process and cannot resolve the rage, depression, and desire to retaliate will not be anywhere near having achieved psychic closure. Often they appear in therapists' offices 10 years after the legal decree was granted and sound as if the divorce just occurred. They are still obsessed by the trauma, have gotten stuck there, and need individual therapeutic assistance to finally let go and work toward achieving a higher level of functioning and a more fulfilling existence.

It is important to differentiate where in the recovery continuum en route to the psychic divorce these clients are when they commence treatment and to help them set realistic goals for modifying their thinking (cognitions), behaviors (actions), and feelings (emotions). Determining a time frame in which they would like this to happen helps them to collaborate in their own treatment planning and to progress more rapidly.

ELIMINATING BATTLEGROUNDS

From our experience, research, and reading of others' studies, it is apparent that a major task for divorcing couples and the professionals who work with them is the reduction of conflict. Whether the conflict is exacerbated by members of the extended families, who seem to "egg on" one or the other party, or results from the parties' feelings of humiliation or guilt, or stems from a "push-pull" situation where one ex-spouse (or both) is miserable living with the other but is also miserable apart from the other, the conflict rages on with negative impact on the adults and on their children (Johnston & Campbell, 1988).

The most negative findings with respect to children of divorce of all ages tend to emanate from continued hostility between the parents. Whether the children become the battleground, as when the parents continue to fight over their custody as if they were prized heirlooms, or are the weapons, in which one parent actively turns the children against the other parent, the children tend to be the losers, no matter which parent apparently wins the war.

When one ex-spouse overreacts to the other's actions by labeling him or her cruel, hostile, or insensitive, then tells the children of these reactions, the children are placed in an impossible position. If they defend the other parent, this is perceived as disloyalty; if they don't defend the other parent, they feel guilty and impotent. Such circular and escalating conflicts, and the accompanying parental alienation behaviors, should bring the parents to a therapist, if only for the sake of the children. The therapist will need to move very delicately in bringing the parent(s) to conflict resolution. Campbell (1993) outlines a multi-session procedure in which the parents are met separately initially, the minor children are interviewed for their views of the continuing conflicts and what they would prefer, and the parents are subsequently seen together in an effort to have them focus on a solution to the sequence of allegations and counter-allegations. The therapist indicates understanding of each parent's position without aligning him- or herself with that position and suggests to each participant that each would like to see the pain of parting reduced, especially as it impacts on the children.

Throughout the treatment sessions, the therapist emphasizes the positive outcomes of working together as parents and of how appreciative their children will be for their mutual support. It is essential that the parents learn to discriminate between their roles as ex-spouses and their coparenting roles and to recognize that neither of them has exclusive wisdom about the children's ongoing relationship with either parent. If they can separate their parental responsibilities from their differences with the ex-spouse, they become what Ahrons (1994) calls "Cooperative Colleagues."

BEYOND LEGALITIES AND ON TO PREVENTION

Continuing litigation after separation and even after the divorce is final may produce a few remedies with regard to child support, perhaps even some taste of "victory," but it prolongs the devastation, delays recovery, and can be financially ruinous. It might be more profitable in the long run, for the sparring partners to learn what impels them to prolong their battles and in what other ways they might resolve differences.

An interactive program sponsored by the American Bar Association, broadcast by the Massachusetts Corporation for Educational Television, and designed by Lynne Gold-Bikin, a family lawyer from near Philadelphia, seeks to teach conflict resolution skills in marriage to high school students in hopes that this will reduce divorce in the future (Dubin, 1994). The curriculum deals with such practical marital matters as budgeting, sustaining loving relationships, how to fight fairly, the art of compromise, divorce laws and their differences among the states, and child custody laws. It is Gold-Bikin's hope, and that of the Family Law section of the American Bar Association which she had chaired, that such preventive learning, telecast to 44 schools across the country in its first offering, will enable these youths to avoid entanglement in divorce as adults. Aspects of the program may also teach youths how to settle *any* differences without violence.

Another factor to be considered in looking at divorce today and tomorrow is that focusing on "traditional nuclear families" in the face of the reality of the high percentage of single-parent and blended families ignores the violence, conflict, and severe disappointment within marriage that lead to divorce and its consequences. "Because children live at the standard of living of their mothers, current divorce policies promote a systematic disinvestment in the next generation" (Kurz, 1995, p. 227). The nation cannot afford this policy. Nor can it expect women to stay at home to care for their children (the traditional view) and at the same time condemn them for being on welfare or for seeking reasonable child support that includes health care for themselves and their children. If, on the other hand, divorced women try to provide their own support, then they need to have adequate job training, good child care at an affordable cost, and equal pay with men for equal work (Kurz, 1995).

ONWARD!

The parting nature of divorce is painful, but it is not and need not be the "end of the world." It should not make victims of children, who will then be impaired as adults in their intimate relationships. Rather, the divorcing adults should focus their energy and efforts on rebuilding their lives, and those of their children if they have any, in constructive ways. This implies acknowledging and correcting, where possible, their weaknesses and enhancing their strengths. Parents continue to be models for their children, whether together or apart. As models, they should point the way for their children to avoid perpetuating a pattern of divorce, or of self-pity, anger, and other negative behaviors, in the future.

Dwelling on the pain of divorce, harboring anger at the former spouse, and focusing on what was instead of what is make the divorcé(e) unnecessarily bitter. Family and friends alike tend to avoid such people, elevating the individual's sense of being abandoned and isolated. As some formerly married individuals have discovered, maintaining such anger also uses a great deal of energy that might better be applied to more constructive (and enjoyable) activities.

Ahrons (1994) has written of the "good divorce." To her:

> [This] is not an oxymoron. A good divorce is one in which both the adults and children emerge at least as emotionally well as they were before the divorce. . . .
>
> In a good divorce, a family with children remains a family. . . . The parents—as they did when they were married—continue to be responsible for the emotional, economic, and physical needs of their children. (pp. 2–3)

Even when the children are older adolescents or adults at the time of their parents' divorce, this concern for their well-being should outrank any hostile feelings the former spouses may continue to have toward each other.

Part of moving forward, according to Cauhapé (1983) is the development of a new social identity. For women, particularly those whose career has been centered on the home, this may be difficult. It is not easy to cease being "Mrs. Doctor," or "Joe's wife." For both women and men who do not remarry immediately, there must be an acceptance of the status of being a single person in the social realm, with the benefits and drawbacks of that position. Some divorced individuals who are no longer primarily responsible for their children have even declared, after a transition period, that the freedom of being able to go and do what they want, when they want, without reporting to someone else is such a pleasure that they would not even think of remarrying.

As time passes, divorced individuals may well find new interests, new friends, and the emergence of latent abilities. In other words, with a healthy perspective, they grow and their world expands again. They may, even in less comfortable situations than when they were married, be able to take their renewed positive orientation into the marketplace and improve their lives. Their relationships with their children, and with others, are healthier for all concerned as they feel more comfortable with their changes. Perhaps initially with slow steps, they will move forward and onward to a different and ultimately more rewarding lifestyle.

Florida Child Support Guidelines Worksheet

STEP 1: TO DETERMINE MONTHLY GROSS INCOME	FATHER	MOTHER
1. Actual Gross Income (Schedule A)		
2. Imputed Monthly Income pursuant to F.S. 61.13, Section 3(2) (b)		
3. Total Gross Income (Add 1 and 2)		
STEP 2: TO DETERMINE MONTHLY NET INCOME		
4. Total Deductions (Schedule B)		
5. Net Income: (Subtract 4 from 3)		
6. Combined Monthly Net Income of both parents		
STEP 3: TO DETERMINE CHILD SUPPORT AMOUNT		
7. Determine applicable amount for number of children (Schedule C)		
8. Child care cost incurred due to employment or job search or education calculated to result in employment or to enhance current employment income of either parent reduced by 25%. Limited to cost for quality care from licensed source.		
9. Health insurance costs ordered pursuant to Section 61.13 (1) (b)		
10. Total needed child support: Add line 7, 8 and 9		
11. Each parent's mathematical proportion of support; divide the parent's monthly net income (Line 5) by the combined monthly net income (Line 6)		
12. Child support shares: (Multiply Line 10 by Line 11)		
13. Adjustment to support award (Schedule D)		
14. **MONTHLY CHILD SUPPORT OBLIGATIONS OF PARENTS**		
15. **CHILD SUPPORT RANGE (±5%)**		

SCHEDULE A	Father/Mon.	Mother/Mon.
Average gross monthly income shall include the following:		
a. Gross salary or wages (AFDC excluded).		
b. Bonuses, commissions, allowances, overtime, tips & similar payments.		
c. Business income from sources such as self-employment, partnership, close corporations, and/or independent contracts (gross receipts minus ordinary and necessary expenses required to produce income).		
d. Disability Benefits.		
e. Worker's Compensation.		
f. Unemployment Compensation.		
g. Pension, Retirements or Annuity Payments.		
h. Social Security Benefits.		
i. Spousal support received from a previous marriage.		
j. Interest and Dividends.		
k. Rental Income (Gross receipts minus ordinary and necessary expenses required to product income).		
l. Income from Royalties, Trusts or Estates.		
m. Reimbursed expenses and in kind payments to the extent that they reduce personal living expenses.		
n. Gains derived from dealing in property (Not including non-recurring gains).		
o. Itemize any other income of a recurring nature or factor considered.		
TOTAL GROSS INCOME		

SCHEDULE B	Father/Mon.	Mother/Mon.

The trier of fact shall deduct the following from
Gross Income:

  a. Federal, state & local income taxes (corrected for
    filing status and actual number of withholding
    allowances).

  b. F.I.C.A. or self-employment tax (annualized).

  c. Mandatory Union Dues.

  d. Mandatory Retirement.

  e. Health insurance payments, excluding payments for
    coverage of minor child.

  f. Court ordered support payments for other children
    actually paid.

  TOTAL DEDUCTIONS

SCHEDULE D	FATHERS Share	MOTHERS Share

1. Extraordinary medical, psychological, educational
   or dental expenses.
2. Independent income of the child.
3. The payment of both child support and spousal
   support to the obligee or payment of regular support
   to parent in need.
4. Seasonal variations in one or both parents' incomes
   or expenses.
5. The age of the child, taking into account the greater
   needs of older children.
6. Special needs that have traditionally been met within
   the family budget even though the fulfilling of those
   needs will cause the support to exceed the
   proposed guidelines.
7. The particular shared parental arrangement, such
   as where:
   a. The children spend a substantial amount of time
      with the secondary residential parent, thereby
      reducing the financial expenditures incurred
      by the primary residential parent, or
   b. The refusal of the secondary residential parent
      to become involved in the activities of the child, or
   c. Giving due consideration to the primary
      residential parent's homemaking services, or
   d. Visitation for more than 28 consecutive days.
8. Total available assets of the obligee, obligor, and the child.
9. Impact of the IRS dependency exemption and
   waiver of that exemption.
10. Application of the child support guidelines
    requiring payment of 55% of gross income for child
    support obligation from a single support order.
11. In a proceeding for increased support, subsequent
    children and income of other parent may
    be considered.
12. Any other adjustment which is needed to achieve
    an equitable result which may include, but not be
    limited to, a reasonable and necessary
    existing expense or debt.

  TOTAL ADJUSTMENTS

Florida Chapter 61: Dissolution of Marriage, Support, Custody* (1994 Supplement)

61.046 Definitions.—As used in this chapter:

(1) "Custodial parent" means the parent with whom the child maintains his primary residence.

(2) "Department" means the Department of Revenue.

(3) "Depository" means the central governmental depository established pursuant to s. 61.181 to receive, record, report,

---

* This is an abridged version, history and notes are omitted. See the statute for your particular state.

disburse, monitor, and otherwise handle alimony and child support payments.

(4) "Income" means any form of payment to an individual, regardless of source, including, but not limited to: wages, salary, commissions and bonuses, compensation as an independent contractor, worker's compensation, disability benefits, annuity and retirement benefits, pensions, dividends, interest, royalties, trusts, and any other payments, made by any person, private entity, federal or state government, or any unit of local government. United States Department of Veterans Affairs disability benefits and unemployment compensation, as defined in chapter 443, are excluded from this definition of income except for purposes of establishing an amount of support.

(5) "IV-D" means services provided pursuant to Title IV-D of the Social Security Act, 42 U.S.C., s. 1302.

(6) "Local officer" means an elected or appointed constitutional or charter government official including, but not limited to, the state attorney and clerk of the circuit court.

(7) "Noncustodial parent" means the parent with whom the child does not maintain his primary residence.

(8) "Obligee" means the person to whom payments are made pursuant to an order establishing, enforcing, or modifying an obligation for alimony, for child support, or for alimony and child support.

(9) "Obligor" means a person responsible for making payments pursuant to an order establishing, enforcing, or modifying an obligation for alimony, for child support, or for alimony and child support.

(10) "Payor" means an employer or former employer or any other person or agency providing or administering income to the obligor.

(11) "Shared parental responsibility" means a court-ordered relationship in which both parents retain full parental rights and responsibilities with respect to their child and in which both parents confer with each other so that major decisions affecting the welfare of the child will be determined jointly.

(12) "Sole parental responsibility" means a court-ordered relationship in which one parent makes decisions regarding the minor child.

61.075 Equitable distribution of marital assets and liabilities.—

(1) In a proceeding for dissolution of marriage, in addition to all other remedies available to a court to do equity between the parties, or in a proceeding for disposition of assets following a

dissolution of marriage by a court which lacked jurisdiction over the absent spouse or lacked jurisdiction to dispose of the assets, the court shall set apart to each spouse that spouse's nonmarital assets and liabilities, and in distributing the marital assets and liabilities between the parties, the court must begin with the premise that the distribution should be equal, unless there is a justification for an unequal distribution based on all relevant factors, including:

(a) The contribution to the marriage by each spouse, including contributions to the care and education of the children and services as homemaker.

(b) The economic circumstances of the parties.

(c) The duration of the marriage.

(d) Any interruption of personal careers or educational opportunities of either party.

(e) The contribution of one spouse to the personal career or educational opportunity of the other spouse.

(f) The desirability of retaining any asset, including an interest in a business, corporation, or professional practice, intact and free from any claim or interference by the other party.

(g) The contribution of each spouse to the acquisition, enhancement, and production of income or the improvement of, or the incurring of liabilities to, both the marital assets and the nonmarital assets of the parties.

(h) The desirability of retaining the marital home as a residence for any dependent child of the marriage, or any other party, when it would be equitable to do so, it is in the best interest of the child or that party, and it is financially feasible for the parties to maintain the residence until the child is emancipated or until exclusive possession is otherwise terminated by a court of competent jurisdiction. In making this determination, the court shall first determine if it would be in the best interest of the dependent child to remain in the marital home; and, if not, whether other equities would be served by giving any other party exclusive use and possession of the marital home.

(i) The intentional dissipation, waste, depletion, or destruction of marital assets after the filing of the petition or within 2 years prior to the filing of the petition.

(j) Any other factors necessary to do equity and justice between the parties.

(2) If the court awards a cash payment for the purpose of equitable distribution of marital assets, to be paid in full or in installments,

the full amount ordered shall vest when the judgment is awarded and the award shall not terminate upon remarriage or death of either party, unless otherwise agreed to by the parties, but shall be treated as a debt owed from the obligor or the obligor's estate to the obligee or the obligee's estate, unless otherwise agreed to by the parties.

(3) In any contested dissolution action wherein a stipulation and agreement has not been entered and filed, any distribution of marital assets or marital liabilities shall be supported by factual findings in the judgment or order based on competent substantial evidence with reference to the factors enumerated in subsection (1). The distribution of all marital assets and marital liabilities, whether equal or unequal, shall include specific written findings of fact as to the following:

(a) Clear identification of nonmarital assets and ownership interests;

(b) Identification of marital assets, including the individual valuation of significant assets, and designation of which spouse shall be entitled to each asset;

(c) Identification of the marital liabilities and designation of which spouse shall be responsible for each liability;

(d) Any other findings necessary to advise the parties or the reviewing court of the trial court's rationale for the distribution of marital assets and allocation of liabilities.

(4) The judgment distributing assets shall have the effect of a duly executed instrument of conveyance, transfer, release, or acquisition which is recorded in the county where the property is located when the judgment, or a certified copy of the judgment, is recorded in the official records of the county in which the property is located.

(5) As used in this section:

(a) "Marital assets and liabilities" include:

1. Assets acquired and liabilities incurred during the marriage, individually by either spouse or jointly by them;

2. The enhancement in value and appreciation of nonmarital assets resulting either from the efforts of either party during the marriage or from the contribution to or expenditure thereon of marital funds or other forms of marital assets, or both;

3. Interspousal gifts during the marriage;

4. All vested and nonvested benefits, rights, and funds accrued during the marriage in retirement, pension, profit-sharing, annuity, deferred compensation, and insurance plans and programs; and

     5. All real property held by the parties as tenants by the entireties, whether acquired prior to or during the marriage, shall be presumed to be a marital asset. If, in any case, a party makes a claim to the contrary, the burden of proof shall be on the party asserting the claim for a special equity.

  (b) "Nonmarital assets and liabilities" include:

     1. Assets acquired and liabilities incurred by either party prior to the marriage, and assets acquired and liabilities incurred in exchange for such assets and liabilities;

     2. Assets acquired separately by either party by noninterspousal gift, bequest, devise, or descent, and assets acquired in exchange for such assets;

     3. All income derived from nonmarital assets during the marriage unless the income was treated, used, or relied upon by the parties as a marital asset; and

     4. Assets and liabilities excluded from marital assets and liabilities by valid written agreement of the parties, and assets acquired and liabilities incurred in exchange for such assets and liabilities.

(6) The cut-off date for determining assets and liabilities to be identified or classified as marital assets and liabilities is the earliest of the date the parties enter into a valid separation agreement, such other date as may be expressly established by such agreement, or the date of the filing of a petition for dissolution of marriage. The date for determining value of assets and the amount of liabilities identified or classified as marital is such date or dates as the judge determines is just and equitable under the circumstances. Different assets may be valued as of different dates, as, in the judge's discretion, the circumstances require.

(7) All assets acquired and liabilities incurred by either spouse subsequent to the date of the marriage and not specifically established as nonmarital assets or liabilities are presumed to be marital assets and liabilities. Such presumption is overcome by a showing that the assets and liabilities are nonmarital assets and liabilities. The presumption is only for evidentiary purposes in the dissolution proceeding and does not vest title. Title to disputed assets shall vest only by the judgment of a court. This section does not require the joinder of spouses in the conveyance, transfer, or hypothecation of a spouse's individual property; affect the laws of descent and distribution; or establish community property in this state.

(8) The court may provide for equitable distribution of the marital assets and liabilities without regard to alimony for either party. After the determination of an equitable distribution of the

marital assets and liabilities, the court shall consider whether a judgment for alimony shall be made.

(9) To do equity between the parties, the court may, in lieu of or to supplement, facilitate, or effectuate the equitable division of marital assets and liabilities, order a monetary payment in a lump sum or in installments paid over a fixed period of time.

61.13 Custody and support of children; visitation rights; power of court in making orders.—

(1) (a) In a proceeding for dissolution of marriage, the court may at any time order either or both parents who owe a duty of support to a child to pay support in accordance with the guidelines in s. 61.30. The court initially entering an order requiring one or both parents to make child support payments shall have continuing jurisdiction after the entry of the initial order to modify the amount and terms and conditions of the child support payments when the modification is found necessary by the court in the best interests of the child, when the child reaches majority, or when there is a substantial change in the circumstances of the parties. The court initially entering a child support order shall also have continuing jurisdiction to require the obligee to report to the court on terms prescribed by the court regarding the disposition of the child support payments.

(b) Each order for child support shall contain a provision for health insurance for the minor child when the insurance is reasonably available. Insurance is reasonably available if either the obligor or the obligee has access at a reasonable rate to group insurance. The court may require the obligor either to provide health insurance coverage or to reimburse the obligee for the cost of health insurance coverage for the minor child when coverage is provided by the obligee. In either event, the court shall apportion the cost of coverage to both parties by adding the cost to the basic obligation determined pursuant to s. 61.30(6).

1. A copy of the court order for insurance coverage shall be served on the obligor's payor or union by the obligee or the IV-D agency when the following conditions are met:

a. The obligor fails to provide written proof to the obligee or the IV-D agency within 30 days of receiving effective notice of the court order, that the insurance has been obtained or that application for insurability has been made;

      b. The obligee or IV-D agency serves written notice of its intent to enforce medical support on the obligor by mail at the obligor's last known address; and

      c. The obligor fails within 15 days after the mailing of the notice to provide written proof to the obligee or the IV-D agency that the insurance coverage existed as of the date of mailing.

    2. The order is binding on the payor or union when service of the notice as provided in subparagraph 1. is made. Upon receipt of the order, or upon application of the obligor pursuant to the order, the payor or union shall enroll the minor child as a beneficiary in the group insurance plan and withhold any required premium from the obligor's income. If more than one plan is offered by the payor or union, the child shall be enrolled in the insurance plan in which the obligor is enrolled or the least costly plan otherwise available to the obligor.

(c) To the extent necessary to protect an award of child support, the court may order the obligor to purchase or maintain a life insurance policy or a bond, or to otherwise secure the child support award with any other assets which may be suitable for that purpose.

(d) 1. Unless the provisions of subparagraph 3. apply, all child support orders entered on or after January 1, 1985, shall direct that the payments of child support be made as provided in s. 61.181 through the depository in the county where the court is located.

    2. Unless the provisions of subparagraph 3. apply, all child support orders entered before January 1, 1985, shall be modified by the court to direct that payments of child support shall be made through the depository in the county where the court is located upon the subsequent appearance of either or both parents to modify or enforce the order, or in any related proceeding.

    3. If both parties request that the court finds that it is in the best interest of the child, support payments need not be directed through the depository. The order of support shall provide, or shall be deemed to provide, that either party may subsequently apply to the depository to require direction of the payments through the depository. The court shall provide a copy of the order to the depository.

    4. If the parties elect not to require that support payments be made through the depository, any party may subsequently file an affidavit with the depository alleging a

default in payment of child support and stating that the party wishes to require that payments be made through the depository. The party shall provide copies of the affidavit to the court and to each other party. Fifteen days after receipt of the affidavit, the depository shall notify both parties that future payments shall be paid through the depository.

5. In IV-D cases, the IV-D agency shall have the same rights as the obligee in requesting that payments be made through the depository.

(2) (a) The court shall have jurisdiction to determine custody, notwithstanding that the child is not physically present in this state at the time of filing any proceeding under this chapter, if it appears to the court that the child was removed from this state for the primary purpose of removing the child from the jurisdiction of the court in an attempt to avoid a determination or modification of custody.

(b) 1. The court shall determine all matters relating to custody of each minor child of the parties in accordance with the best interests of the child and in accordance with the Uniform Child Custody Jurisdiction Act. It is the public policy of this state to assure that each minor child has frequent and continuing contact with both parents after the parents separate or the marriage of the parties is dissolved and to encourage parents to share the rights and responsibilities of childrearing. After considering all relevant facts, the father of the child shall be given the same consideration as the mother in determining the primary residence of a child irrespective of the age or sex of the child.

2. The court shall order that the parental responsibility for a minor child be shared by both parents unless the court finds that shared parental responsibility would be detrimental to the child. The court shall consider evidence of spousal or child abuse as evidence of detriment to the child. The court shall consider evidence that a parent has been convicted of a felony of the second degree or higher involving domestic violence as defined in s. 741.28 and chapter 775, as a rebuttable presumption of detriment to the child. If the presumption is not rebutted, shared parental responsibility, including visitation, residence of the child, and decisions made regarding the child, shall not be granted to the convicted parent. However, the convicted parent shall not be relieved of any obligation to provide financial support. If the court determines that

shared parental responsibility would be detrimental to the child, it may order sole parental responsibility and make such arrangements for visitation as will best protect the child or abused spouse from further harm.

    a. In ordering shared parental responsibility, the court may consider the expressed desires of the parents and may grant to one party the ultimate responsibility over specific aspects of the child's welfare or may divide those responsibilities between the parties based on the best interests of the child. Areas of responsibility may include primary residence, education, medical and dental care, and any other responsibilities which the court finds unique to a particular family.

    b. The court shall order "sole parental responsibility, with or without visitation rights, to the other parent when it is in the best interests of" the minor child.

    c. The court may award the grandparents visitation rights of a minor child if it is in the child's best interest. Grandparents shall have legal standing to seek judicial enforcement of such an award. Nothing in this section shall require that grandparents be made parties or given notice of dissolution pleadings or proceedings, nor shall grandparents have legal standing as "contestants" as defined in s. 61.1306. No court shall order that a child be kept within the state or jurisdiction of the court solely for the purpose of permitting visitation by the grandparents.

    3. Access to records and information pertaining to a minor child, including, but not limited to, medical, dental, and school records, shall not be denied to a parent because such parent is not the child's primary residential parent.

(c) The circuit court in the county in which either parent or the child resides and the circuit court in which the original award of custody was entered have jurisdiction to modify an award of child custody. The court may change the venue in accordance with s. 47.122.

(3) For purposes of shared parental responsibility and primary residence, the best interests of the child shall include an evaluation of all factors affecting the welfare and interests of the child, including, but not limited to:

(a) The parent who is more likely to allow the child frequent and continuing contact with the nonresidential parent.

(b) The love, affection, and other emotional ties existing between the parents and the child.

(c) The capacity and disposition of the parents to provide the child with food, clothing, medical care or other remedial care recognized and permitted under the laws of this state in lieu of medical care, and other material needs.

(d) The length of time the child has lived in a stable, satisfactory environment and the desirability of maintaining continuity.

(e) The permanence, as a family unit, of the existing or proposed custodial home.

(f) The moral fitness of the parents.

(g) The mental and physical health of the parents.

(h) The home, school, and community record of the child.

(i) The reasonable preference of the child, if the court deems the child to be of sufficient intelligence, understanding, and experience to express a preference.

(j) The willingness and ability of each parent to facilitate and encourage a close and continuing parent–child relationship between the child and the other parent.

(k) Any other fact considered by the court to be relevant.

(4) (a) When a noncustodial parent who is ordered to pay child support or alimony and who is awarded visitation rights fails to pay child support or alimony, the custodial parent shall not refuse to honor the noncustodial parent's visitation rights.

(b) When a custodial parent refuses to honor a noncustodial parent's visitation rights, the noncustodial parent shall not fail to pay any ordered child support or alimony.

(c) When a custodial parent refuses to honor a noncustodial parent's visitation rights without proper cause, the court may:

　1. After calculating the amount of visitation improperly denied, award the noncustodial parent a sufficient amount of extra visitation to compensate the noncustodial parent, which visitation shall be taken as expeditiously as possible in a manner which does not interfere with the best interests of the child; or

　2. Award the custody or primary residence to the noncustodial parent, upon the request of the noncustodial parent, if the award is in the best interests of the child.

(d) A person who violates this subsection may be punished by contempt of court or other remedies as the court deems appropriate.

(5) The court may make specific orders for the care and custody of the minor child as from the circumstances of the parties and the nature of the case is equitable and provide for child support in

accordance with the guidelines in s. 61.30. An award of shared parental responsibility of a minor child does not preclude the court from entering an order for child support of the child.

(6) In any proceeding under this section, the court may not deny shared parental responsibility, custody, or visitation rights to a parent or grandparent solely because that parent or grandparent is or is believed to be infected with human immunodeficiency virus; but the court may condition such rights upon the parent's or grandparent's agreement to observe measures approved by the Centers for Disease Control of the United States Public Health Service or by the Department of Health and Rehabilitative Services for preventing the spread of human immunodeficiency virus to the child.

(7) In any case where the child is actually residing with a grandparent in a stable relationship, whether the court has awarded custody to the grandparent or not, the court may recognize the grandparents as having the same standing as parents for evaluating what custody arrangements are in the best interest of the child. . . .

61.16 Attorney's fees, suit money, and costs.—
(1) The court may from time to time, after considering the financial resources of both parties, order a party to pay a reasonable amount for attorney's fees, suit money, and the cost to the other party of maintaining or defending any proceeding under this chapter, including enforcement and modification proceedings and appeals. An application for attorney's fees, suit money, or costs, whether temporary or otherwise, shall not require corroborating expert testimony in order to support an award under this chapter. The trial court shall have continuing jurisdiction to make temporary attorney's fees and costs awards reasonably necessary to prosecute or defend an appeal on the same basis and criteria as though the matter were pending before it at the trial level. In all cases, the court may order that the amount be paid directly to the attorney, who may enforce the order in that attorney's name. In determining whether to make attorney's fees and costs awards at the appellate level, the court shall primarily consider the relative financial resources of the parties, unless an appellate party's cause is deemed to be frivolous. In Title IV-D cases, attorney's fees, suit money, and costs, including filing fees, recording fees, mediation costs, service of process fees, and other expenses incurred by the clerk of the circuit court, shall be assessed only against the nonprevailing obligor after the court makes a determination of the nonprevailing

obligor's ability to pay such costs and fees. The Department of Revenue shall not be considered a party for purposes of this section; however, fees may be assessed against the department pursuant to s. 57.105(1).

(2) In an action brought pursuant to Rule 3.840, Florida Rules of Criminal Procedure, whether denominated direct or indirect criminal contempt, the court shall have authority to:

   (a) Appoint an attorney to prosecute said contempt.

   (b) Assess attorney's fees and costs against the contemptor after the court makes a determination of the contemptor's ability to pay such costs and fees.

   (c) Order that the amount be paid directly to the attorney, who may enforce the order in his name.

61.21 Parenting course authorized; fees; required attendance authorized; contempt.—

(1) All judicial circuits in the state may approve a parenting course which shall be a course of a minimum of 4 hours designed to educate, train, and assist divorcing parents in regard to the consequences of divorce on parents and children.

(2) All parties to a dissolution of marriage proceeding with minor children or a modification of a final judgment action involving shared parental responsibilities, custody, or visitation may be required to complete a court-approved parenting course prior to the entry by the court of a final judgment or order modifying the final judgment.

(3) All parties required to complete a parenting course shall file proof of compliance with the court prior to the entry of the final judgment or order modifying the final judgment.

(4) A reasonable fee may be charged to each parent attending the course.

(5) Information obtained or statements made by the parties at any educational session required under this statute shall not be considered in the adjudication of a pending or subsequent action, nor shall any report resulting from such educational session become part of the record of the case unless the parties have stipulated in writing to the contrary.

(6) The court may hold any parent who fails to attend a required parenting course in contempt or that parent may be denied shared parental responsibility or visitation or otherwise sanctioned as the court deems appropriate.

(7) Nothing in this section shall be construed to require the parties to a dissolution of marriage to attend a court-approved parenting course together.

61.30 Child support guidelines.—

(1) (a) The child support guideline amount as determined by this section presumptively establishes the amount the trier of fact shall order as child support in an initial proceeding for such support or in a proceeding for modification of an existing order for such support, whether the proceeding arises under this or another chapter. The trier of fact, after considering all relevant factors including the needs of the child or children, age, station in life, standard of living, and the financial status and ability of each parent, may order payment of child support which varies, plus or minus 5 percent, from the guideline amount. The trier of fact may order payment of child support in an amount which varies more than 5 percent from such guideline amount only upon a written finding, or a specific finding on the record, explaining why ordering payment of such guideline amount would be unjust or inappropriate.

(b) The guidelines may provide the basis for proving a substantial change in circumstances upon which a modification of an existing order may be granted. However, the difference between the existing order and the amount provided for under the guidelines shall be at least 15 percent or $50, whichever amount is greater, before the court may find that the guidelines provide a substantial change in circumstances.

(2) Income shall be determined for the obligor and for the obligee as follows:

(a) Gross income shall include, but is not limited to, the following items:

1. Salary or wages.
2. Bonuses, commissions, allowances, overtime, tips, and other similar payments.
3. Business income from sources such as self-employment, partnership, close corporations, and independent contracts. "Business income" means gross receipts minus ordinary and necessary expenses required to produce income.
4. Disability benefits.
5. Worker's compensation.
6. Unemployment compensation.
7. Pension, retirement, or annuity payments.
8. Social security benefits.
9. Spousal support received from a previous marriage.
10. Interest and dividends.

11. Rental income, which is gross receipts minus ordinary and necessary expenses required to produce the income.
12. Income from royalties, trusts, or estates.
13. Reimbursed expenses or in kind payments to the extent that they reduce living expenses.
14. Gains derived from dealings in property, unless the gain is nonrecurring.

(b) Income shall be imputed to an unemployed or underemployed parent when such employment or underemployment is found to be voluntary on that parent's part, absent physical or mental incapacity or other circumstances over which the parent has no control. In the event of such voluntary unemployment or underemployment, the employment potential and probable earnings level of the parent shall be determined based upon his or her recent work history, occupational qualifications, and prevailing earnings level in the community; however, the court may refuse to impute income to a primary residential parent if the court finds it necessary for the parent to stay home with the child.

(c) Aid to families with dependent children benefits shall be excluded from gross income.

(3) Allowable deductions from gross income shall include:

(a) Federal, state, and local income tax deductions, adjusted for actual filing status and allowable dependents and income tax liabilities.

(b) Federal insurance contributions or self-employment tax.

(c) Mandatory union dues.

(d) Mandatory retirement payments.

(e) Health insurance payments, excluding payments for coverage of the minor child.

(f) Court-ordered support for other children which is actually paid.

(4) Net income for the obligor and net income for the obligee shall be computed by subtracting allowable deductions from gross income.

Appendix B

SCHEDULE OF CHILD SUPPORT GUIDELINES AWARDS FOR FLORIDA—
RECOMMENDED CHILD SUPPORT AMOUNTS*

Combined Monthly Available Income ($)	One Child	Two Children	Three Children	Four Children	Five Children	Six Children
650	74	75	75	76	77	78
700	119	120	121	123	124	125
750	164	166	167	169	171	173
800	190	211	213	216	218	220
850	202	257	259	262	265	268
900	213	302	305	309	312	315
950	224	347	351	355	359	363
1000	235	365	397	402	406	410
1050	246	382	443	448	453	458
1100	258	400	489	495	500	505
1150	269	417	522	541	547	553
1200	280	435	544	588	594	600
1250	290	451	565	634	641	648
1300	300	467	584	659	688	695
1350	310	482	603	681	735	743
1400	320	498	623	702	765	790
1450	330	513	642	724	789	838
1500	340	529	662	746	813	869
2000	442	686	859	968	1054	1128
2500	547	847	1061	1196	1304	1394
3000	644	1001	1252	1412	1540	1647
3500	738	1149	1438	1620	1768	1891
4000	828	1288	1603	1816	1982	2119
4500	916	1423	1771	2006	2189	2339
5000	1000	1551	1939	2188	2387	2551
5500	1064	1647	2061	2324	2537	2711
6000	1121	1737	2175	2451	2676	2860
6500	1170	1819	2278	2562	2798	2994
7000	1212	1885	2362	2656	2900	3103
7500	1251	1945	2438	2741	2993	3201
8000	1290	2004	2513	2827	3085	3298
8500	1329	2064	2589	2912	3178	3396
9000	1368	2123	2664	2998	3270	3493
9500	1407	2183	2740	3083	3363	3591
10,000	1437	2228	2795	3148	3432	3666

Child support for combined monthly available income over $10,000 is calculated by adding the minimum amount of support to the result obtained by multiplying the following percentages by the amount of combined available income over $10,000:

One Child	Two Children	Three Children	Four Children	Five Children	Six Children
5.0	7.5	9.5	11.0	12.0	12.5

* Selected numbers are shown. For a full table, refer to your particular state.

Child Custody Evaluation Information for Attorneys

INTRODUCTION

THE PURPOSE OF THIS DOCUMENT is to outline the policies and procedures that we normally follow in conducting child custody evaluations. It represents a model that has evolved over many years of professional practice—one that has been used in both public and private settings, that reflects the state of the art in psychological practice, and that has met with widespread acceptance in the courts. Since the issues are important and complex, we want to be explicit about our standard policies and procedures at the outset.

BACKGROUND

At this point, there is general consensus within psychology that a child custody evaluation should focus on parenting. Typically, we identify the needs of the children, the resources of the parents, and what the best match might be between the two. We do not go into evaluations looking for the "better" parent. Instead, we try to develop a good understanding of the family and the factors that are most relevant to the best interest of the children.

Because of the significance of the issues involved in a custody decision, it is necessary to conduct a thorough evaluation, and not just rely on a few brief interviews, or the administration of a few psychological tests. In doing an evaluation, psychologists generally assemble a broad data base and then integrate it in a coherent manner. We usually do not make a specific recommendation as to which home environment might be better suited to meet the needs of the children, rather we focus on what the strengths and weaknesses may be in each parenting situation. In many cases, sharing parental responsibilities—although not necessarily joint custody—is a good way to satisfy everyone's needs. Normally, psychologists also recommend steps that the parents can take to improve their parenting activities and the postdivorce environment of the children.

To assure valid and reliable results, we will conduct an evaluation only under the following conditions: all of the parties agree to undergo the evaluation and to cooperate fully in it; the referral is made by either court order or joint stipulation of the two principal parties; and appropriate payment arrangements are made at the start. Every effort is made to assure that the evaluation conforms to the American Psychological Association's recently adopted Guidelines for Child Custody Evaluations (1994).

To do a good evaluation, it is essential to have access to all of the relevant parties in the case. This would include, at a minimum, the two parents and all of the children in the family. If one or both parents have remarried, then it is also important to evaluate their new spouses. Similarly, if another adult (say, a grandparent or a live-in companion) is acting in a parental role, then they would need to be involved. Psychologists generally agree that it is inappropriate to conduct a child custody evaluation with access to only one parent. We are willing to see a single individual in some very unusual circumstances: for instance, to provide a second opinion on that individual's psychological functioning (if there are concerns about the objectivity or validity of a previous evaluation).

The results of the evaluation are based upon data from a wide variety of sources, including the following: thorough clinical interviews with parties involved; the administration of various psychological tests and questionnaires; behavioral observations of the individuals; review of records of previous contacts with health care professionals, as appropriate; information from the school (about the child's academic performance and behavioral adjustment); and direct observation of parent-child interaction. Our child custody evaluation typically does not involve a visit to the parental home(s).

EVALUATION PROCEDURES

The actual evaluation process consists of four distinct parts.

The first phase involves a *meeting with all of the adult participants.* At this time, the evaluation process is thoroughly reviewed with them:

the relevant ethical and professional issues are discussed, and their *informed consent is obtained*. A thorough interview is then conducted, to obtain some basic information about the family and the couple. Current custody/visitation arrangements are reviewed, and each party's preferences are determined. We carefully explore the possibility of a mutually agreed upon compromise, and try to help the parties reach one, if possible. This *initial interview generally takes two to three hours*. If a compromise is not reached, we continue the evaluation, with the administration of a variety of psychological tests, including the Minnesota Multiphasic Personality Inventory (MMPI), and the completion of several questionnaires. This first portion of the evaluation basically takes an entire day. Arrangements are then made for each adult to return, on their own, for further tests and interviews.

The second phase involves an *individual interview with each adult, lasting about four hours*. This includes a thorough clinical interview and follow up on the psychological tests. The purpose of the tests, questionnaires, and interviews is to assess their general psychological functioning, and specific attitudes and behaviors relevant to parenting.

The third part involves *interviews with, and behavioral observations of, the child or children*. Various *psychological tests* are administered. This part of the evaluation process varies a great deal, depending upon the age of the child and any special needs or characteristics they may have; the contact may be limited with an infant, but involve several hours of interviewing and testing with a teenager.

The fourth phase involves *observing actual parent-child interaction*. This is done in as unobtrusive a manner as possible, to get some data on actual parenting behavior. Each parent is scheduled to come in, individually, and spend about an hour with their child or children in the presence of the evaluator. In all phases, considerable *emphasis is placed on the parent-child relationship*.

The evaluation is a rather lengthy process, often taking the better part of a month and a half to complete. One reason for this is a need to get to know the family and observe the individuals over time, rather than on just one or two occasions; this way, observations can be more accurate. In the most simple case—where only two parents and a very young child are involved—the evaluation typically involves some 15 hours of direct client contact. In more complicated cases (e.g., where one or both parents have remarried, there are several older children, and/or the children have some special needs), *the evaluation can easily take 20 or 25 hours to complete*. It then takes a *considerable amount of time to integrate the data and write the evaluation report*.

At the completion of the evaluation, a *thorough and detailed report is prepared and sent to the referral source or sources*. Unless there are some very specific and limited questions about a portion of the report, we *prefer not to have any further contact with the parties until the court hearing*. Throughout the evaluation process, we do our best to maintain neutrality and objectivity. We prefer to *function as independent expert examiners appointed by the court* wherever possible.

FEES

Forensic work is done on a retainer basis and reflects our customary fees for forensic activities. This fee applies for time spent reading records, drafting reports, as well as for in-office interview and testing time. A comprehensive evaluation will thus usually cost between $2,000.00 and $3,500.00. As soon as we are given some basic information about the case (e.g., whether the parents have remarried, how old the children are, whether any of the children have any special needs, etc.) we can give an approximation as to the total fee. However, it should be stressed that it is impossible to predict exactly how long an evaluation will take; often, unexpected things are discovered that need to be followed up.

Half payment of the estimated fee is needed at the time the first appointment is made. Our preference is that the *payment come in the form of a check from the attorneys, with each party contributing half of the anticipated costs.* The *second half is due two days before the child (children) are to be seen initially.* If it appears the evaluation will take more time than originally expected, we may notify the attorneys and request enough of an additional retainer to cover the anticipated extra cost. If the evaluation takes less time than expected (e.g., if the couple is able to reach a settlement), any unused portion of the payment will be refunded. A time sheet will be maintained.

The estimated charge for the evaluation does not include any depositions or court appearances that might be needed. A retainer is charged and payable 48 hours before the hearing date; any overage is refunded. These are billed at the conclusion of the proceedings, at the same hourly rate. Mileage, per diem, etc. are charged for out of town court appearances.

REFERRAL PROCEDURES

The best way to initiate a referral is to call our office and discuss the particular situation in question. With information about the family, we can give you an estimate of how extensive the evaluation would have to be and what costs would be expected. We can also give you an approximate date when we could start the evaluation. We try to meet any special needs that might be present; for example, to try to cluster appointments if the parties are coming in from far away. Upon receipt of the court order, or letters of agreement from the attorneys, along with the payment, we will contact you with a firm appointment time.

CONCLUSION

Psychologists realize that child custody disputes are difficult for everyone involved. By doing a thorough evaluation, we hope to provide information and insights which the relevant decision makers—whether they be the parents or the court—can use to make the best possible decisions based upon the best interests of the children.

If you or your clients have any questions about our policies or procedures, please feel free to contact this office. There is no cost or obligation for a preliminary telephone discussion of a case. If, for some reason, we are not able to accept a case (e.g., because of a previous the rapeutic relationship with one of the parties), we will try to facilitate a referral to another qualified psychologist.

Again, if you have any further questions or concerns, please do not hesitate to contact our office.

Sincerely,

Florence Kaslow, Ph.D.
FL PY 0002963
FL MT 0000050

ORIENTATION TO FORENSIC EVALUATION

A. Referral
   1. Who initiated it.
   2. Why it was initiated.
   3. Contact with referral source.
B. Purpose of the Evaluation and Contracting for Services
C. Nature of Evaluation Procedures
   1. Orientation.
   2. Interviews.
   3. Tests.

    4. Review of other records and contact with other sources (if relevant).
- D. Time Frame
- E. Outcome
  1. A report to referral source (and/or other parties).
  2. Range of options that may be considered.
- F. Range of Benefits (e.g., possible distress from confronting problematic issues vs. improved case management as a result of better understanding of the situation).
- G. Alternatives
- H. Costs
  1. Time.
  2. Usual fees.
  3. Estimated time and fees.
  4. Fee sheet signed.
- I. Rights
  1. Participation is totally voluntary: can refuse to participate.
  2. To not answer any questions they don't want to.
  3. May discontinue participation at any time.
  4. But exercise of these rights will likely result in a less than adequate evaluation and cause problems for them with the referral source and/or court.
- J. Issues
  1. Honesty necessary if evaluation is to be accurate and useful vs. possible self-incrimination.
  2. Realizing anything you say may be used against you by the other party and/or the court.
  3. May reveal information without knowing it.
  4. Usual limits of confidentiality:
     a. Child abuse reporting law
     b. Possible disclosure if threat of serious risk of harm to self or others.
  5. Usual limits on confidentiality don't apply: anything and everything that comes up may come out.
- K. Roles or "Players"
  1. Attorney for client.
  2. Attorney for other party or parties.
  3. Mediator.
  4. Guardian ad litem.
  5. Judge.
  6. Jury, if any.
  7. Our role as agent of the court (in court ordered evaluation) or the referral source.

8. Our role as an evaluator differs from usual role as therapist and client advocate.

L. Client's response
1. Do they understand the information provided?
2. What questions, comments, or concerns do they have?
3. Are they willing to go ahead?

Adapted from S. Podrygula
March 29, 1995

APPENDIX D

Guidelines for Child Custody Evaluations in Divorce Proceedings

INTRODUCTION

DECISIONS REGARDING CHILD CUSTODY and other parenting arrangements occur within several different legal contexts, including parental divorce, guardianship, neglect or abuse proceedings, and termination of parental rights. The following guidelines were developed for psychologists conducting child custody evaluations, specifically within the context of parental divorce. These guidelines build upon the American Psychological Association's *Ethical Principles of Psychologists and Code of Conduct* (APA, 1992) and are aspirational in intent. *As guidelines, they are not intended to be either mandatory or exhaustive. The goal of the guidelines is to promote proficiency in using psychological expertise in conducting child custody evaluations.*

Parental divorce requires a restructuring of parental rights and responsibilities in relation to children. If the parents can agree to a restructuring arrangement, which they do in the overwhelming proportion (90%) of divorce custody cases (Melton, Petrila, Poythress, & Slobogin, 1987), there is no dispute for the court to decide. However, if the parents are unable to reach such an agreement, the court must help to determine the relative allocation of decision making authority and physical contact each parent will have with the child.

The courts typically apply a "best interest of the child" standard in determining this restructuring of rights and responsibilities.

Psychologists provide an important service to children and the courts by providing competent, objective, impartial information in assessing the best interests of the child; by demonstrating a clear sense of direction and purpose in conducting a child custody evaluation; by performing their roles ethically; and by clarifying to all involved the nature and scope of the evaluation. The Ethics Committee of the American Psychological Association has noted that psychologists' involvement in custody disputes has at times raised questions in regard to the misuse of psychologists' influence, sometimes resulting in complaints against psychologists being brought to the attention of the APA Ethics Committee (APA Ethics Committee, 1985; Hall & Hare-Mustin, 1983; Keith-Spiegel & Koocher, 1985; Mills, 1984) and raising questions in the legal and forensic literature (Grisso, 1986; Melton et al., 1987; Mnookin, 1975; Ochroch, 1982; Okpaku, 1976; Weithorn, 1987).

Particular competencies and knowledge are required for child custody evaluations to provide adequate and appropriate psychological services to the court. Child custody evaluation in the context of parental divorce can be an extremely demanding task. For competing parents the stakes are high as they participate in a process fraught with tension and anxiety. The stress on the psychologist/evaluator can become great. Tension surrounding child custody evaluation can become further heightened when there are accusations of child abuse, neglect, and/or family violence.

Psychology is in a position to make significant contributions to child custody decisions. Psychological data and expertise, gained through a child custody evaluation, can provide an additional source of information and an additional perspective not otherwise readily available to the court on what appears to be in a child's best interest, and thus can increase the fairness of the determination the court must make.

GUIDELINES FOR CHILD CUSTODY EVALUATIONS IN DIVORCE PROCEEDINGS

I. Orienting Guidelines: Purpose of a Child Custody Evaluation
   1. The primary purpose of the evaluation is to assess the best psychological interests of the child.

   The primary consideration in a child custody evaluation is to assess the individual and family factors that affect the best psychological interests of the child. More specific questions may be raised by the court.

2. The child's interests and well-being are paramount.

   In a child custody evaluation, the child's interests and well-being are paramount. Parents competing for custody, as well as others, may have legitimate concerns, but the child's best interests must prevail.

3. The focus of the evaluation is on parenting capacity, the psychological and developmental needs of the child, and the resulting fit.

   In considering psychological factors affecting the best interests of the child, the psychologist focuses on the parenting capacity of the prospective custodians in conjunction with the psychological and developmental needs of each involved child. This involves (a) an assessment of the adults' capacities for parenting, including whatever knowledge, attributes, skills, and abilities, or lack thereof, are present; (b) an assessment of the psychological functioning and developmental needs of each child and of the wishes of each child where appropriate; and (c) an assessment of the functional ability of each parent to meet these needs, including an evaluation of the interaction between each adult and child.

   The values of the parents relevant to parenting, ability to plan for the child's future needs, capacity to provide a stable and loving home, and any potential for inappropriate behavior or misconduct that might negatively influence the child also are considered. Psychopathology may be relevant to such an assessment, insofar as it has impact on the child or the ability to parent, but it is not the primary focus.

II. General Guidelines: Preparing for a Child Custody Evaluation

4. The role of the psychologist is that of a professional expert who strives to maintain an objective, impartial stance.

   The role of the psychologist is as a professional expert. The psychologist does not act as a judge, who makes the ultimate decision applying the law to all relevant evidence. Neither does the psychologist act as an advocating attorney, who strives to present his or her client's best possible case. The psychologist, in a balanced, impartial manner, informs and advises the court and the prospective custodians of the child of the relevant psychological factors pertaining to the custody issue. The psychologist should be impartial regardless of whether he or she is retained by the court or by a party to the proceedings. If either the psychologist or the client cannot accept this neutral role, the psychologist should consider withdrawing from the case. If not permitted to withdraw, in such circumstances, the psychologist acknowledges past roles and other factors that could affect impartiality.

5. The psychologist gains specialized competence.

   A. A psychologist contemplating performing child custody evaluations is aware that special competencies and knowledge are required for the undertaking of such evaluations. Competence in performing psychological assessments of children, adults, and families is necessary but not sufficient. Education, training, experience, and/or supervision in the areas of child and family development, child and family psychopathology, and the impact of divorce on children help to prepare the psychologist to participate competently in child custody evaluations. The psychologist also strives to become familiar with applicable legal standards and procedures, including laws governing divorce and custody adjudications in his or her state or jurisdiction.

   B. The psychologist uses current knowledge of scientific and professional developments, consistent with accepted clinical and scientific standards, in selecting data collection methods and procedures. The *Standards for Educational and Psychological Testing* (APA, 1985) are adhered to in the use of psychological tests and other assessment tools.

   C. In the course of conducting child custody evaluations, allegations of child abuse, neglect, family violence, or other issues may occur that are not necessarily within the scope of a particular evaluator's expertise. If this is so, the psychologist seeks additional consultation, supervision, and/or specialized knowledge, training, or experience in child abuse, neglect, and family violence to address these complex issues. The psychologist is familiar with the laws of his or her state addressing child abuse, neglect, and family violence and acts accordingly.

6. The psychologist is aware of personal and societal biases and engages in nondiscriminatory practice.

   The psychologist engaging in child custody evaluations is aware of how biases regarding age, gender, race, ethnicity, national origin, religion, sexual orientation, disability, language, culture, and socioeconomic status may interfere with an objective evaluation and recommendations. The psychologist recognizes and strives to overcome any such biases or withdraws from the evaluation.

7. The psychologist avoids multiple relationships.

Psychologists generally avoid conducting a child custody evaluation in a case in which the psychologist served in a therapeutic role for the child or his or her immediate family or has had other involvement that may compromise the psychologist's objectivity. This should not, however, preclude the psychologist from testifying in the case as a fact witness concerning treatment of the child. In addition, during the course of a child custody evaluation, a psychologist does not accept any of the involved participants in the evaluation as a therapy client. Therapeutic contact with the child or involved participants following a child custody evaluation is undertaken with caution.

A psychologist asked to testify regarding a therapy client who is involved in a child custody case is aware of the limitations and possible biases inherent in such a role and the possible impact on the ongoing therapeutic relationship. Although the court may require the psychologist to testify as a fact witness regarding factual information he or she became aware of in a professional relationship with a client, that psychologist should generally decline the role of an expert witness who gives a professional opinion regarding custody and visitation issues (see Ethical Standard 7.03) unless so ordered by the court.

III. Procedural Guidelines: Conducting a Child Custody Evaluation

8. The scope of the evaluation is determined by the evaluator, based on the nature of the referral question.

The scope of the custody-related evaluation is determined by the nature of the question or issue raised by the referring person or the court, or is inherent in the situation. Although comprehensive child custody evaluations generally require an evaluation of all parents or guardians and children, as well as observations of interactions between them, the scope of the assessment in a particular case may be limited to evaluating the parental capacity of one parent without attempting to compare the parents or to make recommendations. Likewise, the scope may be limited to evaluating the child. Or a psychologist may be asked to critique the assumptions and methodology of the assessment of another mental health professional. A psychologist also might serve as an expert witness in the area of child development, providing expertise to the court without relating it specifically to the parties involved in a case.

9. The psychologist obtains informed consent from all adult participants and, as appropriate, informs child participants.

In undertaking child custody evaluations, the psychologist ensures that each adult participant is aware of (a) the purpose, nature, and method of the evaluation; (b) who has requested the psychologist's services; and (c) who will be paying the fees. The psychologist informs adult participants about the nature of the assessment instruments and techniques and informs those participants about the possible disposition of the data collected. The psychologist provides this information, as appropriate, to children, to the extent that they are able to understand.

10. The psychologist informs participants about the limits of confidentiality and the disclosure of information.

    A psychologist conducting a child custody evaluation ensures that the participants, including children to the extent feasible, are aware of the limits of confidentiality characterizing the professional relationship with the psychologist. The psychologist informs participants that in consenting to the evaluation, they are consenting to disclosure of the evaluation's findings in the context of the forthcoming litigation and in any other proceedings deemed necessary by the courts. A psychologist obtains a waiver of confidentiality from all adult participants or from their authorized legal representatives.

11. The psychologist uses multiple methods of data gathering.

    The psychologist strives to use the most appropriate methods available for addressing the questions raised in a specific child custody evaluation and generally uses multiple methods of data gathering, including, but not limited to, clinical interviews, observation, and/or psychological assessments. Important facts and opinions are documented from at least two sources whenever their reliability is questionable. The psychologist, for example, may review potentially relevant reports (e.g., from schools, health care providers, child care providers, agencies, and institutions). Psychologists may also interview extended family, friends, and other individuals on occasions when the information is likely to be useful. If information is gathered from third parties that is significant and may be used as a basis for conclusions, psychologists corroborate it by at least one other source wherever possible and appropriate and document this in the report.

12. The psychologist neither overinterprets nor inappropriately interprets clinical or assessment data.

    The psychologist refrains from drawing conclusions not adequately supported by the data. The psychologist interprets any data from interviews or tests, as well as any questions of data reliability and validity, cautiously and conservatively, seeking convergent validity. The psychologist strives to acknowledge to the court any limitations in methods or data used.

13. The psychologist does not give any opinion regarding the psychological functioning of any individual who has not been personally evaluated.

This guideline, however, does not preclude the psychologist from reporting what an evaluated individual (such as the parent or child) has stated or from addressing theoretical issues or hypothetical questions, so long as the limited basis of the information is noted.

14. Recommendations, if any, are based upon what is in the best psychological interests of the child.

Although the profession has not reached consensus about whether psychologists ought to make recommendations about the final custody determination to the courts, psychologists are obligated to be aware of the arguments on both sides of this issue and to be able to explain the logic of their position concerning their own practice.

If the psychologist does choose to make custody recommendations, these recommendations should be derived from sound psychological data and must be based on the best interests of the child in the particular case. Recommendations are based on articulated assumptions, data, interpretations, and inferences based on established professional and scientific standards. Psychologists guard against relying on their own biases or unsupported beliefs in rendering opinions in particular cases.

15. The psychologist clarifies financial arrangements.

Financial arrangements are clarified and agreed upon *prior* to commencing a child custody evaluation. When billing for a child custody evaluation, the psychologist does not misrepresent his or her services for reimbursement purposes.

16. The psychologist maintains written records.

All records obtained in the process of conducting a child custody evaluation are properly maintained and filed in accord with the APA *Record Keeping Guidelines* (APA, 1993) and relevant statutory guidelines.

All raw data and interview information are recorded with an eye toward their possible review by other psychologists or the court, where legally permitted. Upon request, appropriate reports are made available to the court.

BIBLIOGRAPHY

References Accompanying APA Child Custody Guidelines

American Psychological Association. (1985). *Standards for educational and psychological testing.* Washington, DC: Author.

American Psychological Association. (1992). Ethical principles of psychologists and code of conduct. *American Psychologist, 47,* 1597–1611.

American Psychological Association. (1993). *Record keeping guidelines.* Washington, DC: Author.

American Psychological Association, Ethics Committee. (1985). *Annual report of the American Psychological Association Ethics Committee.* Washington, DC: Author.

Grisso, T. (1986). *Evaluating competencies: Forensic assessments and instruments.* New York: Plenum.

Hall, J.E., & Hare-Mustin, R.T. (1983). Sanctions and the diversity of ethical complaints against psychologists. *American Psychologist, 38,* 714–729.

Keith-Spiegel, P., & Koocher, G.P. (1985). *Ethics in psychology.* New York: Random House.

Melton, G.B., Petrila, J., Poythress, N.G., & Slobogin, C. (1987). *Psychological evaluations for the courts: A handbook for mental health professionals and lawyers.* New York: Guilford Press.

Mills, D.H. (1984). Ethics education and adjudication within psychology. *American Psychologist, 39,* 669–675.

Mnookin, R.H. (1975). Child-custody adjudication: Judicial functions in the face of indeterminacy. *Law and Contemporary Problems, 39,* 226–293.

Ochroch, R. (1982, August). *Ethical pitfalls in child custody evaluations.* Paper presented at the 90th Annual Convention of the American Psychological Association, Washington, DC.

Okpaku, S. (1976). Psychology: Impediment or aid in child custody cases? *Rutgers Law Review, 29,* 1117–1153.

Weithorn, L.A. (Ed.). (1987). *Psychology and child custody determinations: Knowledge, roles, and expertise.* Lincoln: University of Nebraska Press.

Other Resources: State Guidelines

Georgia Psychological Association. (1990). *Recommendations for psychologists' involvement in child custody cases.* Atlanta, GA: Author.

Metropolitan Denver Interdisciplinary Committee on Child Custody. (1989). *Guidelines for child custody evaluations.* Denver, CO: Author.

Nebraska Psychological Association. (1986). *Guidelines for child custody evaluations.* Lincoln, NE: Author.

New Jersey State Board of Psychological Examiners. (1993). *Specialty guidelines for psychologists in custody/visitation evaluations.* Newark, NJ: Author.

North Carolina Psychological Association. (1993). *Child custody guidelines.* Unpublished manuscript.

Oklahoma Psychological Association. (1988). *Ethical guidelines for child custody evaluations.* Oklahoma City, OK: Author.

Forensic Guidelines

Committee on Ethical Guidelines for Forensic Psychologists. (1991). Specialty guidelines for forensic psychologists. *Law and Human Behavior, 6,* 655–665.

Pertinent Literature

Ackerman, M.J., & Kane, A.W. (1993). *Psychological experts in divorce, personal injury and other civil actions.* NY: John Wiley & Sons.

American Psychological Association, Board of Ethnic Minority Affairs. (1991). *Guidelines for providers of psychological services to ethnic, linguistic, and culturally diverse populations.* Washington, DC: American Psychological Association.

American Psychological Association, Committee on Women in Psychology and Committee on Lesbian and Gay Concerns. (1988). *Lesbian parents and their children: A resource paper for psychologists.* Washington, DC: American Psychological Association.

Beaber, R.J. (1982, Fall). Custody quagmire: Some psycholegal dilemmas. *Journal of Psychiatry & Law,* 309–326.

Bennett, B.E., Bryant, B.K., VandenBos, G.R., & Greenwood, A. (1990). *Professional liability and risk management.* Washington, DC: American Psychological Association.

Bolocofsky, D.N. (1989). Use and abuse of mental health experts in child custody determinations. *Behavioral Sciences and the Law, 7*(2), 197–213.

Bozett, F. (1987). *Gay and lesbian parents.* New York: Praeger.

Bray, J.H. (1993). What's the best interest of the child?: Children's adjustment issues in divorce. *The Independent Practitioner, 13,* 42–45.

Bricklin, B. (1992). Data-based tests in custody evaluations. *American Journal of Family Therapy, 20,* 254–265.

Cantor, D.W., & Drake, E.A. (1982). *Divorced parents and their children: A guide for mental health professionals.* New York: Springer.

Chesler, P. (1991). *Mothers on trial: The battle for children and custody.* New York: Harcourt Brace Jovanovich.

Deed, M.L. (1991). Court-ordered child custody evaluations: Helping or victimizing vulnerable families. *Psychotherapy, 28,* 76–84.

Falk, P.J. (1989). Lesbian mothers: Psychosocial assumptions in family law. *American Psychologist, 44,* 941–947.

Gardner, R.A. (1989). *Family evaluation in child custody mediation, arbitration, and litigation.* Cresskill, NJ: Creative Therapeutics.

Gardner, R.A. (1992). *The parental alienation syndrome: A guide for mental health and legal professionals.* Cresskill, NJ: Creative Therapeutics.

Gardner, R.A. (1992). *True and false accusations of child abuse.* Cresskill, NJ: Creative Therapeutics.

Goldstein, J., Freud, A., & Solnit, A.J. (1980). *Before the best interests of the child.* New York: Free Press.

Goldstein, J., Freud, A., & Solnit, A.J. (1980). *Beyond the best interests of the child.* New York: Free Press.

Goldstein, J., Freud, A., Solnit, A.J., & Goldstein, S. (1986). *In the best interests of the child.* New York: Free Press.

Grisso, T. (1990). Evolving guidelines for divorce/custody evaluations. *Family and Conciliation Courts Review, 28*(1), 35–41.

Halon, R.L. The comprehensive child custody evaluation. *American Journal of Forensic Psychology, 8*(3), 19–46.

Hetherington, E.M. (1990). Coping with family transitions: Winners, losers, and survivors. *Child Development, 60,* 1–14.

Hetherington, E.M., Stanley-Hagen, M., & Anderson, E.R. (1988). Marital transitions: A child's perspective. *American Psychologist, 44,* 303–312.

Johnston, J., Kline, M., & Tschann, J. (1989). Ongoing postdivorce conflict: Effects on children of joint custody and frequent access. *Journal of Orthopsychiatry, 59,* 576–592.

Koocher, G.P., & Keith-Spiegel, P.C. (1990). *Children, ethics, and the law: Professional issues and cases.* Lincoln: University of Nebraska Press.

Kreindler, S. (1986). The role of mental health professions in custody and access disputes. In R.S. Parry, E.A. Broder, E.A.G. Schmitt, E.B. Saunders, & E. Hood (Eds.), *Custody disputes: Evaluation and intervention.* NY: Free Press.

Martindale, D.A., Martindale, J.L., & Broderick, J.E. (1991). Providing expert testimony in child custody litigation. In P.A. Keller & S.R. Heyman (Eds.), *Innovations in clinical practice: A source book* (Vol. 10, pp. 481–497). Sarasota, FL: Professional Resource Exchange.

Patterson, C.J. (in press). Children of lesbian and gay parents. *Child Development.*

Pennsylvania Psychological Association, Clinical Division Task Force on Child Custody Evaluation. (1991). *Roles for psychologists in child custody disputes.* Unpublished manuscript.

Saunders, T.R. (1991). An overview of some psycholegal issues in child physical and sexual abuse. *Psychotherapy in Private Practice, 9*(2), 61–78.

Schutz, B.M., Dixon, E.B., Lindenberger, J.C., & Ruther, N.J. (1989). *Solomon's sword: A practical guide to conducting child custody evaluations.* San Francisco: Jossey-Bass.

Stahly, G.B. (1989, August). *Testimony on child abuse policy to APA Board.* Paper presented at the meeting of the American Psychological Association Board of Directors, New Orleans, LA.

Thoennes, N., & Tjaden, P.G. (1991). The extent, nature, and validity of sexual abuse allegations in custody/visitation disputes. *Child Abuse & Neglect, 14,* 151–163.

Wallerstein, J.S., & Blakeslee, S. (1989). *Second chances: Men, women, and children a decade after divorce.* New York: Ticknor & Fields.

Wallerstein, J.S., & Kelly, J.B. (1980). *Surviving the breakup.* New York: Basic Books.

Weissman, H.N. (1991). Child custody evaluations: Fair and unfair professional practices. *Behavioral Sciences and the Law, 9,* 469–476.

Weithorn, L.A., & Grisso, T. (1987). Psychological evaluations in divorce custody: Problems, principles, and procedures. In L.A. Weithorn (Ed.), *Psychology and child custody determinations* (pp. 157–178). Lincoln: University of Nebraska Press.

White, S. (1990). The contamination of children's interviews. *Child Youth and Family Services Quarterly, 13*(3), 6, 17–18.

Wyer, M.M., Gaylord, S.J., & Grove, E.T. The legal context of child custody evaluations. In L.A. Weithorn (Ed.), *Psychology and child custody determinations* (pp. 3–23). Lincoln: University of Nebraska Press.

APPENDIX E

Form Requesting Information from Therapist Relevant to Possible Annulment for Diocese of St. Petersburg, Florida, October 1995

CASE NAME:
PROTOCOL NO.:
IN RE:

PLEASE ANSWER THE FOLLOWING questions as fully as possible. If necessary, you may continue your answers on the reverse side or on a separate sheet of paper, numbering your answers according to the question you are answering.

1. Please state your name, address, and professional qualifications:

2. Are you related to either of the parties in this case?

3. Over what period of time was this party in treatment/consultation with you (dates and duration)? If possible, give number of times, duration of each contact and dates of each contact.

4. What was your diagnosis?

5. Did you observe any changes in this party during the course of treatment? Please describe these.

6. What was your prognosis at the end of treatment?

7. Are you able to offer an hypothesis as to the origins of any psychological or emotional difficulties you observed in this party? Please elaborate.

8. How early in life do you feel any symptoms of emotional or psychological difficulties were manifested?

9. Would you offer an opinion as to maturity level and state of mind when this person contracted the marriage in question?

10. At the time of marriage do you believe this party suffered any mental or emotional problems?

11. At the time of your last contact, do you feel this party had achieved sufficient maturity and emotional stability to contract a valid marriage?

12. Do you have any further comments?

Signature: _____

Date: _____

APPENDIX F

Ritual of Release*
(Nontraditional Jewish)

VERSION A: BOTH PARTIES PRESENT

(It is understood that the following ritual will be conducted only after the rabbi has had the opportunity to counsel with one or, preferably, both of the parties involved, and only after the couple has received a civil divorce decree. The rabbi will explain to the participants that this ceremony and the accompanying document do not constitute a halachic get. The ceremony should take place in the presence of witnesses. Participants might invite their children, family, or close friends to be present.)

RABBI
SINCE EARLIEST TIMES JUDAISM has provided for divorce when a woman and a man, who have been joined together in *kiddushin* (sacred matrimony), no longer experience the sacred in their relationship. The decision to separate is painful, not only for the woman and the man (and for their children), but for the entire community. Jewish tradition teaches that when the sacred covenant of marriage is dissolved, "even the altar sheds tears." (Gittin 90b)

W: have you consented to the termination of your marriage?

(W responds.)

---

* From the *Rabbi's Manual*, published by the Central Conference of American Rabbis. Appreciation is expressed to Reform Rabbi Howard Shapiro of Temple Israel, West Palm Beach, Florida, for providing this service to us.

M: have you consented to the termination of your marriage?

(M responds.)

W

I, _____ , now release my former husband, _____ , from the sacred bonds that held us together.

M

I, _____ , now release my former wife, _____ , from the sacred bonds that held us together.

RABBI

W and M: _____ years ago you entered into the covenant of *kiddushin*. Now you have asked us to witness your willingness to release each other from the sacred bond of marriage, and your intention to enter a new phase of life.

What existed between you, both the good and the bad, is ingrained in your memories. We pray that the good that once existed between you may encourage you to treat each other with respect and trust, and to refrain from acts of hostility. (And may the love that you have for your children, and the love that they have for you, increase with years and understanding.)

(Personal words by rabbi.)

This is your Document of Separation, duly signed by you both. It marks the dissolution of your marriage. I separate it now as you have separated, giving each of you a part.

W and M: you are both now free to enter into a new phase of your life. Take with you the assurance that human love and sanctity endure.

May God watch over each of you and protect you as you go your separate ways.

And let us say: Amen.

A similar ceremony can be performed if only one party is present.

DOCUMENT OF SEPARATION

On _____ , the _____ day of _____ , in the year 57_____ (the _____ day of _____ , in the year

19_____ of the civil calendar), according to the calendar that we use here in the city of _____ , state of _____ ,
I, _____ , release my former husband, _____ , from the sacred bonds that held us together. He is free and responsible for his life, just as I am free and responsible for my life.

This is his Document of Separation from me.

or

I, _____ , release my former wife, _____ , from the sacred bonds that held us together. She is free and responsible for her life just as I am free and responsible for my life.

This is her Document of Separation from me.

Signed: _____

_____

Witnesses: _____

_____

Rabbi: _____

References

Abel, S.L., & Neumann, K. (1994, July). *Child support using A/B expenses.* Paper presented at the annual conference of the Academy of Family Mediation, Eugene, OR.

Ackerman, M.J. (1995). *Clinician's guide to child custody evaluations.* New York: Wiley.

Ackerman, N.W., Beatman, F.L., & Sherman, S.N. (1961). *Exploring the base of family therapy.* New York: Family Service Association of America.

Ahrons, C.R. (1981). The continuing relationship between spouses. *American Journal of Orthopsychiatry, 51,* 415–428.

Ahrons, C.R. (1989). After the breakup. *The Family Therapy Networker, 13*(6), 30–41.

Ahrons, C.R. (1994). *The good divorce.* New York: HarperCollins.

Ahrons, C.R., & Rogers, R.H. (1987). *Divorced families: A multidisciplinary developmental view.* New York: W. W. Norton.

Allen, M.L. (1985). Visitation rights of a grandparent over the objection of a parent: The best interests of the child. In G.E. Stollak & M.G. Lieberman (Eds.), *Child custody disputes* (pp. 183–208). New York: Irvington.

Allen, S.F., Stoltenberg, C.D., & Rosko, C.K. (1990). Perceived psychological separation of older adolescents and young adults from their parents: A comparison of divorced versus intact families. *Journal of Counseling & Development, 69,* 57–61.

American Bar Association. (1981). *Model code of professional responsibility.* Chicago: National Center for Professional Responsibility.

American Psychological Association. (1994). Guidelines for child custody evaluation in divorce proceedings. *American Psychologist, 49,* 677–680.

Arditti, J.A., & Keith, T.Z. (1992). Visitation frequency, child support payment, and the father-child relationship postdivorce. *Journal of Marriage and the Family, 55,* 699–712.

Arditti, J.A., & Madden-Derdich, D.A. (1993). Noncustodial mothers: Developing strategies of support. *Family Relations, 42,* 305–314.

Aro, H.M., & Palosaari, U.K. (1992). Parental divorce, adolescence, and transition to young adulthood: A follow-up study. *American Journal of Orthopsychiatry, 62,* 421–429.

Ash, P., & Guyer, M.J. (1991). Biased reporting by parents undergoing child custody evaluations. *Journal of the American Academy of Child and Adolescent Psychiatry, 30,* 835–838.

Atwood, J.D. (1993, Fall). The competent divorce. *The Family Psychologist, 9*(4), 15–19.

Austin, G.W., & Jaffe, P.G. (1990). Follow-up study of parents in custody and access disputes. *Canadian Psychology, 31,* 172–179.

Axelrod, T. (1996, February 23). Beating shocks Monsey out of silence. *The Jewish Week* (New York), pp. 6, 43.

Bank, S.R., & Kahn, M.D. (1982). *The sibling bond.* New York: Basic Books.

Barbero, G.J. (1995). Divorce and the child with cystic fibrosis: The therapeutic and legal implications. *Journal of Divorce & Remarriage, 22*(3/4), 13–23.

Barrasso, R.L. (1995, May). *Gender issues in the legal system: Is there a level playing field?* Address at the annual meeting of the Association of Family & Conciliation Courts, Montreal, Quebec, Canada.

Beer, J. (1989). Relationship of divorce to self-concept, self-esteem, and grade point average of fifth and sixth grade school children. *Psychological Reports, 65,* 1379–1383.

Berger, B.R., Madakasira, S., & Roebuck, V. (1988). Child custody and relitigation: Trends in a rural setting. *American Journal of Orthopsychiatry, 58,* 604–607.

Bernard, J.K. (1994, April 21). Divorce very rarely strikes like lightning; it builds like thunder. *Palm Beach, FL Post.*

Berner, R.T. (1992). *Parents whose parents were divorced.* New York: Haworth Press.

Blaisure, K.R., & Geasler, M.J. (1996). Results of a survey of court-connected parent education programs in U. S. counties. *Family and Conciliation Courts Review, 34,* 23–40.

Blatter, C.W., & Jacobsen, J.J. (1993). Older women coping with divorce: Peer support groups. *Women & Therapy, 14*(1), 141–155.

Blau, T.H. (1984). The role of the grandparent in the best interests of the child. *American Journal of Family Therapy, 12*(4), 46–50.

Blessum, S. (1988). Rituals for healing. *Voices, 24*(1), 58–59.

Blue v. Blue, No. DR.-88-1525 (C.P. Lehigh County, PA 1989).

Bohannon, P. (1970). The six stations of divorce. In P. Bohannon (Ed.), *An analysis of the emotional and social problems of divorce* (pp. 29–55). New York: Doubleday.

Boszormenyi-Nagy, I., & Spark, G. (1973). *Invisible loyalties.* New York: Harper & Row. (Reprinted 1984, New York: Brunner/Mazel)

Bowen, M. (1978). *Family therapy in clinical practice.* New York: Aronson.

Bozett, W.W. (Ed.). (1989). Homosexuality and the family [Special issue]. *Journal of Homosexuality, 18*(12).

Bozett, W.W., & Sussman, M.B. (1989). *Homosexuality and family relations.* New York: Harrington Park Press.

Braver, S.L., Salem, P., Pearson, J., & DeLusé, S.R. (1996). The content of divorce education programs. *Family and Conciliation Courts Review, 34,* 41–59.

Braver, S.L, Wolchik, S.A., Sandler, I.N., Sheets, V.L., Fogas, B., & Bay, R.C. (1993). A longitudinal study of noncustodial parents: Parents without children. *Journal of Family Psychology, 7,* 9–23.

Bray, J.H. (1995). Children in stepfamilies: Assessment and treatment issues. In D.K. Huntley (Ed.), *Understanding stepfamilies: Implications for assessment and treatment* (pp. 59–71). Alexandria, VA: American Counseling Association.

Bricklin, B. (1995a). Getting optimum performance from a mental health professional. *Family Law Quarterly, 29,* 7–17.

Bricklin, B. (1995b). *The custody evaluation handbook: Research-based solutions and applications.* New York: Brunner/Mazel.

Brinig, M.F., & Alexeev, M.V. (1993). Trading at divorce: Preferences, legal rules and transactions costs. *Ohio State Journal on Dispute Resolution, 8,* 279–297.

Brodzinsky, D., Hitt, J.C., & Smith, D. (1993). Impact of parental separation and divorce on adopted and nonadopted children. *American Journal of Orthopsychiatry, 63,* 451–461.

Broman, C.L. (1993). Race differences in marital well-being. *Journal of Marriage and the Family, 55,* 724–732.

Brown, F.H. (1988). The postdivorce family. In B. Carter & M. McGoldrick (Eds.), *The changing family life cycle: A framework for family therapy* (2nd ed., pp. 371–398). New York: Gardner Press.

Buber, M. (1937). *I and thou.* Edinburgh, Scotland: T & T Clark.

Buehler, C., & Legg, B.H. (1992). Selected aspects of parenting and children's social competence post-separation: The moderating effects of child's sex, age, and family economic hardship. *Journal of Divorce & Remarriage, 18,* 177–195.

Buehlman, K.T., Gottman, J.M., & Katz, L.F. (1992). How a couple views their past predicts their future: Predicting divorce from an oral history interview. *Journal of Family Psychology, 5,* 295–318.

Bumpass, L.L., & Sweet, J.A. (1989). Children's experience in single-parent families: Implications of cohabitation and marital transitions. *Family Planning Perspectives, 21,* 256–260.

Buxton, A.P. (1991). *The other side of the closet.* New York: John Wiley & Sons.

Cadigan, P.B. (1994, August 21). Hers: The never wife. *The New York Times Magazine,* p. 22.

Camara, K.A., & Resnick, G. (1989). Styles of conflict resolution and cooperation between divorced parents: Effects on child behavior and adjustment. *American Journal of Orthopsychiatry, 59,* 560–575.

Campbell, T.W. (1993). Parental conflicts between divorced spouses: Strategies for intervention. *Journal of Systemic Therapies, 12*(4), 27–38.

Canadian Charter of Rights and Freedoms, Constitution Act, 1982, Schedule B.

Canadian Human Rights Act, R.S.C. 1985, c. H-6.

Carter, B., & McGoldrick, M. (Eds.). (1988). *The changing family life cycle: A framework for family therapy* (2nd ed.). New York: Gardner Press.

Cartwright, G.F. (1993). Expanding the parameters of parental alienation syndrome. *American Journal of Family Therapy, 21,* 205–215.

Casey, S. (1994). Homosexual parents and Canadian child custody law. *Family and Conciliation Courts Review, 32,* 379–396.

Cauhapé, E. (1983). *Fresh starts: Men & women after divorce.* New York: Basic Books.

Cavaliere, F. (1995, July). Society appears more open to gay parenting. *APA Monitor,* p. 51.

Ceschini, R. (1994). Divorce proceedings in Italy: Domestic and international procedures. *Family Law Quarterly, 28,* 143–149.

Child Support Report. (1994a). *16*(1). Washington, DC: U.S. Department of Health and Human Services, Office of Child Support Enforcement.

Child Support Report. (1994b). *16*(4). Washington, DC: U.S. Department of Health and Human Services, Office of Child Support Enforcement.

Child Support Report. (1994c). *16*(6). Washington, DC: U.S. Department of Health and Human Services, Office of Child Support Enforcement.

Child Support Report. (1995). *17*(11). Washington, DC: U.S. Department of Health and Human Services, Office of Child Support Enforcement.

Child Support Report. (1996). *18*(2). Washington, DC: U.S. Department of Health and Human Services, Office of Child Support Enforcement.

Clarity, J.F. (1995, September 17). Irish cabinet back lifting ban on divorce. *The New York Times*, p. 8.

Clark, B.K. (1995). Acting in the best interest of the child: Essential components of a child custody evaluation. *Family Law Quarterly, 29,* 19–38.

Clay, R.A. (1995, December). Courts reshape image of "the good mother." *APA Monitor*, p. 31.

Close, H. (1977, Spring). Service of divorce. *Pilgramage, 5*(1), 60–66.

Cohen, D.N. (1996, January/February). The plight of the Agunah. *The Jewish Monthly* (B'nai Brith), pp. 8–15.

Colarusso, C.A., & Nemeroff, R.A. (1981). *Adult development: A new dimension in psychodynamic theory and practice.* New York: Plenum.

Coogler, O.J. (1978). *Structured mediation in divorce settlement.* Lexington, MA: Heath.

Cooney, T.M., Smyer, M.A., Hagestad, G.O., & Klock, R. (1986). Parental divorce in young adulthood: Some preliminary findings. *American Journal of Orthopsychiatry, 56,* 470–477.

Cooney, T.M., & Uhlenberg, P. (1990). The role of divorce in men's relations with their adult children after mid-life. *Journal of Marriage and the Family, 52,* 677–688.

Cornille, T.A. (1993). Support systems and the relocation process for children and families. *Marriage & Family Review, 19,* 281–298.

Creasey, G.L. (1993). The association between divorce and late adolescent grandchildren's relations with grandparents. *Journal of Youth and Adolescence, 22,* 513–528.

Crosbie-Burnett, M. (1991). Impact of joint versus sole custody and quality of co-parental relationship on adjustment of adolescents in remarried families. *Behavioral Sciences and the Law, 9,* 439–449.

Crosbie-Burnett, M., & Lewis, E.A. (1993). Use of African-American family structures and functioning to address the challenges of European-American postdivorce families. *Family Relations, 42,* 243–248.

Crosbie-Burnett, M., & Newcomer, L.L. (1990). Group counseling children of divorce: The effects of a multimodal intervention. *Journal of Divorce, 13*(3), 69–78.

Crosby, J.F. (1990). The devitalized marriage: Assessment and treatment. *American Journal of Family Therapy, 18,* 323–333.

Cummings, E.M., & Davies, P. (1994). *Children and marital conflict: The impact of family dispute and resolution.* New York: Guilford.

Curtis v. Kline, 666 A.2d 265, Sup. 1995.

Czapanskiy, K. (1993). Domestic violence, the family, and the lawyering process: Lessons from studies on gender bias in the courts. *Family Law Quarterly, 27,* 247–274.

D'Augelli, A.R., & Patterson, C.R. (1995). *Lesbian, gay and bisexual identities over the lifespan.* New York: Oxford.

Davis, B., & Aron, A. (1988). Perceived causes of divorce and postdivorce adjustment among recently divorced midlife women. *Journal of Divorce, 12*(1), 41–55.

Dell, P.F. (1982). Family theory and the epistemology of Humberto Maturana. In F.W. Kaslow (Ed.), *The international book of family therapy* (pp. 56–66). New York: Brunner/Mazel.

Devlin, A.S., Brown, E.H., Beebe, J., & Parulls, E. (1992). Parent education for divorced fathers. *Family Relations, 41,* 290–296.

DeWalt v. DeWalt, 365 Pa. Super 280, 529 A.2d 508 (1987).

Dillon, P.A., & Emery, R.E. (1996). Divorce mediation and resolution in child custody disputes: Long-term effects. *American Journal of Orthopsychiatry, 66,* 131–140.

Dissolution of Marriage—Children Act, Fla. Stat. Chapter 82–96 (1982).

Dissolution of Marriage; Support; Custody, Fla. Stat. Chapter 61 (1992 Revision).

Dubin, M. (1993, November 17). Over 60 and splitting up. *The Philadelphia Inquirer,* pp. G-1, G-5.

Dubin, M. (1994, October 26). Divorce 103. *The Philadelphia Inquirer,* pp. H-1, H-6.

Dudley, J.R. (1991). The consequences of divorce proceedings for divorced fathers. *Journal of Divorce & Remarriage, 16,* 171–193.

Duncan, G.J., & Hoffman, S.D. (1985). A reconsideration of the economic consequences of divorce. *Demography, 22,* 485–497.

Durkin, C. (1994, May 4). Fathers feel system stacked against them in custody fights. *Times-Chronicle* (Jenkintown, PA), pp. 1, 5.

Ecclesiastes. (1965). *The Holy Scriptures.* Philadelphia: The Jewish Publication Society of America.

Elliot, L.B. (1990, August). Experiencing parental divorce during college. Paper presented at the annual convention of the American Psychological Association, Boston.

Ellis, W.L. (1991). The effects of background characteristics of attorneys and judges on decision making in Domestic Relations court: An analysis of child support awards. *Journal of Divorce & Remarriage, 16,* 107–119.

Ellison, R.A. (1991). Family law. *Syracuse Law Review, 42,* 615–635.

Elrod, L.D. (1993). *Child custody practice and procedure.* Deerfield, IL: Clark, Boardman, & Callaghan.

Elrod, L.D. (1994). Summary of the year in family law. *Family Law Quarterly, 27,* 485–514.

Elrod, L.D. (1995). Family law in the fifty states 1993–94. *Family Law Quarterly, 28,* 573–706.

Elrod, L.D., & Walker, T.B. (1994). Family law in the fifty states. *Family Law Quarterly, 27,* 515–745.

Erickson, S., & McKnight-Erickson, M. (1988). *Mediation casebook.* New York: Brunner/Mazel.

Erikson, E.H. (1950). *Childhood and society.* New York: W.W. Norton.

Facchino, D., & Aron, A. (1990). Divorced fathers with custody: Method of obtaining custody and divorce adjustment. *Journal of Divorce, 13*(3), 45–56.

Farmer, S., & Galaris, D. (1993). Support groups for children of divorce. *American Journal of Family Therapy, 21,* 40–50.

Fassel, D. (1991). *Growing up divorced: A road to healing for adult children of divorce.* New York: Pocket Books.

Fernandes, L.O.L., Humphreys, K., & Fincham, F.D. (1991, Summer). The whole is greater than the sum of its parts: A group intervention for children from divorced families. *The Family Psychologist,* pp. 26–28.

Ferstenberg, R.L. (1992). Mediation vs. litigation in divorce and why a litigator becomes a mediator. *American Journal of Family Therapy, 20,* 266–273.

Fine, M. (1992). Families in the United States: Their current status and future prospects. *Family Relations, 41,* 430–435.

Fisher, H. (1992). *Anatomy of love.* New York: Fawcett Columbine.

Fogas, B.S., Wolchik, S.A., Braver, S.L., Freedom, D.S., & Bay, R.C. (1992). Locus of control as a mediator of negative divorce-related events and adjustment problems in children. *American Journal of Orthopsychiatry, 62,* 589–598.

Folberg, J., & Milne, A. (1988). *Divorce mediation.* New York: Guilford.

Fowler, J.G. (1995). Homosexual parents: Implications for custody cases. *Family and Conciliation Courts Review, 33,* 361–376.

Framo, J.L. (1992). *Family of origin therapy: An intergenerational approach.* New York: Brunner/Mazel.

Frieman, B.B. (1993, September). Separation and divorce: Children want their teachers to know—Meeting the emotional needs of preschool and primary school children. *Young Children, 48,* 58–65.

Furstenberg, F.F., Jr., & Cherlin, A.J. (1991). *Divided families: What happens to children when parents part.* Cambridge, MA: Harvard University Press.

Gabriel, T. (1995, April 23). How marriages unravel when one spouse is gay. *The New York Times,* pp. 1, 22.

Gander, A.M., & Jorgenson, L.A.B. (1990). Postdivorce adjustment: Social supports among older divorced persons. *Journal of Divorce, 13*(4), 37–52.

Garber, R.J. (1990, August). *Long-term effects of divorce on the self-esteem of young adults.* Paper presented at the annual convention of the American Psychological Association, Boston, MA.

Gardner, L.A. (1977). *The parent's book about divorce.* New York: Bantam Books.

Gardner, R. (1985). Recent trends in divorce and custody litigation. *Academy Forum, 29*(2), 3–7.

Gardner, R. (1992). *Parental alienation syndrome: A guide for mental health and legal professionals.* Cresskill, NJ: Creative Therapeutics.

Garfinkel, I., Melli, M.S., & Robertson, J.G. (1994). Child support orders: A perspective on reform. *The Future of Children: Children and Divorce, 4*(1), 84–100.

Garfinkel, I., & Uhr, E. (1984). A new approach to child support. *Public Interest, 75,* 111–122.

Garrity, C.B., & Baris, M.A. (1994). *Caught in the middle: Protecting the children of high-conflict divorce.* New York: Lexington Books.

Gately, D., & Schwebel, A.I. (1992). Favorable outcomes in children after parental divorce. *Journal of Divorce & Remarriage, 18,* 57–78.

Geddes v. Geddes, 530 So. 2d 1011 (Fla. 4th DVA 1988).

Gibson, K., & Lathrop, D. (1988). Ceremony and ritual in psychotherapy. *Voices, 24*(1), 3–12.

Gilligan, C. (1982). *In a different voice.* Cambridge, MA: Harvard University Press.

Gindes, M. (1995). Guidelines for child custody evaluations for psychologists: An overview and commentary. *Family Law Quarterly, 29,* 39–50.

Glass, S.P., & Wright, T. (1994, August). *The trauma of marital infidelity.* Paper presented at the annual meeting of the American Psychological Association, Los Angeles, CA.

Glendon, M.A. (1987). *Abortion and divorce in Western law.* Cambridge, MA: Harvard University Press.

Gold, L. (1992). *Between love and hate: A guide to civilized divorce.* New York: Plenum.

Goleman, D. (1995, March 7). 75 years later, study still tracking geniuses. *The New York Times,* pp. Ca, C9.

Gottman, J.M. (1994). *What predicts divorce? The relationship between marital processes and marital outcomes.* Hillsdale, NJ: Erlbaum.

Gottman, J.S. (1990). Children of gay and lesbian parents. In F.W. Bozett & M.B. Sussman (Eds.), *Homosexuality and family relations* (pp. 177–196). New York: Harrington Park Press.

Gray, J. (1992). *Men are from Mars, women are from Venus.* New York: HarperCollins.

Grayson, J. (1994). International relocation, the right to travel, and the Hague Convention: Additional requirements for custodial parents. *Family Law Quarterly, 28,* 531–540.

Grebe, S.C. (1989). Wearing two hats: Divorce mediation is not just an extension of therapy. *The Family Therapy Networker, 13*(6), 17–20.

Green, G.D., & Bozett, F.W. (1991). Lesbian mothers and gay fathers. In J.C. Gonseorek & J.D. Weinrich (Eds.), *Homosexuality: Research implications for public policy (pp. 197–214).* Newbury Park, CA: Sage.

Greene, D. (1995, August 20). Sparing children the crossfire of divorce. *The New York Times*, Sec. 13.

Greif, G.L., & DeMaris, A. (1991). When a single custodial father receives child support. *American Journal of Family Therapy, 19,* 167–176.

Greif, G.L., & Pabst, M.S. (1988). *Mothers without custody.* New York: Heath.

Guttmann, J. (1993). *Divorce in psychosocial perspective: Theory and research.* Hillsdale, NJ: Erlbaum.

Guttmann, J., Geva, N., & Gefen, S. (1988). Teachers' and school children's stereotypic perception of "The child of divorce." *American Educational Research Journal, 25,* 555–571.

Hahleweg, K., & Jacobson, N.S. (1984). *Marital interaction: Analysis and modification.* New York: Guilford.

Halikias, W. (1994). The *Guardian ad Litem* for children in divorce: Conceptualizing duties, roles, and consultative services. *Family and Conciliation Courts Review, 32,* 490–501.

Hartog, H. (1991). Marital exits and marital expectations in nineteenth century America. *The Georgetown Law Journal, 80,* 95–129.

Haskins, R. (1988). Child support: A father's view. In A.J. Kahn & S.B. Kamerman (Eds.), *Child support: From debt collection to social policy* (pp. 306–327). Newbury Park, CA: Sage.

Haynes, J.M. (1981). *Divorce mediation.* New York: Springer.

Haynes, J.M. (1982). A conceptual mode of the process of family mediation: Implications for training. *American Journal of Family Therapy, 10*(4), 5–16.

Hennon, C.B., & Brubaker, T.H. (1994). Divorce and health in later life. In L.L. Schwartz (Ed.), *Mid-life divorce counseling* (pp. 39–63). Alexandria, VA: American Counseling Association.

Hernandez, R. (1996, March 27). Appeals court lifts restrictions on divorced parents' moving. *The New York Times*, pp. A1, B4.

Hetherington, E.M., Stanley-Hagan, M., & Anderson, E.R. (1989). Marital transitions: A child's perspective. *American Psychologist, 44,* 303–312.

Hetherington, E.M., & Tryon, A.S. (1989). His and her divorces. *The Family Therapy Networker, 13*(6), 58–61.

Heyer, D.L., & Nelson, E.S. (1993). The relationship between parental marital status and the development of identity and emotional autonomy in college students. *Journal of College Student Development, 34,* 432–436.

Hoff, M.K., & Kramer, R.L. (1992, July). A chance for children of divorce. *Adolescent Counselor,* 34–38.

Hoffman, C.D. (1995). Pre- and post-divorce father-child relationships and child adjustment: Noncustodial fathers' perspectives. *Journal of Divorce & Remarriage, 23*(1/2), 3–20.

Hoffman, J. (1996, March 27). New custody rules complicate the task of judges. *The New York Times*, p. B5.

Horbatt, W.R., & Grosman, A.M. (1994). Division of retiree health benefits on divorce: The new equitable distribution frontier. *Family Law Quarterly, 28*, 327–346.

Hughes, S.F., Berger, M., & Wright, L. (1978). The family life cycle and clinical intervention. *Journal of Marriage and Family Counseling, 4*(4), 33–40.

Humphreys, K., Fernandes, L.O.L., & Fincham, F.D. (1992, Spring). The whole is greater than the sum of its parts: II. A group intervention for parents from divorced families. *The Family Psychologist*, pp. 19–20.

Hurley, E.C., Taylor, V.L., Ingram, T.L., & Riley, M.T. (1984). Therapeutic interventions for children of divorce. *Family Therapy, 11*, 261–268.

Hyde, L.M., Jr. (1991). Child custody and visitation. *Juvenile & Family Court Journal, 42*, 1–13.

Imber-Black, E. (1993). Ghosts in the therapy room. *The Family Therapy Networker, 17*(3), 18–29.

Imber-Black, E., Roberts, J., & Whiting, R. (1988). *Rituals in families and family therapy.* New York: Norton.

Isaacs, M.B., & Montalvo, B. (1989). The difficult divorce. *The Family Therapy Networker, 13*(6), 42–50.

Isser, N., & Schwartz, L.L. (1988). *The history of conversion and contemporary cults.* New York: Peter Lang.

Jacobson, D.S. (1995). Critical interactive events and child adjustment in the stepfamily: A linked family system. In D.K. Huntley (Ed.), *Understanding stepfamilies: Implications for assessment and treatment* (pp. 73–86). Alexandria, VA: American Counseling Association.

Jacobson, N.S., & Gurman, A.S. (Eds.). (1986). *Clinical handbook of marital therapy.* New York: Guilford.

Johnson, D. (1996, February 12). No-fault divorce is under attack. *The New York Times*, p. A10.

Johnston, J.R., & Campbell, L.E.G. (1988). *Impasses of divorce: The dynamics and resolution of family conflict.* New York: Free Press.

Johnston, J.R., Kline, M., & Tschann, J.M. (1989). Ongoing postdivorce conflict: Effects on children of joint custody and frequent access. *American Journal of Orthopsychiatry, 59*, 576–592.

Jordan, P. (1988). The effects of marital separation on men. *Journal of Divorce, 12*(1), 57–82.

Kadis, A., & Markowitz, M. (1972). Short term analytic treatment of married couples in a group by a therapist couple. In C. Sager & H.S. Kaplan (Eds.), *Progress in group and family therapy* (pp. 463–482). New York: Brunner/Mazel.

Kahn, A.J., & Kamerman, S.B. (Eds.). (1988). *Child support: From debt collection to social policy.* Newbury Park, CA: Sage.

Kantrowitz, B., Wingert, P., Rosenberg, D., Quade, V., & Foote, D. (1992, January 13). Breaking the divorce cycle, *Newsweek, 119*(2), 48–53.

Kaplan, L., Ade-Ridder, L., & Hennon, C.B. (1991). Issues of split custody: Siblings separated by divorce. *Journal of Divorce & Remarriage, 16,* 253–274.

Kaslow, F.W. (1981a). A diaclectic approach to family therapy and practice: Selectivity and synthesis. *Journal of Marital and Family Therapy, 7*(3), 345–351.

Kaslow, F.W. (1981b). Divorce and divorce therapy. In A. Gurman & D. Kniskern (Eds.), *Handbook of family therapy* (pp. 662–696). New York: Brunner/Mazel.

Kaslow, F.W. (1982). Group therapy with couples in conflict. *Australian Journal of Family Therapy, 3*(4), 199–204.

Kaslow, F.W. (1984). Group therapy with couples in conflict. *Australian Journal of Family Therapy, 3*(4), 199–204.

Kaslow, F.W. (1987). Marital and family therapy. In M.B. Sussman & S.K. Steinmetz (Eds.), *Handbook of marriage and the family* (pp. 835–860). New York: Plenum.

Kaslow, F.W. (1988). The psychological dimension of divorce mediation. In J. Folberg & A. Milne (Eds.), *Divorce mediation: Theory and practice* (pp. 83–108). New York: Guilford Press.

Kaslow, F.W. (1990a). "Diaclectic" psychotherapy. In J.K. Zeig & W.M. Munion (Eds.), *What is psychotherapy?: Contemporary perspectives* (pp. 319–323). San Francisco: Jossey-Bass.

Kaslow, F.W. (1990b). Divorce therapy and mediation for better custody. *Japanese Journal of Family Psychology, 4,* 19–37.

Kaslow, F.W. (1991). Enter the prenuptial: A prelude to marriage or remarriage. *Behavioral Sciences and the Law, 9,* 375–386.

Kaslow, F.W. (1993a). Attractions and affairs: Fabulous and fatal. *Journal of Family Psychotherapy, 4*(1), 1–34.

Kaslow, F.W. (1993b). The divorce ceremony: A healing strategy. In T. Nelson & T. Trepper (Eds.), *101 Favorite family therapy interventions* (pp. 341–345). New York: Haworth Press.

Kaslow, F.W. (1993c). Understanding and treating the remarriage family. In *Directions in marriage and family therapy, 1*(3), 1–16. New York: Hatherleigh.

Kaslow, F.W. (1994). Painful partings: Providing therapeutic guidance. In L.L. Schwartz (Ed.), *Mid-life divorce counseling* (pp. 67–82). Alexandria, VA: American Counseling Association.

Kaslow, F.W. (1995a). Family and clinical family psychology at the end of the twentieth century. *World Psychology, 1*(2), 23–41.

Kaslow, F.W. (1995b). The dynamics of divorce therapy. In R.H. Mikesell, D.D. Lusterman, & S.H. McDaniel (Eds.), *Integrating family therapy: Handbook of family psychology and systems theory* (pp. 271–284). Washington, DC: American Psychological Association.

Kaslow, F.W. (1995c). *Projective genogramming.* Sarasota, FL: Professional Resource Press.

Kaslow, F.W., & Hammerschmidt, H. (1992). Long term good marriages: The seemingly essential ingredients. *Journal of Couples Therapy, 3*(2/3), 15–38; In B.J. Brothers (Ed.), *Couples therapy, multiple perspectives* (pp. 15–38). New York: Haworth.

Kaslow, F.W., Hansson, K., & Lindblad, A.M. (1994). Long term marriages in Sweden: And some comparison with similar couples in the U.S. *Contemporary Family Therapy, 16,* 521–537.

Kaslow, F.W., & Lieberman, E.J. (1981). Couples group therapy: Rationale, dynamics and process. In G.P. Sholevar (Ed.), *The handbook of marriage and marital therapy* (pp. 347–362). New York: SP Medical and Scientific Books.

Kaslow, F.W., & Schwartz, L.L. (1983). Vulnerability and invulnerability to the cults: An assessment of family dynamics, functioning, and values. In D. Bagarozzi, A. Jurich, & R.W. Jackson (Eds.), *Marital and family therapy: New perspectives in theory, research, and practice* (pp. 165–190). New York: Human Sciences Press.

Kaslow, F.W., & Schwartz, L.L. (1987a). Older children of divorce: A neglected family segment. In J. Vincent (Ed.), *Advances in family intervention, assessment, and theory* (pp. 99–120). Greenwich, CT: JAI Press.

Kaslow, F.W., & Schwartz, L.L. (1987b). *The dynamics of divorce.* New York: Brunner/Mazel.

Kelly, J.B. (1994, July). *Parent-child alienation: Divorce-related distortions and alienation.* Paper presented at the annual conference of the Academy of Family Mediators, Eugene, OR.

Kelly, J.B, & Olin, S. (1992). Research shows that divorce mediation really works. *The Family Law Commentator, 17*(2), 1.

Kernberg, O. (1975). *Borderline conditions and pathological narcissism.* New York: Jason Aronson.

Kessler, S. (1975). *The American way of divorce: Prescription for change.* Chicago: Nelson Hall.

Kessler, S., & Bostwick, S. (1977). Beyond divorce: Coping skills for children. *Journal of Clinical Child Psychology, 6,* 38–41.

Kirschner, D.A., & Kirschner, S. (1986). *Comprehensive family therapy.* New York: Brunner/Mazel.

Kirschner, S., & Kirschner, D.A. (1994). Male mid-life issues and divorce. In L.L. Schwartz (Ed.), *Mid-life divorce counseling* (pp. 29–38). Alexandria, VA: American Counseling Association.

Kissman, K., & Allen, J.A. (1993). *Single-parent families.* Newbury Park, CA: Sage.

Kitson, G.C., & Morgan, L.A. (1990). The multiple consequences of divorce: A decade review. *Journal of Marriage and the Family, 52,* 913–924.

Kitzmann, K.M., & Emery, R.E. (1994). Child and family coping one year after mediated and litigated child custody disputes. *Journal of Family Psychology, 8,* 150–159.

Kohlberg, L. (1969). Stage and sequence: The cognitive development approach to socialization. In D.A. Goslin (Ed.), *Handbook of socialization theory and research* (pp. 347–480). New York: Rand McNally.

Kohlberg, L. (1981). *The philosophy of moral development.* San Francisco: Harper & Row.

Kompass, F. (1989). After the shouting stops. *The Family Therapy Networker, 13*(6), 62–64.

Koopman, E.J., & Hunt, E.J. (1988). Child custody mediation: An interdisciplinary synthesis. *American Journal of Orthopsychiatry, 58,* 379–386.

Koopman, E.J., Hunt, E.J., & Favretto, F.G. (1994). Accomplishing the multiple tasks of divorce and separation: Checklists for professionals and couples. *Family and Conciliation Courts Review, 32,* 84–92.

Kressel, K. (1985). *The process of divorce: How professionals and couples negotiate settlements.* New York: Basic Books.

Kruk, E. (1994). Grandparent visitation disputes: Multi-generational approaches to family mediation. *Mediation Quarterly, 12,* 37–53.

Kurta, L. (1994). Psychosocial coping resources in elementary school-age children. *American Journal of Orthopsychiatry, 64,* 554–563.

Kurz, D. (1995). *For richer, for poorer: Mothers confront divorce.* New York: Routledge.

Laosa, L. (1988). Ethnicity and single parenting in the United States. In E.M. Hetherington & J.D. Arasteh (Eds.), *Impact of divorce, single parenting, and stepparenting on children* (pp. 23–49). Hillsdale, NJ: Erlbaum.

Leipziger, D. (1996, February 16). Keep your distance. *The Jewish Week* (New York).

Levinson, D. (1978). *The seasons of a man's life.* New York: Knopf.

Levy, R.J. (1993). Rights and responsibilities for extended family members? *Family Law Quarterly, 27,* 191–212.

Lewin, T. (1990, June 4). Father's vanishing act called common drama. *The New York Times,* p. A18.

Lima, L.H., & Harris, R.C. (1988). The child support enforcement program in the United States. In A.J. Kahn & S.B. Kamerman (Eds.), *Child support: From debt collection to social policy* (pp. 20–44). Newbury Park, CA: Sage.

Lopez, F.G. (1987). The impact of parental divorce on college student development. *Journal of Counseling and Development, 65,* 484–486.

Lund, M. (1995). A therapist's view of parental alienation syndrome. *Family and Conciliation Courts Review, 33,* 308–316.

Maccoby, E.E. (1991, Spring). After the divorce: The Stanford Child Custody Project. *Newsletter,* American Psychological Association, Division 7 (Developmental Psychology), pp. 1–2.

Maccoby, E.E., Buchanan, C.M., Mnookin, R.H., & Dornbusch, S.M. (1993). Postdivorce roles of mothers and fathers in the lives of their children. *Journal of Family Psychology, 7,* 24–38.

Maccoby, E.E., & Mnookin, R.H. (1992). *Dividing the child: Social and legal dilemmas of custody.* Cambridge, MA: Harvard University Press.

Magid, K., & Oborn, P. (1986). Children of divorce: A need for guidelines. *Family Law Quarterly, 19,* 331–341.

Mahoney, K. (1995, May). *Gender issues in the legal system: Is there a level playing field?* Address at the annual meeting of the Association of Family & Conciliation Courts, Montreal, Quebec, Canada.

Maltas, C. (1991). The dynamics of narcissism in marriage. *Psychoanalytic Review, 78,* 567–581.

Maltas, C. (1992). Trouble in paradise: Marital crises of midlife. *Psychiatry, 55,* 122–131.

Marlow, L., & Sauber, S.R. (1990). *The handbook of divorce mediation.* New York: Plenum.

Marr, N. (1993). Introduction to the issue. *Child Support Report, 15*(9), 1. Washington, DC: U.S. Department of Health and Human Services, Office of Child Support Enforcement.

Mason, M.A., & Simon, D.W. (1995). The ambiguous stepparent: Federal legislation in search of a model. *Family Law Quarterly, 29,* 445–482.

Matza, M. (1995, July 19). Who has rights when gay parents split? *The Philadelphia Inquirer,* pp. C1, C3.

McCullough, M. (1996, March 17). Gay-rights leaders cry judicial bias as a lesbian loses custody of her son. *The Philadelphia Inquirer,* p. E3.

McIntyre, D.H. (1994). Gay parents and child custody: A struggle under the legal system. *Mediation Quarterly, 12,* 135–149.

Meierding, N.R. (1993). Does mediation work? A survey of long-term satisfaction and durability rates for privately mediated agreements. *Mediation Quarterly, 11,* 157–170.

Minuchin, S. (1974). *Families and family therapy.* Cambridge, MA: Harvard University Press.

Minuchin, S., & Fishman, H.C. (1981). *Family therapy techniques.* Cambridge, MA: Harvard University Press.

Monahan, S.C., Buchanan, C.M., Maccoby, E.E., & Donenbusch, S.M. (1993). Sibling differences in divorced families. *Child Development, 64*, 152–168.

Morgan, L.A., Kitson, G.C., & Kitson, J.T. (1992). The economic fallout from divorce: Issues for the 1990s. *Journal of Family and Economic Issues, 13*, 435–443.

Mundy v. Mundy, 498 So. 2d 538 (Fla. 1st DCA 1986).

Mussen, P.H., Conger, J.J., & Kagan, J. (1979). *Child development and personality.* New York: Harper & Row.

Myers, J.E., & Perrin, N. (1993). Grandparents affected by parental divorce: A population at risk? *Journal of Counseling & Development, 72*, 62–66.

Myers, M.F. (1989). *Men and divorce.* New York: Guilford.

National Center for Health Statistics. (1985, December 26). Advance report of final divorce statistics, 1983 (DHHS Publication No. PHS 86-1120). *Monthly Vital Statistics Report, 34*(9, Suppl. 9). Hyattsville, MD: U.S. Public Health Service.

National Center for Health Statistics. (1993). Annual summary of births, marriages, divorces, and deaths: United States, 1992. *Monthly vital statistics report, 41*(13). Hyattsville, MD: U.S. Public Health Service.

National Center for Health Statistics. (1994a). Births, marriages, divorces, and deaths for 1993. *Monthly vital statistics report, 42*(12). Hyattsville, MD: U.S. Public Health Service.

National Center for Health Statistics (1994b). Annual summary of births, marriages, divorces, and deaths: United States, 1993. *Monthly vital statistics report, 42*(13). Hyattsville, MD: U.S. Public Health Service.

National Center for Health Statistics (1996). Births, marriages, divorces, and deaths for July 1995. *Monthly vital statistics report, 44*(7). Hyattsville, MD: U.S. Public Health Service.

Nazareno, A. (1995, December 25). Denied visitation rights, grandparents revisit the law. *The Philadelphia Inquirer*, pp. B1–B2.

Nelson, G. (1994). Emotional well-being of separated and married women: Long-term follow-up study. *American Journal of Orthopsychiatry, 64*, 150–160.

Nelson, R. (1989). Parental hostility, conflict and communication in joint and sole custody families. *Journal of Divorce, 13*, 145–157.

Neumann, D. (1992). How mediation can effectively address the male-female power imbalance in divorce. *Mediation Quarterly, 9*, 227–239.

Nicholson, A. (1994). The Family Court of Australia. *Family and Conciliation Courts Review, 32*, 138–148.

Nicholson, A. (1995, May). *Gender issues in the legal system: Is there a level playing field?* Address at the annual meeting of the Association of Family & Conciliation Courts, Montreal, Quebec, Canada.

Nielsen, L. (1993). Students from divorced and blended families. *Educational Psychology Review, 5,* 177–199.

O'Brien v. O'Brien, 66 NY 2d 576 (N.Y. Ct. of Appeals 1985).

Oppawsky, J. (1991). Utilizing children's drawings in working with children following divorce. *Journal of Divorce & Remarriage, 15,* 125–141.

Palmer, N.S. (1988). Legal recognition of the parental alienation syndrome. *American Journal of Family Therapy, 16,* 361–363.

Parents, Families, and Friends of Lesbians and Gays (PFLAG). (1994). *Opening the straight spouse's closet.* Washington, DC: Author.

Pasley, K., & Dollahite, D.C. (1995). The nine Rs of stepparenting adolescents: Research-based recommendations for clinicians. In D.K. Huntley (Ed.), *Understanding stepfamilies: Implications for assessment and treatment* (pp. 87–98). Alexandria, VA: American Counseling Association.

Pasley, K., & Healow, C.L. (1988). Adolescent self-esteem: A focus on children in stepfamilies. In E.M. Hetherington & J.D. Arasteh (Eds.), *Impact of divorce, single parenting, and stepparenting on children* (pp. 263–277). Hillsdale, NJ: Erlbaum.

Patterson, C.J. (1995). Lesbian mothers, gay fathers and their children. In A.R. D'Augelli & C.J. Patterson (Eds.), *Lesbian, gay, and bisexual identities over the lifespan* (pp. 262–292). New York: Oxford University Press.

Penn. Cons. Stat. Ann. Title 23, § 4327 (1993).

Petersen, V., & Steinman, S.B. (1994). Helping children succeed after divorce: A court-mandated educational program for divorcing parents. *Family and Conciliation Courts Review, 32,* 27–39.

Phillips, C.P., & Asbury, C.A. (1993). Parental divorce/separation and the motivational characteristics and educational aspirations of African American university students. *Journal of Negro Education, 62,* 204–210.

Phillips, R. (1993, July). Divorced, beheaded, died . . . . *History Today, 43,* 9–12.

Piaget, J. (1926). *The language and thought of the child* (M. Worden, Trans.). New York: Harcourt, Brace & World.

Piaget, J. (1951). *Play, dreams and imitation in childhood.* New York: W. W. Norton.

Piaget, J. (1981). *Intelligence and affectivity: Their relationship during child development.* T.A. Brown & C.F. Kaege, trans. & eds. Palo Alto, CA: Annual Reviews Monograph.

Pittman, F. (1989). *Private lies: Infidelity and the betrayal of intimacy.* New York: W. W. Norton.

Portes, P.R., Howell, S.C., Brown, J.H., Eichenberger, S., & Mas, C.A. (1992). Family functions and children's postdivorce adjustment. *American Journal of Orthopsychiatry, 62,* 613–617.

Public Act 93-319. (1993). Parenting Education Programs, Connecticut.

Public Law 97-252. (1982). Uniformed Services Former Spouses' Protection Act.

Public Law 98-378. (1984). Child Support Enforcement Amendments of 1984. *United States Statutes at Large, 98,* 1305–1331.

Public Law 102-521. (1992). Child Support Recovery Act of 1992.

Radanovic, H., Bartha, C., Magnatta, M., Hood, E., Sagar, A., & McDonough, H. (1994). A follow-up of families disputing child custody/access: Assessment, settlement, and family relationship outcomes. *Behavioral Sciences and the Law, 12,* 427–435.

Ray, D. (1994, August 28). About men: The endless search. *The New York Times Magazine,* p. 32.

Rhodes, S.L. (1977). A developmental approach to the life cycle of the family. *Social Casework, 58,* 301–311.

Ricci, I. (1980). *Mom's house, Dad's house: Making shared custody work.* New York: Macmillan.

Roberts, T.W., & Price, S.J. (1987). Instant families: Divorced mothers marry never-married men. *Journal of Divorce, 11*(1), 71–92.

Roizblatt, A., Garcia, P., Maida, A.M., & Moya, G. (1990). Is Valentine still doubtful? A workshop model for children of divorce. *Contemporary Family Therapy, 12,* 299–310.

Rosenberg, E.B. (1992). *The adoption life cycle: The children and their families through the years.* New York: Free Press.

Rosenberg, E.B., & Hajal, F. (1985). Stepsibling relationships in remarried families. *Social Casework, 66,* 287–292.

Rothman, B. (1991). *Loving and leaving: Winning at the business of divorce.* Lexington, MA: Lexington Books.

Sager, C.J., Brown, H.S., Crohn, H., Engel, T., Rodstein, E., & Walker, L. (1983). *Treating the remarried family.* New York: Brunner/Mazel.

Saposnek, D.T. (1983). *Mediating child custody disputes.* San Francisco: Jossey-Bass.

Satir, V. (1964). *Conjoint family therapy.* Palo Alto, CA: Science and Behavior Books.

Sauer, L.E., & Fine, M.A. (1988). Parent-child relationships in stepparent families. *Journal of Family Psychology, 1,* 434–451.

Schackman, W.M. (1994). Mid-life divorce: A judge's perspective. In L.L. Schwartz (Ed.), *Mid-life divorce counseling* (pp. 117–122). Alexandria, VA: American Counseling Association.

Schupack, D. (1994, July 7). "Starter" marriages: So early, so brief. *The New York Times*, pp. C1, C6.

Schutz, B.M., Dixon, E.B., Lindenberger, J.C., & Ruther, N.J. (1989). *Solomon's sword: A practical guide to conducting child custody evaluations*. San Francisco: Jossey-Bass.

Schwartz, L.L. (1992). Children's perceptions of divorce. *American Journal of Family Therapy, 20*, 324–332.

Schwartz, L.L. (1993). What *is* a family? A contemporary view. *Contemporary Family Therapy, 15*(6), 429–442.

Schwartz, L.L. (1994a). Enabling children of divorce to win. *Family and Conciliation Courts Review, 32*, 72–83.

Schwartz, L.L. (1994b). Separation and divorce in mid-life: Variations on a theme. In L.L. Schwartz (Ed.), *Mid-life divorce counseling* (pp. 89–98). Alexandria, VA: American Counseling Association.

Schwartz, L.L. (1994c). The challenge of raising one's nonbiological children. *American Journal of Family Therapy, 22*, 195–207.

Schwartz, L.L. (1996). Adoptive families: Are they non-normative? In M. Harway (Ed.), *Treating the changing family: Handling normative and unusual events* (pp. 97–114). New York: John Wiley & Sons.

Schwartz, L.L., & Kaslow, F.W. (1985). Widows and divorcees: The same or different? *American Journal of Family Therapy, 13*, 72–76.

Seltzer, J.A. (1991). Legal custody and children's economic welfare. *American Journal of Sociology, 96*, 895–929.

Shapiro, J.L. (1984). A brief outline of a chronological divorce sequence. *Family Therapy, 11*, 269–278.

Silverstein, M. (1994, April 1). New egalitarian "get" aims to humanize bitter process. *Jewish Exponent* (Philadelphia), pp. 6, 16–17.

Singer-Magdoff, L.J. (1988). May-December marriages: Dynamics, structure, and functioning. In F.W. Kaslow (Ed.), *Couples therapy in a family context* (pp. 133–146). Rockville, MD: Aspen.

Slipp, S. (1988). *The technique and practice of object relations family therapy*. Northvale, NJ: Jason Aronson.

Smith, D.F., & Allred, G.H. (1990). Adjustment of women divorced from homosexual men: An exploratory study. *American Journal of Family Therapy, 18*, 273–284.

Smith, L. (1995, June 4). In a divorce, joint custody of the children is not always the perfect solution. *The Philadelphia Inquirer*, p. M3.

Stahl, P.M. (1994). *Conducting child custody evaluations: A comprehensive guide*. Thousand Oaks, CA: Sage.

Stake, J.E. (1992). Mandatory planning for divorce. *Vanderbilt Law Review, 45*, 397–454.

Starnes, C. (1993). Divorce and the displaced homemaker: A discourse on playing with dolls, partnership buyouts and dissociation under no-fault. *University of Chicago Law Review, 60*, 67–139.

Stone, L. (1990). *Road to divorce: England 1530–1987*. Oxford, England: Oxford University Press.

Storaasli, R.D., & Markman, H.J. (1990). Relationship problems in the early stages of marriage: A longitudinal investigation. *Journal of Family Psychology, 4*(1), 80–98.

Strommer, E.F. (1989). "You're a what?" Family member reactions to a disclosure of homosexuality. *Journal of Homosexuality, 18*(1/2), 37–58.

Stuart, A. (1991). Australia's new child support scheme. *Journal of Divorce & Remarriage, 16,* 139–151.

Sullivan, J.F. (1995, February 15). State Supreme Court reviews child support. *The New York Times,* p. B6.

Swartzman-Schatman, B., & Schinke, S.P. (1993). The effect of mid-life divorce on late adolescent and young adult children. *Journal of Divorce & Remarriage, 19*(1/2), 209–218.

Tannen, D. (1990). *You just don't understand: Women and men in conversation.* New York: Ballantine Books.

Tavris, C., & Offir, C. (1977). *The longest war: Sex differences in perspective.* New York: Harcourt Brace Jovanovich.

Thoennes, N., Salem, P., & Pearson, J. (1994). *Mediation and domestic violence: Current policies and practices.* Madison, WI: Association of Family and Conciliation Courts.

Thompson, R., Tinsley, B., Scalora, M., & Parke, R. (1989). Grandparent's visitation rights: Legalizing the ties that bind. *American Psychologist, 44,* 1217–1222.

Thompson, R.A. (1994). The role of the father after divorce. *The Future of Children, 4*(1), 210–235.

Tompkins, R. (1995). Parenting plans: A concept whose time has come. *Family and Conciliation Courts Review, 33,* 286–297.

Turner, N.W. (1980). Divorce in mid life: Clinical implications and applications. In W.H. Norman & T.J. Scaramella (Eds.), *Mid life: Developmental and clinical issues* (pp. 149–177). New York: Brunner/Mazel.

Umberson, D., & Williams, C.L. (1993). Divorced fathers: Parental role strain and psychological distress. *Journal of Family Issues, 14,* 378–400.

Umberson, D., Wortman, C.B., & Kessler, R.C. (1992). Widowhood and depression: Explaining long-term gender differences in vulnerability. *Journal of Health and Social Behavior, 33,* 10–24.

Uniform Child Custody Jurisdiction Act, 9 ULA 123.

Veum, J.R. (1993). The relationship between child support and visitation: Evidence from longitudinal data. *Social Science Research, 22,* 229–244.

Visher, E.B., & Visher, J.S. (1995). Avoiding the mind fields of stepfamily therapy. In D.K. Huntley (Ed.), *Understanding stepfamilies:*

Implications for assessment and treatment (pp. 25–34). Alexandria, VA: American Counseling Association.

Vobejda, B. (1994, August 30). Half of U.S. children not in nuclear family. *The Philadelphia Inquirer*, p. A4.

Wagner, R.M. (1988). Changes in extended family relationships for Mexican American and Anglo single mothers. *Journal of Divorce*, *11*, 69–87.

Wah, C.R. (1994). Religion in child custody and visitation cases: Presenting the advantage of religious participation. *Family Law Quarterly*, *28*, 269–287.

Wallerstein, J.S. (1991). The long-term effects of divorce on children: A review. *Journal of the American Academy of Child and Adolescent Psychiatry*, *30*, 349–360.

Wallerstein, J.S., & Blakeslee, S. (1989). *Second chances: Men, women, and children a decade after divorce*. New York: Ticknor & Fields.

Wallerstein, J.S., & Blakeslee, S. (1995). *The good marriage: How and why love lasts*. New York: Houghton Mifflin.

Wallerstein, J.S., & Corbin, S.B. (1989). Daughters of divorce: Report from a ten-year follow-up. *American Journal of Orthopsychiatry*, *59*, 593–604.

Wallerstein, J.S., & Kelly, J.B. (1980). *Surviving the breakup: How children and parents cope with divorce*. New York: Basic Books.

Wardle, L.D. (1995). International marriage and divorce regulation and recognition: A survey. *Family Law Quarterly*, *29*, 497–517.

Weingarten, H.R. (1988). The impact of late life divorce: A conceptual and empirical study. *Journal of Divorce*, *12*(1), 21–39.

Weissman, H.N. (1994). Psychotherapeutic and psycholegal considerations: When a custodial parent seeks to move away. *American Journal of Family Therapy*, *22*, 176–181.

Weitzman, L.J. (1985). *The divorce revolution: The unexpected social and economic consequences for women and children in America*. New York: Free Press.

Werblowsky, R.J.Z., & Wigoder, G. (Eds.). (1965). *The encyclopedia of the Jewish religion*. New York: Holt, Rinehart and Winston.

Whitaker, C.A., & Miller, M.H. (1969). A re-evaluation of psychiatric help when divorce impends. *American Journal of Psychiatry*, *126*, 57–64.

White, L.K. (1990). Determinants of divorce: A review of research in the Eighties. *Journal of Marriage and the Family*, *52*, 904–912.

Wilks, C., & Melville, C. (1990). Grandparents in custody and access disputes. *Journal of Divorce*, *13*, 1–14.

Wright, R. (1994, August 15). Our cheating hearts. *Time*, 44–52.

Yura, M.T. (1987). Family subsystem functions and disabled children: Some conceptual issues. *Marriage and Family Review*, *11*(1/2), 135–151.

Zelder, M. (1993). The economic analysis of the effect of no-fault divorce law on the divorce rate. *Harvard Journal of Law & Public Policy,*
16, 241–267.

Zill, N., Morrison, D.R., & Coiro, M.J. (1993). Long-term effects of
parental divorce on parent-child relationships, adjustment, and
achievement in young adulthood. *Journal of Family Psychology, 7,*
91–103.

Zollinger, M., & Felder, W. (1991). Children of divorce and their view-
points on visiting-rights. *Journal of Divorce & Remarriage, 16,*
275–290.

Author Index

Subject Index